The Master Banquet and Party Book

The Master Banquet and Party Book

By

BEATRICE PLUMB

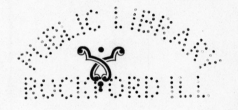

Publishers

T. S. DENISON & COMPANY, INC.

Minneapolis, Minnesota

Printed in the U. S. A.
By THE BRINGS PRESS

Acknowledgments

The author wishes to express her appreciation to the following publishers and editors for their kind permission to reprint material prepared by her and first published in their magazines, and to the New England Mutual Life Insurance Company of Boston, Massachusetts, for permission to reprint Alan Beck's "What Is a Girl?"

The Curtis Publishing Company: A Souvenir Spoon Party, A Get-Your-Man Party for Leap Year, A Spring Spoof Banquet, A Waist-Whittling Banquet, A Go-Getter Garden Banquet, Let's Go A-Maying, A Sunset Tea for the Fourth, A Piece-ful Fourth, A Tea-Totally Free Affair, Porch-Preferred Parties, Merry Meanders, A Funny-Bone Banquet, The Siren Charm School Party, Assorted Christmas Box Socials.

(The above originally appeared in *Country Gentleman* or in *Country Gentlewoman* League Leaflets.)

Christian Herald: A Pioneer Banquet, A New Spud Shindig, A Junior-Senior Blossom Banquet, A Fan-ciful Banquet, A Many-Thanks Banquet, A Boxy Banquet, A You'll-Remember Party, A Twelfth Night Revel.

The Party Magazine, Dennison Manufacturing Company, Framingham, Massachusetts: A Time's-Up Social for the New Year, A Chop and Chips Banquet, A Bird of a Banquet.

The author also wishes to express her appreciation to the food or household editors of these magazines, whose menus and recipes are included in her material; and to the friends who contributed the few additional recipes. Since these bore no date or credit line, no more formal acknowledgement is possible. But to all, the author's heartfelt thanks.

—THE AUTHOR

Music of the Book

The music used in the book consists of old, familiar songs, practically all of which will be found in Denison's song book, "Songs Worth While," and in "Get Together Songs," published by the Lorenz Publishing Company.

PUBLISHER'S NOTE ON DECORATIONS: The publishers of this book handle the crepe paper and other materials used in the decorations for various banquets and parties. They may, however, be obtained at the stores of practically all towns of ordinary size throughout the country.

Foreword

Banquets, dinners, socials, teas
Picnics, parties, planned to please.

The author can think of no better greeting to her readers than the title of her first party book, "Here's for a Good Time!"

She believes in play and its power. Her first "big boss," a city recreation commissioner, sent her out on her first major assignment with the plea, "Teach them to play as well as to pray. One is almost as necessary for their salvation as the other."

In the many years and places in which she has organized and directed recreation, in two countries, in community centers, churches, schools, libraries, city slums and exclusive country clubs, on city parks and town playgrounds, even in three reform schools, she has seen the spirit of play, through many mediums, work miracles.

Here, in this book, is an assortment of good times. The author has frequently given a surplus of suggestions for decorations, entertainment, menus, etc., so that hostess and director can select what best meets their own needs, bearing in mind number, type, and age of guests, and facilities and space available.

She also has purposely included several old-time favorites, agreeing with Amos R. Wells that "A poorer game, in which all can heartily join, is far better than a better game that appears only to a few." Once get the shy guest playing a game he knows, and he will gain confidence to try a new one.

Finally, the author gives you this couplet to hold in your heart as you plan your next gay, good time:

"God bless everyone who strives
To keep the laughter in our lives."

—The Author

CONTENTS

BANQUETS

Bird of a Banquet, A 57

Boxy Banquet, A 120

Chops and Chips Banquet, A 29

Fan-ciful Banquet, A 80

Funny-Bone Banquet, A 104

Gay Nineties Mother-and-Daughter Banquet 73

Go-Getter Garden Banquet, A 49

Junior-Senior Blossom Banquet 66

Many-Thanks Banquet, A 112

Pioneer Banquet, A 20

Rattling Good Banquet, A 11

Spring Spoof Banquet, A 38

Waist-Whittling Banquet, A 95

World-of-Fun Banquet, A 87

PARTIES, SOCIALS, SUPPERS, PICNICS, AND TEAS

Assorted Christmas Box Socials 297

Beat-the-Jinx Dinner, A 259

Christopher Robin's Outdoor Fete 246

Do Tell (Announcement parties) 264

Family Christmas Bazaar, A 300

Get-Your-Man Party for Leap Year, A 137

Kid 'Em Along Social, A 235

Let It Pour (Bridal showers) 191

Let's Go a-Maying 181

Merry Meanders 220

New Spud Shindig, A 173

Note-able Evening, A 272

Piece-ful Fourth, A 205

Porch-Preferred Parties 199

Procedure Pointers 283

Program Trimmings 279

Siren Charm School Party, The 250

Snow Ball, A 157

Souvenir Spoon Party, A 163

St. Patrick's Day Tea, A 170

Stunts for the Fellers 293

Suggestions for Church Suppers 290

Sunset Tea for the Fourth, A 227

Tea-Totally Free Affair, A 213

Time's-Up Social for the New Year, A 129

Twelfth Night Revel, A 146

You'll-Remember Party, A 153

BANQUETS

A RATTLING GOOD BANQUET

Of all festive occasions, New Year's celebrations are undoubtedly the noisiest. For at such social affairs, it is not only permissible to raise the roof, but it is the proper thing to do. Then why not welcome the baby New Year with "A Rattling Good Time," featuring the baby's first noisemaker?

RATTLING GOOD INVITATIONS—These show the New Year as a chubby cherub of a baby, wearing little else but a toothless smile and a wisp of chiffon on which are the golden numerals of the New Year.

An easy way to make the invitation is to decorate a tinted correspondence card with a gummed seal or sticker of the baby New Year. In one hand is sketched an outsize baby's rattle, or a picture of one may be cut from a catalog and pasted in place. Below, the following is written or printed:

> This plump little person is Baby New Year,
> Without a layette! What a crime!
> Let's all get together and welcome the dear
> With one jolly, rattling good time!

Below, the name, place of banquet, day, date, and the usual fib, "From nine to twelve," may be added. The time deceives nobody, since all the world knows a New Year's celebration breaks out, not up, at midnight!

OTHER RATTLING GOOD BABIES—A picture gallery showing baby portraits of invited guests is always a howling success. To help in the collection of exhibits, a postscript may be added to the invitation, reading, "Please bring—or, better still, send in advance—the earliest existing portrait or snapshot of yourself as a baby. To preserve secrecy, please do not show your picture to other guests."

If wished, the request may be telephoned.

RATTLING GOOD DECORATIONS—Christmas is still in the air, and the holly, mistletoe, evergreens, and colored lights are not yet taken down, so all that is required is a little New Year touch here and there.

11

Since a circle is the symbol of all time—eternity—this could be featured. Not only in wreaths of evergreen, but as the frame for fancier forms of decoration.

Wooden hoops, from embroidery hoops to the wooden ones rolled by children, which are wrapped around with strips of crepe or tissue paper or tinfoil, make a solid foundation on which to build all sorts of decorative effects.

Hung flat in doorways or from arches or chandeliers, the curved rims of the hoops make an ideal circle on which to tie seasonal symbols, such as tiny calendars, diaries, toy watches, hourglasses, or wee kewpie dolls, wearing the numerals of the New Year.

Or the hoops can be decorated with a misty fringe of finely-cut crepe or tissue paper, sparked with tinsel "rain." Colored balloons fastened to strings of various lengths can be tied to the rim of a suspended hoop, thus forming a circle of gay balls in constant motion.

A decorated hoop can be hung directly over the banquet table, with balloons floating from it, each bearing one figure of the numeral of the New Year. Or, if wished, from its rim can dangle a noisemaker for every guest.

The hoop, in an upright position, has just as many decorative possibilities. Tacked securely to a block of wood to steady it, it can be decorated and then placed, in all its glory, on mantel shelf, piano top, or hall table. A kewpie doll, dressed as the baby New Year, with a huge safety pin securing his three cornered diaper, can be set swinging in a flower-trimmed hoop, hung upright in doorway or arch.

RATTLING GOOD TABLE DECORATIONS—Paper tablecloths and napkins, especially designed for New Year entertaining, may be used, or a gaily-colored linen cloth may be made even more festive by decorating the top and skirt with cutouts from colored construction paper or crepe paper, and then spreading over all a sparkling white cellophane cover.

The cutouts can be circles of various colors, to match the confetti sprinkled on the table top under the cellophane. Or they can be cutouts of rattles, teething rings, pacifiers, safety pins, or cuddly baby animals.

RATTLING GOOD CENTERPIECE—The baby New Year, being the center of attraction for all the world tonight, has a right to the center of the table. A good-sized kewpie doll, wearing a sash, dated with the numerals of the New Year, and with a rattle wired to one hand, stands in—or on—a circle of rolls of serpentine.

Other such rolls stand in colorful piles down the length of the table, carefully spaced so that the top roll of each pile can carry one letter of the greeting, "Happy New Year!"

The letters forming the word "Happy" are on one side of the baby New Year centerpieces, and those spelling "New Year" on the other. These letters can be cut from colored cardboard, or purchased at a store selling such holiday novelties, or spelled out with toy alphabet blocks.

RATTLING GOOD FAVORS—The favors may be noisemakers, such as rattles, trumpets, drums, harmonicas, squawker balloons, bells, bird whistles, crickets, etc.

Strict instructions should be given that guests must not try out their noisemakers before midnight.

Other favors may be confetti cutie dolls, which are easy to make and are just as much fun as a pillow fight and make almost as great a litter.

The cutie's head is made of a paper napkin, stuffed with confetti. Features are marked on the round ball, and the corners and surplus paper of the napkin then brought down to form a neck. This neck is padded with paper and strengthened by wrapping it around a few times with spool wire.

The infant is then dressed in a simple, full garment of combined hood and cloak, cut from crepe paper.

When it is grabbed by its robes, and its head is bashed against that of some merry reveler, it spills its sawdust—or, rather, its confetti—all over the place!

Games and Stunts

The program for a New Year's Eve banquet varies according to what hour the meal is to be served.

Usually there is time after the guests arrive for some sort of informal entertainment. In which case, any of the following games and stunts would be suitable:

THE INFANTRY—When the guests arrive, the official greeter tells them he wants them all to be as young as the New Year. Then men are ushered into their cloak room and asked to doff their wraps—and put on their baby bonnets! Sure enough, on the dressing table is a row of little white bonnets made of lacy shelf paper, with long tissue paper strings. They are in assorted head sizes, and there is an assistant there to help fit bonnets to heads and tie the strings in a fetching bow under each strong, disapproving chin. Each bonnet has a numbered circle glued to one string, no two numbers being alike.

Meanwhile, the girls have been ushered into their cloak room, and are encouraged to choose and don one of the baby bibs displayed on their dressing table. These are made of be-frilled crepe paper, and bear such sweet lettering as "Mamma's Pet," "Ickle Precious," "Angel Child," "Sweetie Pie," and so on. They, also, are numbered to agree with the numbers on the men's bonnets.

THE BABY SHOW—A sign, in bold letters, reads "To the Bigger and Better Baby Picture Gallery." The hand on the directing sign is that of a plump little baby, holding a rattle to point out the way.

The exhibit is either in a separate room, or in some screened-off appropriate spot. Each baby picture has been given a distinguished number, and hung on the wall. In the center of the collection, and numbered one, is a particularly attractive picture of the baby New Year. One often finds just the thing on a magazine cover, which can be mounted to resemble a tinted photograph.

Each guest, as he enters to view the pictures, is handed a catalog. This is merely a colored correspondence card, made decorative by a sticker of the Baby New Year, and useful by taping a tiny pencil to one corner. On these cards, guests jot down against each number the name of the guest they think the photo bearing that number portrays.

PRIZES—The guest who succeeds in correctly naming most baby pictures deserves a handsome prize. But awards of merit should go to every person who recognizes any beside his own and those of his immediate family. Guests can also be asked to vote for the prettiest baby, the best, the brightest, and the one most likely to succeed, prizes being given to those securing most votes.

These awards should be babyishly appropriate. Thus, the grown-up prettiest baby could receive a can of much advertised baby powder; the best baby, a silver (tin) cup labeled, "A gift for a good child;" the brightest baby, a set of rubber alphabet blocks, and the baby most likely to succeed, a pacifier labeled "Good for stomach ulcers."

BABY TALK—After the baby show, each man is told to find his first partner by searching for the girl whose bib number corresponds with that on his own bonnet string. When all are paired off, the couples are told to stand in a large conversational circle and, at the sound of the rattle instantly start to talk on whatever subject the leader announces.

But all the conversation must be carried on in baby talk, and all who break the rule must pay a heavy forfeit. At the next sound of the rattle, each man must leave his first partner and find another with whom to discuss the second subject announced.

Subjects for discussion could be: "Measles," "My Teething Troubles," "Colic," "My Favorite Cradle Toy," "Reasons for Not Growing Up," and "Why Is a Choo-Choo a Train?"

Two "nursemaids" are on hand to listen in on all conversations and jot down all the names of babies lapsing from baby talk. Those who lapse are afterwards made to pay a forfeit by reciting any nursery rime and using baby talk throughout.

Or they are required to caricature or dramatize in melodramatic manner Little Bo-Peep and her lost sheep, Little Jack Horner and his pie, or Little Miss Muffet and her spider.

DINNER IS SERVED—When the time comes for guests to be seated at the table, they may march there, singing any suitable childhood song or parody, such as the following chorus to the tune of "Ten Little Indians."

> One little, two little, three hungry babies,
> Four little, five little, six hungry babies,
> Seven little, eight little, nine hungry babies,
> Ten hungry baby boys.

The second verse ends, "Ten hungry baby girls."

RATTLING GOOD MENU—Any good dinner menu, suitable for holiday hospitality extended to old friends, can be chosen. The following are samples:

Menu No. 1
Consomme

Crown Roast Pork   Baked Apple Rings

String Beans   Scalloped Potatoes

Stuffed Celery Salad

Vanilla Ice Cream with Caramel Sauce

Salted Nuts   Macaroons   Spiced Raisins

Coffee

Menu No. 2
Oyster Cocktail

Toasted Oyster Crackers

Roast Duck   Peanut Stuffing

Parsnips baked with Duck

Applesauce   Southern Sweet Potatoes

Cauliflower au Gratin

Plum Pudding with Hard Sauce   Pumpkin Pie

Assorted Salted Nuts   Mints

Coffee

RATTLING GOOD SOUVENIR PROGRAM—The cover design shows the Baby New Year, rattle in hand, shyly looking over his shoulder. The numerals of the New Year are printed on the rear of the only garment he is wearing. Above the sketch is printed, "A Rattling Good Banquet," and below, the time and place. The inside pages carry the menu and the program of table entertainment.

PROGRAM

Chief Baby Sitter .... (Name of Toastmaster)
Cradle and Nursery Songs   Nursery Pass
Nursery Rime Quiz   Baby's Bottle
Baby Cries   Safety Pin Chain

CRADLE AND NURSERY SONGS—The Chief Baby Sitter (the emcee), using a baby's rattle as a gavel, announces that there will be a contest between rival teams to see which can give the best rendering of the old nursery song, "Rock-a-bye, Baby, on the Tree-top." He designates the teams—as guests on one side of a long banquet table being the "Rockers," those on the other, the "Byers." Or, if guests are seated at several small tables, he chooses the tables and assigns the teams' respective names.

Most people know the tune of "Rock-a-bye" but if memories need to be refreshed, the simple air can be first played on the piano.

"Now," beams the emcee, "we'll soon see which team has the best voices. There is one important rule: The ladies must all sing bass; the men, soprano. Ready, Rockers? I will direct with my rattle. Sing!"

The emcee decides that it is a draw; each team gave a terrible performance. "So let us try it with an orchestra! The men will whistle the tune, while the ladies hum it, at the same time tapping time to it with their dinner knives against their water glasses. The Byers will perform first. Ready? Begin!"

NURSERY RIME QUIZ—Odd lines are taken from a dozen nursery rimes. The emcee recites each line in turn, and the guest who first shouts out the name of the nursery rime from which it was quoted scores one for his team.

BABY CRIES—Guests count in turn around the table—one, two three, etc.—but when they reach the number 7, or a multiple of seven, they give a quick little baby cry instead of the number. When a player makes a mistake, he crosses his arms over his chest to show he is out of the game. After each mistake, the counting starts with one again.

NURSERY PASS—Two baby baskets are brought in. In each is an identical collection of baby objects—as teething ring, rubber doll, card of safety pins, sponge, pacifier, etc.

At the word "Go," the first player at the head of each side of the table passes one of the objects down the line to the foot of the table. Each article must be passed behind the backs of the players.

Should an object be dropped, that team is stymied until it is recovered and taken back to the starter to be passed again.

BABY'S BOTTLE—Each side picks a contestant. Two baby's feeding bottles are filled with watered milk. On the word to start, the contestants see which one can first empty the bottle by suction.

SAFETY PIN CHAIN—Duplicate sets of safety pins of very assorted sizes are distributed to competing teams. On the word, "Pin!" the leader of each line hands his pin to the next in line, who clasps his own pin in the one handed to him, and then passes them on to Player Three who adds his pin, and so the chain of pins grows until the last player adds the last pin.

The side which first succeeds in finishing its chain of linked safety pins, with none dropped, wins the contest.

When the leader distributes the safety pins to the players, it adds to the suspense and difficulty of the race if he will give the first player a huge pin, the next player a tiny one, and so on, so that it takes time to pin one to the other.

FORFEITS—Sometimes several forfeits can be paid at one time. For instance, a group of men may be asked to display its knowledge of dressmaking before the rest of the company.

Each is given a clothespin—the sort with a round head—and told to dress it as a baby in long clothes. The men share a box containing pins, thread, needles, string, a tube of library paste, black and red crayons, and odds and ends of pale pink and pale blue tissue paper.

A mischievously "helpful" director can add to their discomfiture by such questions as, "Do you put the selvage side up or down? How many gussets in the neck, Mr. Smith? Tom, do you intend to gather the hem or just smock it?"

To get forfeits all paid off in a hurry, offenders are divided into two groups and given just ten minutes in which to compose not only words, but the tune of an original nursery rime or lullaby.

When called, they must instantly come forward and sing their composition with appropriate actions. If it fails to win a sufficient volume of applause from the audience, the singers must retire and work up another with more popular appeal.

AN OUTSIZED BABY NEW YEAR—Some hefty young man is chosen for the part of the Baby New Year. He is dressed in a close-fitting bonnet and long night dress and given an enormous feeding bottle and rattle.

Just before the stroke of midnight, he is trundled into the room, either in a wheelbarrow or in a huge improvised baby carriage, to wish the hilarious company "a rattling good New Year."

Some guest with a good singing voice, who has been previously notified, now starts singing, "For he's a rattling good fellow" to the well-known old tune. All the guests join hands to form a singing circle around the fat "baby." Later, if wished, he can leave his baby carriage to lead the revels.

A PIONEER BANQUET

The "Let's remember" theme is a richly-rewarding one for banquets, dinners, suppers, and even serve-selves and "potlucks." Since it is based on reminiscences, it can be adapted to almost any occasion or season, and is a delightful way to entertain senior citizens and honor them and include them in the program.

When, where, why? Some organizations find the banquet theme especially appropriate for the New Year, when we pause on the threshold of the new to glance back at the old.

Others consider it a February affair, since that month seems to lend itself naturally to historic memories.

Others prefer it as a feature of their Memorial Day programs, sometimes to stimulate interest in a fund for placing permanent markers at historic places in the community, city, county, or state, or for erecting memorials to local heroes of the armed forces.

A pioneer banquet, however, is its most popular form, staged to celebrate the birthday, or the pioneer days, of the local home town. The word "staged" is used advisedly, for, however unpretentious, the banquet needs showmanship.

RESEARCH COMMITTEE—This is an important committee on which most of the success of the undertaking depends. Its members visit old inhabitants and learn local history firsthand. They search yellowed newspaper files, read old books of minutes and records, visit old graves to get epitaphs and dates, haunt local museums, and ask the help of any existing old-timers' clubs.

PIONEER MEMENTOS—This committee begs from the descendants of early settlers relics of those old days to display in the banquet room or in an adjoining safe room. The committee asks them to ransack attic and cellar for old-time costumes and their accessories—bonnets, hats, dolmans, fichus, fans, shawls, parasols, uniforms—and to bring or wear these costumes to the banquet.

The committee asks them to search for pioneer household or farm utensils or tools—oil lamps, lanterns, old pieces of harness, candlesticks and candle molds, etc. Sometimes a proud owner will lend a precious heirloom quilt or a prized cross-stitch sampler. Old family Bibles and other valuable old books, if loaned, should be kept under glass.

The research committee assumes complete responsibility for all the relics borrowed. The committee collects them, tickets each with a card, giving the name or exhibit, the approximate date when in use, and by whom lent, and appoints curators to guard and display the treasures on the night of the banquet. It sees that they are safely returned, unharmed, to their owners.

If there are fine specimens of old attire, such as shawls or the elegant creations of velvet and silk that were once the best gowns of a past generation, this committee arranges to have them modeled by local beauties who will show them to advantage.

ENTERTAINMENT COMMITTEE — This committee visits old-timers to gather names of the songs they used to sing, the readings grandma memorized—she will still know them!—and the oldest jokes grandpa remembers; also the "play games" and folk and square dances that were popular when the settlement was young.

Is there an old fiddler who remembers the old tunes? The committee puts him down for his best selections. It also arranges for the songs—solo, quartet or group—which are to accompany the showing of the living portraits in the Old Family Album tableau.

If the plans call for banquet toasts and a short inspirational talk, this committee secures the speakers, giving them several weeks' notice and explaining that the theme of the banquet is "The Present Honors the Past." Elder Brewster's message to the Pilgrims, in which he adjures them to be true to their promises, strikes the right note for the main after-dinner speech: "Generations to come will look back . . . to this day of small things, and say, 'Here was our beginning as a people. These were our forefathers. Through their trials we inherit our blessings. Their faith is our faith; their hope, our hope; their God, our God.'"

A FOOD COMMITTEE—The food committee does research along its own line. What was the menu on festive occasions in those old days? Who made the best cake? From what recipe? What was the main dish? The committee gets an old-timer good cook to help make the banquet menu as true to the old days as possible.

The food the early settlers found in this country was game of almost every kind, fish, oysters, shad, lobsters; corn, squash, pumpkins, beans; berries, honey, maple sugar, and syrup. The menu could be planned around these foods, with the addition of old-type cakes—pound, spice, marble, and ginger.

STAGE AND PROPERTIES COMMITTEE—This committee plans and carries out the pioneer setting for the banquet room, not only the stage, with its frontier scenery, and the prairie schooner encampment display, but also the old family album which frames the living portraits of past days.

PRIZE AND GIFT COMMITTEE—Suitable prizes and gifts are important at a pioneer banquet, when the usual "joshing" souvenir is often out of place. The selection of such prizes takes time and taste. Gifts could be presented to the oldest settler in the community, the oldest person present, the couple longest married; or, if a church banquet, to the oldest charter member; or, if a club banquet, to the oldest living president.

There could be prizes for the most interesting pioneer relic; the quaintest old-time costume worn or exhibited; the oldest pioneer tool, household or farm; the oldest gun, snuff box, daguerreotype, spinning wheel, etc.; or for the most graphic eye-witness account of some historic, exciting, or amusing local incident of the past.

Suitable prizes would be any gift related to memory, such as memorandum, note, address, or telephone number books, diary, budget book, snapshot album; or any keepsake or article that would bring to mind the community's early days, such as old photographs of the town as it was, with its old dirt road.

This committee might also select and buy the banquet favors.

FLOOR COMMITTEE—Since there will be things of value on display, this committee is needed to help keep a protective eye on them. It is responsible for keeping order, guarding against fire, vandalism, and the like.

RECEPTION COMMITTEE—The friendliest and sunniest members should be chosen for this important "first impression" group. They greet the incoming guests, giving their best in courtesy and consideration to the old-timers. They give directions and guidance to those asking where they can find this exhibit or that. When the affair is over, they are at the door to give each parting guest a kind word.

PUBLICITY COMMITTEE—Local newspapers are always happy to make old times news. This committee reports all historic and human interest "finds" to community papers, with photographs, if required.

This committee could also be responsible for designing, making and distributing posters or invitations.

OTHER COMMITTEES—A pioneer banquet is not usually a pay affair. But should it be, then a finance committee is a must; also a ticket committee, and an office committee to take care of telephone calls and correspondence pertaining to the banquet and program. Many such banquets require a good check room committee.

PIONEER POSTER—The poster or invitation to the banquet shows a sketch of an ox-drawn covered wagon from the rear, bumping down the trail. The dilapidated cover has many stitched-on patches, and at the rear a card is tacked. An old lantern is the tail light.

On the rounded end of the wagon's cover, above the opening which serves as the door, is printed "A Pioneer Banquet," with day, date, time, and place of banquet. All other necessary information is printed on the patches on the prairie schooner's cover and on the card tacked at the rear. The inscriptions could read: "Award to the oldest settler present;" or "Prize for the best pioneer costume worn;" or "Prize for the best true story of local pioneer days."

PIONEER INTERIOR DECORATIONS—The banquet hall must go early American. The modern furniture and fancy lamps are removed. A rough fireplace can be made of real field stones, or by covering crates with rock-design crepe paper and filling it with logs. A flashlight behind flames of red and yellow fireproof paper gives it a realistic glow. An imitation crane is swung above the fire and a huge pot hung on it. There should be ancient fire irons and bellows, and a high-backed bench on each side of the hearth and an oval rag rug before it.

The high-backed chimney seats can be made on a church bench foundation, with strips of thin board tacked on to raise the backs.

If the fireplace builders can add a long mantel shelf, old guns and swords can be hung above it, and old brass candlesticks, pewter dishes, and horn glasses stood upon it.

HITTING THE TRAIL—On the stage, or somewhere in the hall, is a rough replica of a prairie schooner encampment. The covered wagon can be built on a light cart or wagon, or of a framework of arched bamboo canes and cardboard. It is given high sides, and so built overhead that a tarpaulin can be thrown over the top, hanging down over the sides.

A few men, women and children, dressed as early settlers, rest beside a make-believe fire. The girls wear old-fashioned calico dresses, with tight waists and full, long skirts. The boys wear big hats and gaily-colored bandannas around their necks. One boy sits on the tongue of the wagon, playing old-time songs on his banjo or ukulele. Little children in old style garb play with wooden-headed dolls.

PIONEER TABLE DECORATIONS—To be true to the times, tables should be boards laid on sawhorses, covered with a homespun cloth, with a large pewter saltcellar as a centerpiece. Plates should be wooden trenchers, but since the latter are now collector's items, china of an early pattern, such as willow ware, could be substituted. Pewter plates and pitchers, leather tankards, if procurable, should have a place of honor in the service, but coffee served from a punch bowl into pewter (tin) cups might take the place of the common tankard from which the early settlers drank.

For favors, toy drums or toy pistols may be given or water pistols filled with toilet water of some old-fashioned fragrance, as lavender or lilac.

PROGRAM AND ENTERTAINMENT—The cover of the banquet program could show an old sampler, or a row of little prairie schooners in silhouette. Inside pages give the menu, the table program—mostly music, toasts and the main speech —and the words of the theme song, composed if possible, for the occasion by a local versifier and sung to some time-honored old tune.

String music is featured in both background and entertainment. A string quartet in early American attire could apparently wander in and serenade the guest of honor, or play a medley of old-time songs.

For between-courses, some old-timer could come prepared to tell about a famous "first"—the first time he used a telephone, the adventure of riding in his first automobile, his first gramophone, his first ear-muff radio.

Suggested toasts: To the early colonizers; To the old-time fiddler; To early American explorers; To the everbeckoning trail.

THE OLD FAMILY ALBUM—There are many ways of making the skeleton album which is to stand on the stage, or at the end of the room. The wooden frame, covered with black, should stand out from the wall about twelve feet or so, and be held in place by long laths or sticks running back on either side from the top of the frame to the wall. These laths form the skeleton framework for the covering of top and sides by anything dark that is handy, such as drapes or blankets.

The front of the frame is covered with mosquito netting. A light is placed inside the inclosure, so that it will shine on the people posing for the living photograph.

The frame is curtained, and two pretty girls, dressed in early American costumes, pull the curtain aside when each photograph is ready to be shown, and close it again at a signal.

All other lights are turned off except the one in the album.

One verse of some suitable song accompanies each picture. These may be solo, quartet, or chorus numbers. Singers are either hidden from view, or grouped, in costume, around the camp fire.

Actual family albums may be consulted for authenic reproductions of photographs, poses, photographers' props, etc.

Tableaux could be arranged after this pattern:

1. The Family Group .... Music, "Auld Lang Syne"

2. Grandmother .... Music, "Love's Old Sweet Song"

3. Children with Schoolbooks .... Music, "Coming Through the Rye"

4. The Bride and Groom .... Music, "Believe Me, if All Those Endearing Young Charms"

5. Uncle Noah and Aunt Maggie .... Music, "When You and I Were Young, Maggie"

6. Our Graduate (with diploma .... Music, "Schooldays" in hand)

7. The Village preacher and the Choir of (early date of first church meeting) .... Music, A line out of some old hymn, as was the custom, choosing one that fits the theme. For example:

> When I can read my title clear
> To mansions in the skies,
> I'll bid farewell to every fear,
> And wipe my weeping eyes.

MORE PICTURED MEMORIES—This is another idea for a "Let's Remember" stage number. It can be presented in a series of tableau or stage scenes, as preferred. If the latter, then just enough action or dialogue to tell the story is given.

The purpose of the Memories is to show the church, choir, Sunday School, club, library, schoolhouse, or community as it was in its earliest days.

Many a noble church started out as a humble group, meeting in a barn, stable, abandoned shed or mill, on a sagging porch, or over a saloon. This lowly beginning maybe presented in a simple tableau, or as a dramatic scene, with a character—possibly a descendant—taking the part of the pioneer preacher who helped found the church.

THE PIONEER SUNDAY SCHOOL—Old timers will tell of the plain, dark room, the hard wooden benches, what was taught, and how. The scene on the stage should be made true to history or traditions. The curtain goes up to show the old-fashioned schoolma'am and a few children, all dressed in the costumes of that day. There are no hymn books or lesson helps. There is nothing to help with the singing but a tuning fork.

The children sing, "O God, Our Help in Ages Past," in high sweet voices, and then one of them prays a children's prayer of those days, as "Gentle Jesus, Meek and Mild," while all the rest, with the teacher, stand with bowed heads and folded hands.

THE PIONEER DAY SCHOOL—The children may present a tableau of the first little day school of which there is any record or tradition, showing the stern schoolmistress, birch rod in hand.

If a dramatic scene, a few children could rise, when called on by some old pioneer's name, to repeat verses from the New England Primer, such as: "Letter L. The lion bold, the lamb doth hold." Or:

> "Zaccheus, he
> Did climb a tree
> His Lord to see."

THE PIONEER HOME—A tableau may be presented showing the interior of an early settler's home. A spinning wheel is beside the open fire. Guns and traps and skins are on the wall.

Every member of the family is occupied, busily weaving, knitting, kneading bread, whittling, molding candles, or making soap. The locality of the community will determine what pioneer activities should be pictured.

If a dramatic scene, grandpa or a visiting neighbor can enter, carrying his fiddle. He can be coaxed to play, which he does; first, some lively air, as a jig or one of the play-party tunes—"Jim Along Josie," "Skip to My Lou," etc.

Then the weary mother asks for something "more quiet-like," and the old fellow gives her, "Home, Sweet Home."

PIONEER HOUSE CHORES—Here is a dramatic scene, showing the family doing the work as it was done in pioneer days. Mother is taking loaves of bread from the ancient oven, while grandma is sweeping the floor with a broom such as the witches ride! One daughter bends over a wooden tub, doing the family wash with an outsize scrub brush on a corrugated washboard. Another daughter has a board laid across the backs of two kitchen chairs and is ironing with old heavy hand irons, heated against the bars of an antiquated coal fireplace.

The sons, of school age, are lugging in pails of water from an improvised handle pump or wind-up well, while they sing, "The Old Oaken Bucket."

PIONEER COMMUNITY SING—The audience is divided into rival singing societies, competing in the singing of old songs, such as: "Old Oaken Bucket;" "Good-bye, My Lover, Good-bye;" "Aunt Dinah's Quilting Party;" "Old Black Joe," etc.

OTHER PROGRAM EVENTS—The old games, Spin the Platter, Going to Jerusalem, Looby Lou, London Bridge, Round and Round the Village, may be played and the evening may be ended by the singing of "Auld Lang Syne" and "Good Night, Pioneers" to the tune of "Good Night, Ladies."

A CHOP AND CHIPS BANQUET

After we have said "Cheerio!" with cherries, and "Hell-o, old thing" with one of those devastating "Tell the truth" affairs, there seems little left of Washington to celebrate but his hatchet. Then hew to the line and let the chips fall where they may at a chop and chips banquet for Washington's Birthday.

INVITATIONS—Chipper posters or invitations show a hatchet doing it. The log is almost hacked in two, and chips are flying furiously to the four corners of poster or correspondence card. Somewhere amidst the melee, is written or printed the following:

Small sands make the mountains,
Moments make the year;
And chips could make a banquet
For Washington; that's clear!

Please come to our Chop and Chips Banquet at .... on .... from .... o'clock to .... (Place day and hour added.)

CHOPPY DECORATIONS—When in doubt, use a hatchet! Scores of them, cut from red, white, and blue cardboard, or bought ready made may dangle from the chandeliers, across the room in festoons and in archways and open doorways. They may alternate with a few curly wood shavings. A couple of large hatchets, crossed, make an impressive-looking crest over the mantel, piano, speaker's table, or other prominent spot. A smaller hatchet cut from wood can be attached to the door, to serve as a knocker. Other hatchets can be wired to the window; a frieze of tiny cardboard ones around the shades of floor lamps; a couple tied to the post of the stairway. In short, shout it with hatchets!

CHOPPY TABLE TRIM—Paper cloth and napkins that fairly drip hatchets can be used. A flaxen-haired baby doll can be dressed as the illustrious boy who chopped down his daddy's pet cherry tree and got away with it, and has been famous ever since! A toy hatchet is placed in his hand and a few severed logs at his feet. The rest of the logs may be distributed around the table, one for each guest. Those for the men can be a few cigarettes wrapped in brown crepe paper to resemble a log; those for the girls, packages of chocolate mints, similarly wrapped. A small cardboard hatchet may be wedged by one sharp corner of its blade into each log. If wished, names can be written on the handles of the hatchets, thus making them serve as place cards as well as favors.

CHOPPY REFRESHMENTS—The refreshments can be actually "choppy," with chop suey, chicken salad, lamb chops—anything in pieces—as the main course, with potato chips or French fries on the menu, and a dessert of fresh chopped fruits served with coconut chips.

CHOPPY POETRY—First comers are made to feel at ease by being presented with a cardboard hatchet and a fancy red, white and blue pencil and invited to write a clever last line—or any old line—to the following little gem, which is plainly printed in big letters on a hatchet-trimmed card, and posted in a prominent position:

> "My!" said the 'ousemaid, 'Won't you catch it!
>   Wot in the world 'ave you been hat?
> Choppin' that narsty, 'orrid 'atchet
>   Right through a cherry tree! My 'at!"

> "No," murmured George, "I shan't catch it;
>   I have been making his-tor-ee!
> This is a patriotic hatchet.
> ....

Finding a wise-cracking last line to that stanza, jotting it down on their little hatchets and proudly signing it should keep the guests from feeling homesick.

NOTHING BUT THE TRUTH—This game is an ice-breaker that needs no preparation. The guests form a circle, girls and men alternating, with the leader in the center. He swings around unexpectedly and points an accusing finger at somebody in the ring, at the same time snapping in a stern voice, "Who did it?"

The flustered player at whom he is pointing must immediately notice whether the leader is pointing with a finger of his right or left hand. If with the right, the player must say, "I cannot tell a lie. So-and-so did it," naming as the culprit the player who stands on his right. If the leader is pointing with the left, he must blame the whole thing on his left-hand neighbor. He must do it, too, before the leader counts ten.

The idea is to get the players so rattled that the smartest of them cannot tell his left hand from his right, or, under the threat of that menacing finger, the names of friends with whom he went to school. Frantic players who stammer, "I cannot t-tell a l-lie. Er-er-hem-Thingamagig, here, did it!" must pay a forfeit. Those who fail to tell right from left or fail to answer correctly or at all, are penalized.

As a forfeit, the culprits are lined up, and each in turn is made to tell a true hatchet story about himself. This is an account of some occasion when he "got it in the neck" and, no doubt, richly deserved it.

An other forfeit is for the players to stand up and say three nice things about himself. They must be quite true. A third forfeit is to answer truthfully four personal questions asked by anyone.

UNEARTHING BURIED HATCHETS—This game needs a little preparation. First of all, a four-inch square of cardboard is provided for every invited man. They are numbered from one up. A hatchet is lightly sketched on each and the outline perforated. A sewing machine makes a quick, easy job of it. The needle is unthreaded, the stitch is lengthened and the needle sews around the outlined hatchet until it is neatly pricked out with evenly-spaced little holes.

For each girl, an oblong, jagged piece of cardboard or crisp yellow paper shaped like a chip is prepared. In the center of each a darning needle is thrust, threaded with enough red or blue yarn to sew around the hatchet. These "chips" are numbered also from one up.

Before the first guest arrives, the hatchets and needle "chips" are hidden not too carefully—about the room.

When ready for the hunt, the hostess announces that she has "buried the hatchet" for every man present, and a "chip" for every girl; that no matter how many hatchets the girls find, they must neither pick them up nor disclose their hiding-places. Their specialty is chips. Likewise, the men must stick to their hatchets.

When a girl finds one chip, she must instantly join the ranks of the unemployed until some man unearths the hatchet which carries the same number as does her chip. Having found his first hatchet, the man, too, comes under the same rule. He must wait patiently for the chip which has his number.

As soon as a couple come together, the girl hands the man the yarn-threaded needle from her chip. He then begins to sew clumsily around the outlined hatchet on his card, a referee adding to his difficulty by telling him that on no account must he skip a hole. His partner stands by to deride or encourage him, according to her disposition.

A prize goes to the one who first finishes his hatchet to the satisfaction of the referee. But all must stick to their embroidery lesson, even if this "glorifying of the American hatchet" takes all evening. At the conclusion of the job, the girl is given the hatchet.

MORE HATCHERY—The leader now displays a poster on which have been sketched with crayon fifteen fallen logs, explaining that George is responsible. The cherry tree may have been his first offense, but not his last. Each log is numbered and lettered as follows:

1. Bark; 2. Can; 3. Chest; 4. Drop; 5. Dumpling; 6. Hock; 7. Lozenge; 8. Needle; 9. Oil; 10. Pillow; 11. Pudding; 12. Rum; 13. Stick; 14. Sunday; 15. Syrup.

"Each little log," explains the leader, "belongs to a different sort of tree, and it is up to you to name them all correctly. The word on each log is the clue. It suggests the name of the tree it once was, before George Washington made it what it is today. Thus the poor little thing here marked 'bark' was, of course, birch. Now go on with the story."

The guests are given cards and pencils and, if they turn in a correct list, it reads as follows:

1. Birch; 2. Ash; 3. Cedar; 4. Gum; 5. Apple; 6. Holly; 7. Elm; 8. Pine; 9. Olive; 10. Balsam; 11. Plum; 12. Bay; 13. Hickory; 14. Palm; 15. Maple.

SOMETHING NEW IN HATCHETS—Each guest is given a circle of red tissue paper and told to tear out a hatchet from it.

Anything that remotely resembles a hatchet is numbered and pinned on the wall. Guests vote for the best. Any hatchet that receives even one vote other than that of its owner makes the prize-winning class.

Did They Bury the Hatchet?—The big question before the house is "What became of George Washington's hatchet?" The investigation goes into the matter thoroughly, with nation-rocking disclosures. The players sit in a circle. The leader starts the probe by demanding of his left-hand neighbor, "What became of George Washington's hatchet?"

Before ten can be counted, the questioned one must make a reply—the more insane the better!—always using a last word for which a rime can be found. Such as, for instance, "It's in the pastor's cellar." And next it is the questioner's turn to think fast, for he must comment on this with a line that rimes and yet makes sense as "Oh, you story-teller!"

The player who attempted to cast allegations at the pastor's cellar, now turns questioner and sternly asks his left-hand neighbor, "What became of George Washington's hatchet?" The answer could be: "It fell in the ocean," which calls for the pat comment, "An outlandish notion!;" or, "Our leader wore it out," to which an easy reply would be, "No doubt! No doubt!"

Thus the probe goes merrily on, around the circle. Anyone who finds himself stumped for a riming reply can be helped by any of the other players, but must pay a stiff forfeit for this service.

A qualified "judge" sits in the circle to rule out lines too difficult for riming such as, "It's stored in mothballs;" or riming errors which come thick and fast as forfeits mount. For example, when the reply, "It's in the Smithsonian," draws the excited comment, "Marked 'Early Colonian.'"

Three forfeits put a player out.

Ax Me Another—This is a game that reduces players and onlookers alike to helpless laughter.

The rival teams line up in column formation, about ten feet apart, with a captain heading each column. Each captain is given a cardboard hatchet. A bowl is on the floor at the foot of each line, and at the opposite end of the course stand homemade "cherry trees," one for each team, on chairs or platforms. These trees are branches of any thorny shrub, with one cranberry for each player thrust on the thorns.

On the word "Go!" the leader of each team rushes up to his team's cherry tree, picks a cherry, puts it on his hatchet and hurries back with it to the starting line, where he deposits it in the bowl. He then hands his hatchet to Player Two. This business is repeated until every player has brought home his cherry and the tree is bare. The first side to finish with no errors wins.

The fun of the game rests largely in that each player must repeatedly chant, "Ax me another. Ax me another," as he races over the course to the tree. When the cherry is safely on his hatchet, he changes his tune to, "I did it with my little hatchet!" and must continue this song of exultation until the cherry is safely in the bowl. If he drops the cherry, he must immediately revert to "Ax me another," and keep up his melancholy chant all the time he is groping for the lost treasure. Having discovered it and placed it on his hatchet, he must burst forth again into, "I did it with my little hatchet!"

Every time a runner laughs, it is counted an error for his side. It adds to the hilarity for the men to assume a high falsetto for the contest and the girls a deep bass.

CHIPPER PRIZES—The prizes may be anything amusingly consistent, from a glass of chipped beef to a package of soap chips.

CHIPSY CHANCE—The theme of the banquet provides an excellent chance for making a collection for any persons or cause. The hostess simply announces it, then passes George's three-cornered hat, with a cherry "Now, chip in, everybody!"

CHOP SUEY OF IDEAS—In Washington's day, it was the custom to enjoy an old-fashioned supper. Invitations could be written on large, legal-size paper and sealed with wax as they were in the days of old before envelopes were used.

The supper might be served, as it was then, with everything on the table. It might consist of:

Raw Oysters on the Half Shell

Fried Chicken

Warm Biscuits   Cold Virginia Ham

Lettuce Salad Garnished with Hard-boiled Eggs

Cheese   Frozen Custard   Pound Cake

Tea   Coffee

Or the hostess can make any menu conform to colonial times by confining it to strictly American dishes, such as baked beans, brown bread, scalloped oysters, corn muffins, and ice cream.

A THIRTEEN-COLONIES MENU—Some organizations have favorite menus which they have tried in the past with marked success and like to repeat. These can be made to fit the occasion by simply naming the various dishes for the thirteen original colonies. For instance:

Connecticut Cocktail

New Jersey Capon with Massachusetts Poultry Stuffing

New York Creamed Onions   New Hampshire Spinach

Maryland Celery Curls   Rhode Island Radish Roses

Pennsylvania Bread and Butter Sandwiches
(hatchet shaped)

Virginia Martha Washington Pie

Delaware Candy Hatchets and Cherries

South Carolina Salted Nuts   North Carolina Mints

Georgia Coffee

Recipes

MARTHA WASHINGTON PIE WITH CANDIED CHERRY TRIM

1/3 cup shortening

1 cup sugar

2 eggs

1 1/2 cups flour

2 teaspoons baking powder

1/2 pint cream

Citron

1/2 cup milk

1 teaspoon vanilla

3/4 cup chopped nuts,
    walnuts or pecans

1/4 teaspoon salt

Candied cherries

Cream the shortening and sugar together. Add the eggs beaten until light. Sift the flour, baking powder, and salt together and add, alternating with milk, to the first mixture. Beat thoroughly and add the vanilla and nuts. Bake in two-layer cake pans in a hot oven (375 to 400 F.) When cool, put whipped cream, sweetened and flavored, between the layers and on top. Decorate with candied cherries, and citron cut in thin strips.

AN EASY WASHINGTON PIE

Use any layer cake recipe. Bake in pie plates and put together with thick raspberry jam, having four layers of cake. Dust thickly on top with powdered sugar. Place twenty-two candles around cake, alternating red, white and blue candles. In the center of cake, and around the base of the plate, arrange a few sprays of artificial cherries.

CHERRY PIE

Roll the pastry one fourth of an inch thick and use to line a small, deep pie plate. Trim off extra pastry. Strain the juice from one can of cherries and remove the stones, if they are not already stoned. Put the fruit in a pie plate. Mix one half a cup of juice with two tablespoons of sugar, one tablespoon of quick-cooking tapioca and few grains of salt and pour over the fruit. Roll the pastry one fourth of an inch thick.

Wet the edges of the under crust, cut small gashes to resemble a tree on the upper crust, and lay on top of the pie. Trim the edges and turn under the under crust. Brush with water, milk, or slightly beaten egg and bake ten minutes in a hot oven at 450 F. Then reduce the heat and bake at 325 F. until the pastry is brown, or about thirty minutes in all.

FRENCH CHERRY TARTLETS

This is a more "partified" dessert. Bake the pastry on the outside of four individual tins. Put three fourths of a cup of juice from canned cherries in a saucepan, add two tablespoons sugar mixed with one tablespoon of cornstarch and stir until the boiling point is reached and the mixture is thick. Cook ten minutes over hot water and cool slightly.

Fill the tartlet shells with cherries, cover with thickened juice, and chill. Serve with whipped cream sprinkled with chopped pecans.

MOCK CHERRY PIE

Mix one and a half cups of cranberries cut in halves, three fourths of a cup of seeded and shredded raisins, one cup of sugar and one tablespoon of flour. Pile this mixture in a pie pan lined with flaky pastry. Dot over with one table-spoon of butter, add two tablespoons of orange juice. Cover with the upper crust, crimp the edges, and bake thirty-five minutes in a hot oven. The initial heat should be strong to set the pastry, after which the heat may be reduced.

A SPRING SPOOF BANQUET

"When daffodils begin to daff and pussy willows purr," the whole world turns skittish and wants to play. Spring is in the very air. One sniff, and—tra-la-la!—we have caught springitis so badly that we are likely to break out any minute! Then is the time to play safe and spring a profit-making or purely social for church or club "banquet."

The quotation marks on "banquet" signify that this need not be a formal banquet or even an informal dinner. The menu can be as simple, spoofed, or serve-self as wished. Instead of being the usual heavy feature, the meal may be little more than light refreshments.

SPRING SPOOF MONEY-RAISER—Perhaps the club's treasury is depleted, and while members do not feel equal to putting on an ambitious money-making project like a bazaar, yet they would like to give a social affair that not only pays its way, but makes a little profit besides. So they plan a few easy attractions, "free for a dime," and a booth or two selling spring-like trifles, and watch the money roll in.

DATE OF BANQUET—A spring spoof banquet in its main features, is suitable for March twenty-first, the beginning of spring, clear through to summer. If one particular month is to be stressed, all that is necessary is to add to the invitation, decorations, program, and refreshments a few individual touches symbolic or characteristic of the chosen month, such as kites for March, rainbows for April, and birds for May.

SPRING SPOOF POSTERS—The posters may be either springy or spoofy. They may be fancy with daffodils, apple blossoms, tulips; or funny with a sketch of a chirping bird, with "Tweet-tweet! Spring is here!" issuing from its ecstatic throat, above a cavorting lamb with "Bleat, bleat! Spring is here!" coming from its woolly throat. For an April first banquet, "Cuckoo!" can come from the bird's foolish throat. For Easter, "chirp, chirp!" may issue from a fluffy little chick on the half shell; and for May, when bird banquets are the thing, a warbler on a flowering twig may be sketched with its song caroling from an open beak in tiny music notes.

If the spring banquet is given in March, a roaring lion may be added to the bleating lamb.

SPRING SPOOF INVITATIONS—If invitations are in order, tinted correspondence cards may be decorated with one of the intriguing little spring favors with which the stores abound. The favors may be: sprig of pussy willow glued in one corner of a soft gray, silver-edged card; a couple of artificial violets, their stalks thrust through a double slit cut in a lavender card; a mite of a garden tool glued to the top of a green card; a downy yellow chick to a purple one; or a wee cotton bunny, bereft of his carrot and hugging instead a capsule holding a rolled slip of paper on which is written an absurd prescription for spring fever or a rosy prophecy for the spring romance.

The "pome" for both poster and invitation may be as follows:

> Oh, spring is in the treetops,
> And spring is in the heart;
> We want to turn an handspring,
> But don't know how to start.
>
> We want to sing the spring song,
> But don't know how to sing it;
> We want to spring spoof banquet;
> Hurrah! Come on; let's spring it!

The last line but one of the invitation can be changed to suit the occasion; for example, "We want an Easter banquet, a foolish banquet (April first), a May move banquet, a birdhouse banquet, a rainbow, hobo, umbrella" etc.

All the necessary information is added. If it is a pay affair, the price of the ticket is clearly marked, also if wished, the postscript, "Prizes awarded for the springiest costume and manner."

This postscript, also, can be changed to suit the banquet theme; as, "Prizes offered for the most eggs-traordinary costume," or the craziest, trickiest, most moving and so on.

SPRING SPOOF DECORATIONS—Every season has its mile-a-minute decorations, and, undoubtedly, Spring's is the apple blossom bough. A group of girls can make a whole orchard in a jiffy, and have the banquet room a froth of pink and white blossoms in another. All they need is some tissue paper, in white and two shades of pink, a few leafless boughs, a spool of florist's wire, a pair of scissors and a spare evening.

Scores of little paper circles are cut and each is folded from the center to resemble a wee, half-closed parasol. These "blossoms" are wired singly or in clusters on a bushy bough, and the effect is natural and lovely. In addition to the boughs, a few twigs are made small enough to be used in vases, bowls, and baskets, banked on radiators, piano, or tables, twisted around chandeliers, or tied to window catches or chair backs.

A few pink and green balloons may be added, also a caged canary that warbles, regardless of whether the brightness around it is natural sunshine or electric light; and an effect is achieved that is guaranteed to inspire the Spring Poet to add another stanza.

TABLE DECORATIONS—If there are several tables, each can feature a different well-known sign of spring. The head table, presided over by the emcee, is where the Spring Poet holds forth. His wife, Spring Cleaning, presides at another table, and may serve as pianist when required. He wears a velveteen coat, a soft shirt with a picturesque flowing tie, a long haircut, and a distraught expression, and scribbles sonnets on a huge writing tablet, which may carry the printed program for table events and after-banquet entertainment.

Spring Cleaning wears a dust cap and bungalow apron, and carries a broom and dustpan in her hand. She is constantly "ridding up" the apple orchard, stuffing into her wastebasket the "pomes" that her inspired husband begins, despairs of, tears off his writing tablet, and flings on the floor.

Her table, placarded, "Spring Cleaning," can have as a centerpiece a feather brush blooming in a small new pail. The favors can be guest-size tablets of soap. The covers of menu and program are decorated with cutouts of cleaning aids and utensils.

Spring millinery can be featured at another table, the centerpiece being a hatbox on which rests a wierd new spring hat. Ribbons radiate from the box to the place of each guest, terminating in a tiny hat made over a nut cup foundation, holding candies of rainbow hues.

Spring fever can be spoofed at another table. Here the centerpiece is an array of large bottles, each labeled "spring tonic," with boxes of vitamin pills—round, white candies as big as mothballs and patent medicine advertising matter.

At the head of the table is a guest, dressed as an intern, with "Spring Fever Specialist" lettered on his white coat. He gravely takes each fellow guest's temperature with an individual thermometer—a peppermint stick.

"Hold that in your mouth for three and a half minutes. Ah, just as I expected. You're low; very low down—subnormal. In fact, not quite but nearly imbecile!"

He then directs them to take a spring spoof vitamin, guaranteed to give them perpetual pep.

Spring Sports can be the theme at another table, featuring spring baseball or the seasonal pastimes of the youngsters—tops, kites, or marbles. In this case, the centerpiece could be a freak "pet," made up of the makings of whatever game is most popular with the group.

Are they golf enthusiasts? Then the place of honor is given to a fine specimen of the "Putter-fly," set on a raised green. Its body is made up of a row of mangy golf balls; old score cards form its wings, the intricate markings of which are merely the golfer's prayer, "Hole in one!" printed in various designs and bright colors. Its nondescript legs and bristling antennae are made of cigarettes and used matches. Its expression—either winning or losing—is inked on the head golf ball.

If the younger set prefers tennis, a Tennis Bird centerpiece is easily made. Its body is a tightly-rolled tennis net; its head, a tennis ball, with inked-in eyes; its wings, tennis rackets. If, in tune with spring, a nest is required, it can be made of a circle of new tennis shoes, in which is a hatching of tennis ball eggs.

MENU—If the banquet is to be "springy," any seasonal menu is in order, such as roast lamb with mint sauce as the main dish, served with new potatoes and garden peas; peach ice cream, or pink jello with a spring bonnet of whipped cream, accompanied by little pink, green, and white frosted cakes, each decorated with cut gumdrop flowers. A crab-meat cocktail, arranged to form a rose, radish roses, and little rose cakes tie in with the theme. Favors can be pink and white Jordan almonds in containers appropriate to the month, as, in April, in nut cups hidden under fool's caps; for a May affair, in dainty flower baskets or in nests.

SPRING THAW—A game or contest may be provided for first-comers, so that they don't get frozen past all hope of a spring thaw. Here is one suitable for any spring program.

As the guests arrive, they are greeted by the Spring Poet and his wife, who hand each a card and pencil, and direct them to a wall on which is thumbtacked an unfinished spring "pome." The poet's wife explains that this is the product of her husband's frenzied genius; that he wrote three lines and then got stuck. Will they help him out by supplying a fourth line, correct in line and meter, if possible, but, in any case, a fourth line? Prizes are to be awarded the writers of the winning last lines.

The unfinished verse reads:

> Oh, Spring is here! And out of doors
> The seeds grow better every day;
> I know that spring is here, because

Winning last lines might be: "My feet, they always ache this way," or, "My wife cleans house the livelong day!"

SPRING BONNETS—Here is a merry game that gets any crowd going. Each girl is given a roll containing two lengths of crepe paper, in contrasting shades, and then directed to a table on which are scissors, papers of pins, and spools of thread with a big-eyed needle tied to the end.

It is then announced that on the word to start, she is to make her partner a spring bonnet, which he must wear for the rest of the evening. A fine of ten cents is levied each time the unfortunate model is found hatless. For an April banquet, a prize may be offered for the most decorative fool's cap.

SPRING MIXER—This is an old favorite in a new spring dress. A number of slips are prepared on each of which is written a different sign of spring. One of these is pinned to the back of each guest so that he does not see what is written.

The announcement is made that each guest is a walking sign of spring, and every player is to find out what his particular sign is. He may get the information by quizzing fellow guests, but no questions are allowed except those which can be answered by "Yes," "No," or "I don't know." Should he discover his sign, he is to whisper it to the Spring Poet's wife, and if correct, she will remove the card from his back and pin it on his chest. He can then drop out of the game, or remain to answer the questions of his still unenlightened friends.

The signs might read: spring fever, spring cleaning, spring chicken, spring showers, spring thaw, spring lamb, spring frogs, spring romances, spring hats. If more are needed, baseball, tops, kites, skipping ropes, marbles, birds' nests, rainbows, etc., may be added.

Spring Poets—The program committee previously types on oblongs of pink-tinted paper several four-lined spring "pomes," one for every couple attending. When all are typed, they cut the last line from each, putting all last lines in one basket and the shorn verses in another.

Girls draw from the last line basket, men from the other. The girls especially are warned to keep their lines a secret. No hints are allowed.

When all have drawn, it is announced that every man is to find his partner by going to each girl in turn and reciting his three-line verse—with gestures, please! If she has the missing line, she will say so; if not, she will smile indulgently at his rhapsody and shake her head, which means that he must inflict his poem on the next girl, and so on until his last line is found.

With all the poets doing their stuff at the same time, there can be no question but what the banquet is out to tell the world that Spring is here.

More Poetry—As the poets find partners, they are asked to select a cozy corner where the girl can memorize the verse—the man will probably know it well enough to say it backwards! Then they are to invent a tune for it, because when the banquet is served, the cards are to be collected, and between courses, or after the banquet, couples are to be asked to sing their spring poem, "with actions."

The dissected poems are simple, all the first lines being the same. If more are needed, a ready jingler on the program committee can easily compose them, being sure to choose rhymes that have not the same sound as those already used, otherwise two poets will be claiming the last line of the same lady, resulting in the "infernal triangle!"

The poems could run as follows:

> The thing I like about the spring
>   Is not a new-found thirst;
> I love to plant some early peas
>   And have 'em come up first.

> The thing I like about the spring
>   Is not spring fever—No!
> I like to study summer trips,
>   And wonder where I'll go.

> The thing I like about the spring
>   Is not my throbbing bunions;
> I do not like the way they act
>   But oh, you young spring onions!

> The thing I like about the spring
>   Is not last winter's bills;
> I like to play-pretend they're paid
>   And buy some daffodils.

> The thing I like about the spring
>   Is not the baseball star;
> I love to watch the little lambs
>   And listen to them baa.

> The thing I like about the spring
>   Is not that itching rash;
> I like to get new ties and socks
>   That match—and cut a dash!

SPRING SPOOF MILLINERY SHOW—Attics and rummage sales may be ransacked for enough ancient ladies' hats to outfit the models. Each atrocity is put in a paper bag, on the outside of which is written the name of the man whom the hat is to adorn.

On the night of the banquet, each "manikin" is given a name for the creation he is to model, as "breath o' spring." Each girl takes the first bag her hand touches, searches for the man whose name is on the bag, and then leads him off to some secluded nook where she can dress him up in his new spring bonnet.

When all are ready, the style show is announced. The viewers are asked to show their approval of the new styles in hats by their applause.

This stunt may become a contest as well as a show by telling each model to assume the expression and pose pantomiming the adjective handed to him with the hat. These can be haughty, coy, delicate, frivolous, dreamy, vivacious, queenly, tender, hard-boiled, scornful, elusive, intellectual, etc.

The viewers are given cards and pencils and asked to jot down the adjective the model seems to be trying to pantomime. The guesses will be woefully wide. For example, the man who demonstrated the words "intellectual" and fancied he did it rather well, will be cut to the quick because one viewer thought he was seasick and another thought he was feeble-minded!

Spring Choir—A quartet in costume could sing from the stage good spring numbers such as: "I'm Always Chasing Rainbows," "April Showers," "Wishing on a Star," then give ridiculous little take-offs as encores. For instance, the prima donna could bow her acknowledgment of applause for a really fine number, then announce that she will now give a spring selection, entitled, "The Lost Lamb."

A most elaborate introduction is given by her accompanist. Then the singer inflates her chest, opens her mouth, and bleats out the one word, "Ba-a-a-a!"

Another good encore piece is to have a soulful tenor sing with great expression:

> In the s-s-spring-time, when I hold somebody's hand;
> In the s-s-spring-time, oh, then I understand.

He pauses for effect, while the pianist picks out a few exquisite notes to prepare audience for the next rhapsody, and then continues:

> Why all the little bears-es, and all the little bees-es,
> Always go in pairs-es, and never go in threes-es,
>   (With much feeling)
> In the s-s-spring-time when I hold somebody's hand!

Spring Spoof Money-makers

BROOMS FOR SALE—The Spring Poet's wife can sell these brooms for a dime each. They are all-day suckers, with fringed paper arranged over the flat candy end to resemble the bristles of a broom.

MARCH BOOTH—March is a pretty blonde, dressed as an Irish maiden in green crepe paper. Under one arm she carries a woolly lamb, under the other a toy lion, both on wheels, so that she can drag the lion after her when she walks up the room, and the lamb when she walks down toward the exit.

When the guests have arrived, she takes her place behind the March booth, which is hung with Japanese windbells, pussy willows, balloons, and toy kites. A huge box kite, covered with yellow paper, makes a shade over the light. To its tail are tied scores of little twists of yellow and green paper, on each of which is typed a spring fortune, such as:

> In the spring a young girl's fancy
> Lightly turns to hats and frocks;
>
> Ponder this! 'Twill keep your bark off
> Many matrimonial rocks!

Fortunes for the girls are typed on yellow paper; for the men, on green; and these may be sold for a dime each.

March also sells other souvenirs such as: blow-out toys and whistles; collapsible balloons; china cats, with tiny bunches of pussy willow tied with a green ribbon bow around their necks; rabbit's foot charms; inexpensive copies of "Alice In Wonderland," marked "Introducing the March Hare."

The lion may be represented by a toy, or a small reproduction of the Barye lion or the famous Perry picture of a lion. A Dresden china shepherdess can be prominently displayed, surrounded by a flock of fluffy little lambs, either purchased at a dime store, or made at home out of cotton wool, pipe cleaners, and mucilage.

SPRING SPOOF BOOTH—This booth is in charge of a jester in traditional King's fool costume: a red blouse with full bishop sleeves and long-pointed yellow cuffs and a double skirt gathered full halfway to the knees and made in pointed scallops of alternating yellow and red, with a little bell at each point; odd stockings, one yellow, the other red, with a red sandal on the yellow leg, and vice versa. The sandals have sharply pointed toes with a bell at the tip. A red leather belt fits snugly around the waist, and the cap is peaked, yellow and red, with bells on the hood. A yellow-lined red cape completes the costume, which can be made of crepe paper, with sandals of canton flannel.

The jester sells spring or "spoof" novelties, such as a jack in-the-box; rubber pencils that bend as one writes; small wooden boxes, out of which spring long green snakes when the covers are lifted; beanies or lapel flowers that flash a light when a bulb, concealed in the pocket, is squeezed; and so on.

The jester has an extra cap, which every so often he slyly slips on some unsuspecting person's head. This unfortunate must then mount the platform and tell a joke on himself or relate the most foolish thing he ever did in his life.

He can buy his release by paying a dime or a forfeit. The forfeit may place him in a worse predicament. For instance, he may find himself in the spotlight, with the whole roomful of guests breathlessly listening to his floundering attempts to answer the Spring Poet's question, "Do you always like your girl friend's new hats? If not, why not?" Or, "Describe in detail any hat worn by your wife when you were courting her."

The girls may fare no better when confronted with Spring Cleaning's question: "Does your husband keep his temper during house-cleaning time?" Or, "Does he take down the storm windows and put in the window screens the first time you ask him? What is his most annoying excuse?"

LADY APRIL'S BOOTH—This booth is placed under a beautiful rainbow cut from compo board, covered with crepe paper in prismatic colors, and veiled with cheesecloth splashed with silver. Lady April wears a raincoat and a slouch hat in one of the dainty new colors, and stands in a shower of silver raindrops. The raindrops are clear glass beads strung on fine threads and knotted in place at irregular intervals. An occasional irridescent one catches the light and sparkles like the real thing. The strings of raindrops are tied to concealed wires overhead. Out in front of the booth is a little "rain barrel," its top filled with a circle of cardboard, covered with silver paper. A hole is cut in it just large enough to admit a hand and pull out a gift. The charge is a dime a grab.

Toy watering cans are also sold, the tiny ones being lined with waxed paper and filled with pretty little candies, the larger ones with silver confetti with which to shower other guests.

A GO-GETTER GARDEN BANQUET

A seed catalog in the mail! Hoe! Hoe! Spring is here! And suddenly everybody is out to say it with flowers or early radishes. Country acre, suburban backyard, or city window box—all must go get a garden. Well, this banquet is that way, too!

INVITATIONS—Each invitation is written on a sheet of tinted note paper, then folded small and clipped to a small package of flower seeds—they come in tiny envelopes—which is then placed in the envelope matching the note paper.

The invitation can be decorated with a small colored picture of a spring flower or vegetable, cut from a seed catalog and pasted in place. These lines below may be written or typed:

> Oh, gardener or gardenette,
> Pray, can you grow gardenias,
> And violets and mignonette,
> And string and other beanias,
>   And mushrooms and azaleas,
>   With hardly any faileas?
> Our banquet's full of helpful hints
> To experts and beginnias
> On how to raise in tony tints
> Green onions, snails, and zinnias.
>   Attend this grand go-gettera
>   In garden hat, et cetera!

The day, date, time, and place and the words, "Go-Getter Garden Banquet," should be added.

GO-GETTER GARDEN DECORATIONS—The decorations need not cost a cent. All the committee need do is go get 'em: their own garden tools, and the neighbors'; house plants, home-grown and borrowed; seed catalogs; porch and garden furniture; green ferns, vines, and branches; and a few oddments from potting shed and workshop. A piece of old tarpaulin can masquerade as the good earth. Laid on the floor, it will represent "the soil" of the garden banquet, in fact as well as in fancy. If there is a stage, artificial grass mats can be used to make a lawn, with potted geraniums here and there to suggest a flower garden.

GO-GETTER GARDEN—The banquet hall represents a spring garden in the making. The committee should work for laughs rather than loveliness. They should move out as much stuffy good furniture as posible, and bring in the open-air wicker set. The family goldfish may swim around in an improvised lily pond, made from a child's rubber wading pool, or by placing a washtub on several fruit crates and covering all crudities with green moss, vines, small growing plants, the hall fern, or what have you? A shallow, white china bowl looks enough like a water lily—and agrees with the goldfish better than a paraffin-waxed flower! A tin basin, set on the vacated fern stand, makes a birdbath. A celluloid bird on the rim cinches it. A taller fern stand topped by a small, round tray, with almost anything for a pointer, becomes the sundial.

The hall tree, a leafy branch tied to each peg, and topped with a small birdhouse, becomes a glad omen of spring. Watering cans make suitable vases, the flower stems of small flowers being thrust into the holes of the rose sprinkler. Tennis nets, with vines threaded through the mesh, are invaluable as verdant backgrounds, as screens to hide the radiators or ugly spots, as garden hedges, and so forth.

THE GO-GETTER GARDEN ENTRANCE—First impressions mean a lot, so the committee in charge of decorations should use its ingenuity to make a clever gate in the doorway of the vestibule or reception room, where early birds assemble to await the summons to the banquet hall. A wicket gate is easily made of cardboard or plywood palings, or a more substantial one of rustic tree branches. Vines can fall from the door frame, and a wheelbarrow, rake, and hoe can flank the sides for atmosphere.

A less fancy but funnier entrance is achieved by simply draping lengths of garden hose in a circle in the doorway, so that guests must worry through it to enter.

GO-GETTER GARDENERS—The gardeners are members of the receiving committee, the girls being dressed in decorative smocks and pretty shade bonnets, the men in disreputable overalls and torn straw hats. The official greeting of the men is a jolly, "Well, what do you hoe?" The girls hand to each guest a pencil and a double card, the cover of which is decorated with a bright seed catalog flower, under which is printed, "Go and guess the exhibits in the flower show."

If preferred, guests who have arrived without the head-gear requested in the invitation may be led to a table on which there are all the makings for hats—crepe paper, scissors, pins, thread, needles, a made-up model hat—and told to "go getter garden hat."

Go-Getter Flower Show—First arrivals are directed to the fake exhibit by a freckled lad in faded overalls. The show is arranged on card tables, and each entry has been given a distinguishing number. The freckled boy explains that each entry represents some flower, and guests are to write down opposite its number on their cards the name of the flower which they think that particular exhibit represents.

These entries should not be too difficult to guess, for the object of the starter game is to amuse rather than absorb the first-comers.

The show could contain such exhibits as: 1. Two pictures, each of a flock of sheep (phlox); 2. Several rows of buttons, toothpicks, matches (rose); 3. A clock with the hands stopped at 4 (four o'clock); 4. Fox fur, or a picture of a fox, and one glove (foxglove); 5. A cup, with a pat of butter in it (buttercup); 6. A safety pin (bachelor's button); 7. A few dried peas in a saucer of sugar (sweet peas); 8. A toy oar and old kid glove (orchid); 9. A dress snap and picture of a dragon (snapdragon); 10. A picture of a steaming cup of coffee (morning glory).

Other flowers easily represented are: jonquil, hollyhock, dogwood, dandelion, lady's slipper, bluebell, sweet William, sunflower, larkspur, snowball, bridal wreath, pansy, tulip, poppy, marigold, Johnny-jump-up, etc.

When all the guests have arrived, Freckles collects the cards and pencils, after making sure that all guests have signed their cards.

Go-Getter Garden March—The song, led by a peppy song leader, can be rehearsed while the guests are waiting for the dinner bell. Copies of the words may be handed out, or the leader can sing the verses, while the guests join him in the simple chorus. It is sung to the well-known tune of "My

Bonnie Lies Over the Ocean," and guests, in couples, march into the banquet hall as they sing. The words are:

> Oh, come to our Go-Getters' Banquet;
> It's just what its title implies;
> And dressed in your best garden outfit,
> Compete for the best garden prize.

The chorus, to which all give their roaring best, goes:

> Com—pete,
> Com—pete,
> Compete for the best garden prize, yes, prize!
> Com—pete,
> Com—pete,
> Compete for the best garden prize!

TABLE DECORATIONS—Nothing fancy! Instead of the usual vases of flowers, pyramids of little red flower pots adorn the tables, with tassels of gardener's raffia streaming out of the holes in the base of the pots.

The place cards are the wooden labels used to mark where the carrots should come up.

The favors are sets of the miniature garden tools—rake, spade and hoe, to be found in most dime stores; or tiny hand-sewn gardening gloves, each with a wee green thumb.

MENU CARD—The menu card may be an earth-brown folder, tied with spring-green ribbon, the cover decorated with any colored cutout of garden needs or equipment, from wheelbarrows to weed killers. The menu follows:

> All the birds left us
> (Fruit Cocktail)
> A Garden Interloper, Caught and Cooked
> (Chicken a la King)

Gold Medal Award	Blue Ribbon Award
Grown by (name of guest)	Grown by (name of guest)
(Buttered New Peas)	(Potatoes)

> First Prize, County Fair
> Raised by (name of guest)
> (Rolls)
> All the rabbits left us (Spring Salad)
> Evergreen (Olives)   All the mice left us (Cheese Straws)
> Go-Getter Garden Plant
> (Chocolate Ice Cream)

| Nosegay | The Grind | Candytuft |
| (Flower-shaped Cookies) | (Coffee) | (Bonbons) |

The chocolate ice cream is served in sanitary drinking cups. They are placed in tiny flowerpots which can be purchased from the florist. A sweet pea is stuck in the top of each pot. The happy effect is that of a tiny potted plant.

The nosegay cookies, shaped like flowers, may be made gay with different colored icings.

GO-GETTER PRIZES—A daintily-wrapped box, labeled "Head Prize," contains a head of cabbage. Another, expensively small, contains a dime package of Japanese water flowers labeled, "All you have to do to raise a garden is drop a few in a glass of water."

Leis of radishes and onions or corsages of carrots and turnips with salad greens foliage, may be presented to the speakers.

BANQUET PROGRAM—If music is needed, live or recorded, any song with a flowery title is suitable, such as "It's Raining Violets," "Lilac Time," "Moonlight and Roses," and "Tiptoe Through the Tulips with Me."

GARDEN PESTS—The guests are given pencil and paper, and asked to draw any sort of garden pest. They are to sign their sketches, but not name the "critter." These drawings are collected, and later hung in a rogues' gallery for others to guess what they are supposed to be.

KNOW YOUR VEGETABLES—This game is a verbal quiz, so requires no paper or pencils. One of the speakers listed on the program may ask the questions. Any guest at the table may shout the answer.

1. What vegetable does a policeman walk on?
2. What vegetable is a plumber's delight?
3. What vegetable is found in the laundry?
4. What vegetable do you find on bargain day at . . . ? (Insert the name of a well-known store.)
5. What vegetable is an invitation?
6. What vegetable has been through fire?
7. What herb is full of regret?

8. What herb is most learned?
9. What herb is most comforting?
10. What herb is most dreaded by women?
11. What herb is found in the stable?
12. What herb is a money-maker?

The answers are: 1, beet; 2, leek; 3, mangel; 4, squash; 5, lettuce; 6, chard; 7, rue; 8, sage; 9, balm; 10, thyme; 11, sorrel; 12, mint.

MOCK LECTURE—The speaker has been chosen because he knows nothing at all about gardening and admits it. He speaks from notes so vague that even when viewed intently through a large, round magnifying glass they leave him lost. He begins in a hesitant manner to give his formal speech, as follows:

"Fellow Gardeners: Have you ever thought of your life without spring? Without the return of the robin or the green in the trees?" Here he loses his place; peers through the magnifying glass; hunts through his pockets for the paper containing his notes; comes up with the milk bill, laundry slip, theater tickets, etc., but no notes.

He clears his throat, and begins again: "Fellow gardeners, have you ever thought of your life without spring? Without the return of the robin or the green in the trees?"

Again, he bogs down. He whispers to the guest next to him, who, after a few pretended failures to hear him, finally stumbles up to bring him a glass of ice water. The speaker gulps it down.

He begins for the third time: "Fellow gardeners, have you ever thought of your life without spring? Without the return of the robin or the green in the trees?"

It's no good! His prepared speech has left him. Abandoning all attempts to be an orator, he thrusts his hands into his pockets and begins just to talk as follows:

"Look, folks! Remember how that invitation promised you 'helpful hints on how to raise in tony tints, green onions, snails, and zinnias'? Well, they picked on me to give those helpful hints. I ask your sympathy. It could have been you! As you know, I'm no authority on how to raise anything. I can't even raise the roof. And as to growing a garden, well,

I have a little notebook here in my pocket—a book in which I jotted down my garden report for last year. Here it is: I planted a pussy willow, and up came a catnip. I planted a rambler, and up came a hobo. I planted an iris, and up came a doll's eye. I planted some thyme, and up came a century plant. I planted a Jack-in-the-pulpit, and up came the calling card of the Rev. John Johnson. I planted a forget-me-not, and up came an old unpaid doctor's bill. I planted a date, and up came a calendar. I planted a trumpet vine, and up came a tin horn.

"By this list of garden failures, you will see I am not the person to give you hints on how to raise in tony tints, green onions, snails, and zinnias. Once I did sow some green onions. Nothing came up but this . . ."

He produces from his pocket, or from under the table, if the specimen is large, any appropriate trick toy insect or garden pest, such as a snake that pops out of some harmless-looking box, or one of those slithering, wiggling green and yellow pull-toys—the sort of caterpillar one might see in a nightmare—called a cata-puller.

If he can sing, he can warble to the tune of "Polly-Wolly Doodle" the following words:

> Said a thousand-legged worm,
> As he gave a little squirm,
> "Has anybody seen a leg o'mine?
> If it can't be found, I'll have to hop around
> On the other nine hundred and ninety-nine.
>
> "Hop around, hop around, on the other
> Nine hundred and ninety-nine;
> If it can't be found, I'll have to hop around
> On the other nine hundred and ninety-nine."

MIXED FRUITS AND VEGETABLES—This game is a good after-dinner teaser. The guests are divided into equal classes. A blackboard is set up so that all have a good view of it. The "professor" writes down the name of a fruit or vegetable, with all the letters jumbled. Perhaps he had better print it.

"What is it?" he asks the class. The one who first calls out the correct name scores one for his class, and the class with most scores to its credit may ask any stunt of the losers. The list follows:

1. Oomatt; 2. Nabaan; 3. Abbhurr; 4. Shiard; 5. Pishcan; 6. Groane; 7. Unpirt; 8. Porcati; 9. Ahussq; 10. Pagrusasa; 11. Culteet; 12. Leeyrc; 13. Klomnumse; 14. Rustcran; 15. Rafelluwoci; 16. Leetnowarm; 17. Hockerati; 18 Breyarrnc; 19. Engreatin; 20. Ciborloc; 21. Nilpeeppa; 22. Craylkrebb; 23. Brumuecc; 24. Ansiri.

The answers are: 1. Tomato; 2. Banana; 3. Rhubarb; 4. Radish; 5. Spinach; 6. Orange; 7. Turnip; 8. Apricot; 9. Squash; 10. Asparagus; 11. Lettuce; 12. Celery; 13. Muskmelon; 14. Currants; 15. Cauliflower; 16. Watermelon; 17. Artichoke; 18. Cranberry; 19. Tangerine; 20. Broccoli; 21. Pineapple; 22. Blackberry; 23. Cucumber; 24. Raisin.

A BIRD OF A BANQUET

There's a bobolink singing in the poplar and a canary in a cage, and they're both deliriously trilling to a sensibly stodgy world that spring is here and summer just around the corner, and that the month of May is to be merrier than usual this year!

The season for indoor merry meals will soon be over, and for that reason many young people's societies look for a rather special sort of affair to which they can invite parents, older church members, or maybe the young people of another church—something that lends itself to lovely decorations, all sunshine and song, in short, a bird of a banquet. And here it is!

INVITATIONS—The invitation, "a bird of a poster," shows either bluebirds or a bird house, with a family of birds dining off bird seed, and the words:

It's a bird of a banquet! Tweet-tweet!
From bird house to bird seed complete.
Since birds of a feather
Should all flock together,
Come, birdy! Come early! Tweet-tweet!
Birdhouse—(location of banquet)   Bird call—(date and time)
Admission, One Bird Whistle—Do It Yourself.

THE BIRD PRESERVE—Any decorating committee should chortle with glee at such a marvelous chance of turning a drab, prosaic hall into an exquisite bower of spring flowers, brilliant-hued birds, and flitting butterflies. For the chairman whose style is cramped without a definite color scheme, the gorgeous blue of the bluebird may be tried against the pale yellow of primroses, with the pink of apple blossom to give it that Parisian touch.

The ceiling lights can be shaded with primrose yellow paper cut into a fringe of about two feet in length. Branches of blossoming acacia or forsythia can be made by sticking hundreds of little bits of shaped yellow paper on branches brought in from garden or woods. When these branches are banked in corners on or around the stage, and a few choice twigs are placed over windows or doorways and arranged in blue bowls, that stuffy hall has already become a bit of the great outdoors.

A BIRD OF A STAGE—Whoever saw a spring bird perched against any other background but a blossoming bough? So the stage should resemble an apple orchard in the spring. Apple blossoms can be little circles of tissue paper in two tints of pink, crushed in the hand to resemble the real thing and wired on branches.

The barest twig can be made a glory of blossoms in a second by smearing it with a little good library paste, and then dipping it in a tray of vari-colored confetti. A few latticed arches and some pieces of wicker furniture complete the garden on the stage. Or two flower-twined arbors could grace the corners at the back of the stage, where sit pretty girls in mob caps and aprons fashioned of paper or cretonne of bluebird design. These girls could serve as waitresses or as assistants to the director of games, or take part in the program at the table, on the stage or the floor.

A few picturesque birdhouses made of composition board add to the picture, as also do birdbaths which, for all their look of stony solidity, are merely construction paper bowls glued on mailing tube stands, the whole being covered with paste and rolled in sand to give them that built-for-the-ages appearance.

BIRD DECORATIONS—The bird decorations are everywhere and of all sorts and sizes. Some are cut from blue construction paper, others from a decorated paper of bluebird design, mounted on cardboard. They fly from the ceiling and from doorways and dart from between the yellow fringe around the ceiling lights. They are attached to an invisible wire or thread, and since the slightest draft keeps them in motion, they are always on the wing.

Even more delightfully realistic are those cut from any of the decorated papers on which are printed gorgeously plumed birds. By pasting two identical birds together, after padding with cotton to a certain shapeliness, and outlining the underside of one with wire, a most life-like result is attained. Perched on a "tree," they would almost deceive the cat.

But, of course, they won't sing. To offset this, pet canaries are borrowed and their cages hung beneath real branches, in hopes they will sing. However, like all singers, they may prove temperamental. So behind some flowering shrub a phonograph with a bird record on should be hidden, all ready for such emergencies.

Other bird music can be produced on "canaries," clever novelties purchased at toy shops for a few cents. Several girls hidden behind a vine-covered lattice screen can fill the air with bird music whenever the signal is whistled to them from the Bird Warden or one of his deputies.

A BIRD OF A BANQUET TABLE—The speaker's table is centered with a lawn of artificial grass on which is a low birdbath, twined with real flowers matching the color scheme. On the rim, perch a few toy birds. Other tables may have, as centerpieces, small, well-branched trees, on which are four or five paper birds. Another idea is to make a birdhouse of construction paper, with two prospective feathered tenants carefully inspecting it. Paper napkins and cloth with a bluebird motif may be used.

BIRD FAVORS—A good favor is a life-saver roll covered with gray paper to form the pedestal. The bowl-shaped top, made of construction paper, is lined with silver paper, and the circle of cardboard—or lid of a small round box—which forms the base, with green paper.

A bird of a lollipop is an edible favor. The candy top is wrapped in blue paper to form the bird's body, which can have a splashy old-rose breast, if wished. A bird's head and perky tail, cut from orange paper, are added. Then the stick of the lollipop is wrapped in yellow paper, so that the bird has a leg to stand on. This leg is stuck into a large chocolate-covered mint which serves as the base and stands on a frilly, round doily of grassy green.

The just-for-a-lark favor is simply any small candy, such as hundreds-and-thousands, packed in a little paper sack, which is lettered "Just-for-a-Lark Bird Seed." These sacks may be used as place cards, if around the neck of each sack is tied a label bearing the name of the guest.

Thirsty birds are the simplest of all favors. A small celluloid parrot is perched on the rim of each water glass.

A bird of a program has as a cover design a colored sketch of a funny mother bird, feeding a nestful of five rav-

enous youngsters, all of which have their beaks wide open.
From each beak floats a "chirp balloon," bearing one word
of "A Bird of a Banquet." The mother bird has their banquet held down on the branch, by one claw. It is a long,
juicy worm. Her beak is wide open, too, and from it balloons a big-lettered "Tweet-tweet!"

The inside pages carry the menu and the program. For
example:

Menu
Fruit Cocktail
Individual Chicken Pie

Mashed Potatoes   Buttered Peas and Carrots
Rolls   Olives   Pickles
Bird's Nest Salad
Bird's Egg Gelatine with Whipped Cream
Coffee   Fruit Punch

Recipes for some of these items are given at the end of
this section.

Program
Bird Warden .... (Name of Toastmaster)
Bird Blessing
Bird Whistlers
Bird Quiz
It's for The Birds
Bluebird for Happiness

BIRD BLESSING—A little child with a clear voice sings the
well-known kindergarten blessing, "Thank You For the
World So Sweet," repeating the last two lines, one of which
is "Thank you for the birds that sing."

BIRD WHISTLERS—There will be time between the cocktail
and main course to have whistling contest among tables,
the group at each table, in turn, whistling a tune of their
own choice.

Or, instead of having his birds whistle a whole tune, the
Bird Warden may ask all to inhale deeply, and then let the
breath out in one long, drawn-out whistled note.

He then divides the group into three parts, telling one group to whistle on the note C, another on the note E, and another on the note G. Then he asks all "flocks" to whistle their respective notes in unison. If done correctly, the musical result is a bird of a whistle!

BIRD QUIZ—Between the main course and the salad, the Bird Warden conducts a rapid quiz. The table that answers his question first scores a point for that team. He starts with an easy one. He asks, "What bird is the first sign of spring?"

Everyone knows the answer, but a quick-speaking girl shouts, "Robin!" before anyone else can open his mouth. "Correct!" calls the Bird Warden, giving her table credit for it on his scorecard. Other questions are:

What bird is a symbol of happiness? ....Bluebird
What bird is a symbol of vanity? ....Peacock
What bird is a symbol of peace? ....Dove
What bird is a symbol of wisdom? ....Owl
What bird is a symbol of grace? ....Swan
What bird is a symbol of a chatterbox? ....Magpie
What bird wants a cracker? ....Parrot
What bird is a subject of a poem by Poe? ....Raven
What bird is a message bearer? ....Carrier-Pigeon
What bird is named for a group of islands? ....Canary
What bird hides its head in the sand? ....Ostrich
What bird sings by "Hallie's grave"? ....Mocking Bird
What bird is a black robber of cornfields? ....Crow
What bird is an early riser? ....Lark
What bird is credited with increase of population? ....Stork
What bird suggests a clock? .... Cuckoo
What bird suggests speed? ....Swift
What bird suggests the hereafter? ....Paradise Bird
What bird is most useful at banquets? ....Swallow
What bird sings its glorious song at night? ....Nightingale

When all questions have been answered, the Bird Warden checks his scorecard and announces results.

IT'S FOR THE BIRDS—Between the salad course and the dessert, the Bird Warden introduces Polly, a neighbor's parrot, borrowed for the evening. The cage stands on a box in which is concealed a young man who supplies the parroty voice

which proceeds to cast discretion and gossip to the winds—
and also juicy tid-bits of neighborhood scandal. The "voice"
has been notified beforehand that he has been cast in this
role, and is prepared to give a star performance. If the box
stands on the stage, far removed from the table, a micro-
phone placed inside insures that all the "dirt" will be heard!

BLUEBIRD FOR HAPPINESS—The speech of the evening can be
based on Maeterlinck's "Bluebird."

If a program of musical numbers, toasts, and speeches is
in order, rather than one of all fun, toasts can be based on
bird proverbs or phrases, such as: "Birds of a feather flock
together;" "Killing two birds with one stone;" "One swallow does not make a summer;" "Taking a bird's eye view of
things," etc.

Background music can be anything that suggests spring,
such as Mendelssohn's "Spring Song," or "It Might as Well
Be Spring."

A BIRD IN THE HAND—This is a game for the early birds. First
comers to the banquet are led by a guide to the "aviary"
and asked to write down on their cards the name of every
bird there which they recognize. The aviary is a large bush
on which hang twelve cards, each card bearing a colored
picture of some well-known bird. Dime stores sell books of
such pictures. The names of the birds are not given, but
under each illustration is a number, the highest numbers
being under the less known of the collection. Thus the
robin might be numbered one, the catbird, twelve.

The bird students are asked to keep secret their finds
from fellow students and to write on their cards the numbers one to twelve, and then against each number their guess
as to the name of the bird so numbered.

At the end of a given time, the guide reads off the correct
list and students score double the "catalog" number of each
bird. Thus a guest who correctly guesses that number twelve
is a catbird receives twenty-four for his superior intelli-
gence, while those who accurately name the robin receive
only two. The lady who totals the highest score might be
awarded a tiny boudoir pillow with the hope that she will
now start to feather her nest. The first prize for the top
man could be any bit of masculine finery, such as a flashy

tie, bearing a card reading, "Fine feathers make fine birds."
The consolation prize could be a long, black licorice "worm."

BIRD LECTURE—This number can be used on the program at
the banquet table, or later. By its previous build-up, the
audience is led to expect something educational from the
Audubon Club. Instead, the talk turns out to be advice on
how to select a wife! The overly-academic professor makes
elaborate, slow preparations before he starts. He fusses about
the lights being just so; asks that this window be opened,
and that one closed; smells the glass of iced water before
him on the desk, and asks that it be replaced by a soft drink;
searches in all pockets for his box of throat lozenges, clears
his throat noisily, and finally starts. The lecture may be as
follows:

For those in search of a wife, many things should be taken into
consideration. Women are like birds in many ways—they have
sweet voices, bright eyes; some have very long bills, and all like
gay plumage. Do not expect too many good qualities in one creature, and remember that "a bird in the hand is worth two in the
bush."

If you want a harmless, affectionate wife, consider the dove,
which is always cooing.

The crow makes a sensible wife, for she never does anything
without caws.

The goose is a simple creature, but do not arouse her anger,
or she will fly at you with hisses.

Hens make good helpmeets, if you do not mind a little peck-
ing, for they will scratch for their living, but beware of the chickens, for they are apt to be wild.

The English sparrow is a chatterbox, always quarreling with
her neighbors.

A parrot is noisy and would repeat what you tell her.

If you have a roving disposition, a swallow would make a good
companion, for she likes to be on the wing. But treat her gently or
she will homeward fly.

The peacock is a fine dresser, but vain.

The bluejay always looks well, but her voice is harsh, and she
chatters a good deal.

The catbird is soberly dressed, but she always looks neat and
trim, and she will keep you guessing as to what she will say.

A canary is a cheerful companion, and she will sing about the
house all day.

A warbler is a good singer, too, but she likes to go south for
the winter.

The swan is **recommended for grace.**

If you are fond of a lark, do not marry a stay-at-home like the cheerful wren.

Beware of the turkey that would gobble your living in no time. The eagle, too, would prey on you.

Avoid hawks lest their wildness lead you astray, and if you are not clever, keep away from owls, or they may hoot at you.

Have nothing to do with lyres.

And after you are married, beware lest you transform your bird-of-paradise into a turkey buzzard.

WHAT'S THAT BIRD?—A prize is offered to the flock which pantomimes in the most original way any member of the bird family, living, literary, or dead. The entire flock may perform, or a few "gay birds" be chosen by the Bird Warden to represent the rest. They need not confine themselves to impersonating a swallow (with castor oil as the only stage property) or the bluejay (with an imaginary corn). They can turn themselves loose on such impersonations as: the cuckoo in the clock; quail on toast; Poe's "Raven;" the four-and-twenty blackbirds baked in a pie; the cat that ate the canary; or the little bird that told me.

Recipes

BIRD NEST SALAD

Work a very little green color paste into a cream cheese until the desired tint is obtained. Season with salt and cayenne. Press the quarter of a pecan nut meat in a rounded teaspoon of the mixture; then roll with the smooth sides of butter "paddles," into egg shapes and sprinkle them with paprika. Arrange three eggs in each individual nest, made of the fine, bleached leaves of chicory or head lettuce heart leaves.

If wished, eggs can be made of cottage cheese, mixed with chopped nut meats, moistened with French dressing, shaped like eggs, and then sprinkled with parsley dust— parsley dried in the warming oven and then rubbed fine between the fingers.

TWEET-TWEET SALAD

Have a tiny bird peeping out of a broken egg in a nest of lettuce leaves. Take a shelled hard-boiled egg and cut a wedge-shaped opening in one side—not end—through the thin part of the white. Take out the yolk and mix with an equal amount of chopped cooked chicken, moisten with melted butter, season with salt and shape like a bird just coming out of a shell. A bit of peppercorn can be used for the eyes and a kernel of unpopped corn for the beak. Serve with saltines.

BIRD NEST ICE CREAM

Bake good-sized cupcakes from sponge cake batter. Hollow out the centers, and shape the outside like nests. Ice thickly and sprinkle with crumbed centers, shredded coconut, or slivers of finely-cut orange peel to give a natural rough appearance. Put a scoopful of ice cream in each nest. Serve with "yellow canaries"—birds cut from cooky dough rolled thin and frosted yellow. Ordinary white icing will do, colored with a bit of egg yolk.

BIRD'S EGG JELLO

Make lemon jello in egg molds, standing the flat end of the mold on a slice of sponge cake and smothering the cake and jello in whipped cream.

JUNIOR-SENIOR BLOSSOM BANQUET

A flower garden motif is adaptable to any sort of class flower, be it poppy or pansy, and to any class color. Sometimes the ladies of a church will undertake the giving of a flower banquet as a money-making venture.

FLOWERY INVITATIONS—The invitations show a high-handled florist's basket, full to overflowing of flowers, and the written invitation as follows:

(Name of organization)
requests your presence at the
Junior-Senior Blossom Banquet
Friday night (date)
(Place)   (Time)

DECORATIONS—Green branches and vines have magical power to transform even an ugly gymnasium into a dream of loveliness. They may be aided by flower-twined, lattice-work arbors, screens, arches, rural fences, and swinging gates, all made of whitewashed laths, with gray walls of stonewall crepe paper. An old wishing well can be added; also a sundial, a fountain, a birdbath, white garden furniture, and cages of singing canaries.

BLOSSOM-DECKED TABLES—The tables are set to form an open square, in the center of which is the loveliest bit of garden. Real flowers—the class flower, if possible—grow in it, picked out by a spotlight.

The class flower decorates the tables. Place cards can be attached to the backs of chairs. The cards are decorated in the Seniors' class colors and in keeping with the theme. Thus they could be May baskets of one color, containing place cards of the other; or large butterflies, the crepe paper wings of one color, the clothespin body painted another, could be attached to chairs with spiralled wire. The place card of one color could be tied with a ribbon of the other.

FAVORS—A tiny bottle of perfume makes a sweet bud vase favor. A hole is pierced in the cork and the stem of a wee artificial flower, such as a forget-me-not, is thrust through.

Or an adorable doll-size growing plant is made by thrusting cardboard stems of flower cutouts into a soft cream-filled chocolate-coated candy, which makes convincing soil. Finished off with a florist's frill of crepe paper in the class colors, this favor is amusingly real.

The menus can be flowery booklets, the cover decorated with flower stickers or seals, the booklet containing the menu and the program, tied with class colors.

TOASTS—Toasts could be based on the legends of three or four well-known flowers, or around the meaning each flower is supposed to have, such as: red rose, true love; daisy, innocence; carnation, courage; poppy, peace; violet, loyalty.

For group singing at the table, songs about flowers should be selected, such as "My Wild Irish Rose." For a serious reading, a beautiful poem by Grace Noll Crowell, "I Planted a Rose," to be found in her book, "Silver in the Sun."

Games and Stunts

SING IT WITH FLOWERS—Here is an amusing stunt in which the decidedly mixed chorus renders any flower song in voices alien to their natural range. Thus the girls sing bass or tenor and the boys high soprano or worse. Moreover, each vocalist is disguised, the boys with false mustaches, wigs, whiskers, bushy eyebrows, false noses, monocles, etc. The girls wear their hair in curlers, with orange-peel teeth, freak earrings, false red braids, etc.

Those in the flowery chorus quietly leave the group on some pretended errand, then go to a dressing room to don their disguises. In this room, tacked to a light frame, is a large paper screen, on which has been painted the stems and leaves of some flowers which has a round center circled with petals, such as the sunflower or daisy. The place where the "hub" of the flower would be has been carefully cut out and left vacant for a human head. Each vocalist has to put his or her face in one of these openings and keep it there while singing.

Having the paper screen in the dressing room gives a chance for a swift dress rehearsal, to see if outsize paper ears or paper-stuffed cheeks need a little more opening allowed among the painted flower petals.

When the time for the stunt arrives, the screen is brought on the stage, then the flower faces bloom on the painted stalks and sing their flower song.

The stunt may be used as a guessing contest, if each unknown vocalist, in turn, sings a solo line, with much wide mouthing and frenzied expression, while the audience tries to guess who this wild flower can possibly be.

HEAR! HEAR!—This game is an old-time favorite, easily adapted to fit almost any banquet theme. The emcee connives with two good speakers to come prepared to make a short speech composed entirely of opinions that are insultingly opposed to those held by the outraged audience.

For instance, at the blossom banquet, the first speaker waxes eloquent on how he loathes flowers—always has and always will; how there should be a law to abolish every flower-bed in the world and turn it into a cabbage patch.

The emcee warns the guests that no matter what the speaker says, every listener must applaud and shout, "Hear! Hear!" after his every statement. It may be hard to take, but any who fail to do so will be called on to make the next speech.

Scared by this threat, the audience applauds and loudly cheers, "Hear! Hear!" after such statements as "Not only hay fever, but every known disease, can be traced to some obnoxious flower!"

When the first orator is almost at the end of his speech, he gives a secret sign to the speaker who is to follow him, who then forgets to applaud and cheer, and so is called upon to pay the penalty by making the next speech.

He feigns dismay, but is pushed to his feet. The emcee warns the guests that the same proviso prevails. No matter what this second speaker says, they must applaud and shout, "Hear! Hear!" after his every statement or take the consequences.

He may eulogize the early frost that kills the flowers, the bugs that eat them, the weeds that choke them. "Hear! Hear!" the audience must shout, clapping furiously whenever he pauses for breath.

Sometimes this second speech has a surprise ending. For instance, the speaker may wind up with, "Honestly, folks, I love flowers. Always have. They're my weakness. To prove it, look what I have for you! Grew 'em myself in my own garden."

Whereupon, he signals for a waiter to bring in a tray or basket of flower souvenirs for every guest, or perhaps an orchid corsage for a guest of honor.

FLOWER BASKET—This game is played like fruit basket, except that each guest is given the name of a different flower.

The florist stands in the center of the circle, and calls, for instance, "Lily and Lilac," and instantly the two persons so named, jump up and try to exchange chairs before the florist can seat himself in either one of them. If he succeeds, then the flower which is crowded out becomes the florist.

At the call, "Flower exchange," all must change chairs, giving the florist a good chance to be seated.

PAPER AND PENCIL GAMES—Guests may be asked to make as many words as possible out of the name of the class flower, or lily of the valley, chrysanthemum, or forget-me-not. They may list while drinking a glass of water, three pink flowers, three white ones, and three blue ones; or they may unscramble such mixed-up flower names as lllbbeeu (bluebell) or untie pa (petunia).

Other scrambled flowers are: they all love lify, (lily-of-the-valley); weep esta, (sweet pea); ring moon gyrl, (morning glory); list came, (clematis); get note for m, (forget-me-not); a girldom, (marigold); me in a rug, (geranium); cant hum rhymes, (chrysanthemum); name one, (anemone); wi is a rat, (wistaria).

Any protests that "wistaria" is properly spelled "wisteria" may be squelched with the weighty fact that the former spelling is approved by the International Code of Botanical Nomenclature.

Guests may be asked to name their birth month flower. The flowers are: January, snowdrop; February, primrose; March, violet; April, daisy; May, hawthorn; June, rose; July, poppy; August, water lily; September, morning glory or goldenrod; October, aster; November, chrysanthemum; December, poinsettia.

MENU—Some husky dishes are on the menu, but boys come to the junior-senior banquet to eat as well as to admire the sweet girl graduates and other flower-like decorations. The menu follows:

Shrimp Roses

Chicken Saute

Boiled Parisian Potatoes with Parsley

Asparagus Buca Lapi

Clover Rolls   Quince Jelly

Hawaiian Salad

Flower Molded Ice Cream

Flower Wafers   Salted Nuts

Coffee

Recipes

SHRIMP ROSES
(For 50 servings)

8 cans (5¾oz.) shrimp	4 teaspoons of salt
16 large ripe tomatoes	4 cups of cocktail sauce
8 hearts of celery	5 bunches loose leaf lettuce
2 teaspoons cayenne pepper	1 pint jar stuffed olives

Drop fresh shrimps into boiling salted water and cook for twenty minutes. When cool, remove the shells and set aside the shrimps to chill. Peel ripe tomatoes and chop fine. Also finely chop a heart of celery. Combine the shrimps, chopped tomatoes and celery. Season highly with cayenne pepper and salt. Add cocktail sauce and mix well. Chill. Serve one heaping tablespoon full for each guest. Cut lettuce strips the long way of leaf and arrange on each plate like flower petals. The shrimp is served on this leaf garnished with slices of stuffed olives.

CHICKEN SAUTE

7 young chickens	1 cup sherry jelly
7 cups raw diced mushrooms	1½ quarts cream

7 egg yolks

Have the young chickens cut into eight pieces; wash them in cold water and dry thoroughly. Season with salt and pepper and saute in clarified butter until lightly browned. Cover each chicken with one cup of raw mushrooms which have been chopped into dice, cover the pan and place in a moderate oven to finish cooking—about twenty-five minutes. Keep the pan tightly covered while in the oven. Remove the pan from the oven and place it over a low flame, add two tablespoons full of sherry jelly and stir three quarters of a cup of scalded cream. Thicken the sauce with one egg yolk. Pour the sauce over the chicken and sprinkle over the sauce two tablespoons of finely chopped truffles or of stuffed olives. Makes fifty servings.

BOILED PARISIAN POTATOES

25 pounds potatoes	½ pound butter

4 cups finely chopped parsley

Wash and pare large potatoes. Cut in small balls, using a French vegetable cutter. Cook them in boiling salted water, drain, add a piece of fresh butter and carefully shake pan until the potatoes have absorbed the butter. Sprinkle with finely chopped parsley. If no French cutter is available for shaping the balls, use tiny new potatoes. Makes fifty servings.

ASPARAGUS BUCA LAPI

12 pounds fresh asparagus	½ pound butter

1 cup grated Parmesan cheese (5 oz. package)

This is a specialty of the Buca Lapi restaurant in Florence, Italy. Wash the asparagus in cold water, trim the lower part of stalks and arrange in small bunches, tying them together with a piece of white string. Cover with boiling salted water and cook until soft, about twenty minutes.

Drain, arrange the asparagus on hot plates, pour hot melted butter over the tips, sprinkle with grated Parmesan cheese, and serve. Makes fifty servings.

HAWAIIAN SALAD

1 No. 10 can shredded pineapple
5 cups grated coconut

1 quart mayonnaise
6 bunches leaf lettuce
2 cups chopped peanuts

Either cut up or shredded pineapple is used in this recipe. To the pineapple add the grated coconut and moisten and mix with mayonnaise. Arrange the individual portions on crisp lettuce leaves and sprinkle the top with finely chopped peanuts. Makes fifty servings.

MOLDED ICE CREAM

This you can buy ready molded from local confectioner. If he has not flower molds, he may be willing to get some to use for the occasion, if he receives the order well in advance. The ice cream may be made up in the class colors. Use personal judgment here.

MISCELLANEOUS SUPPLIES

6 glasses or 3 pints jelly
7 dozen rolls
2½ pounds salted nuts
3 pints coffee cream, or 2 pints Grade A milk mixed with
1 pint heavy whipping cream (Many guests will prefer their after dinner coffee black.)
150 mints, made to order in two colors
2½ gallons ice cream
Each makes fifty servings.

GAY NINETIES MOTHER-AND-DAUGHTER BANQUET

Many a church would prefer to give its annual Mother-and-Daughter Banquet in its own dining room, rather than in a local hotel, were it not for the work involved.

When we celebrate Mother's Day, is it right to expect her to spend it in the church kitchen, helping to prepare and cook her own banquet? Is it right to expect a daughter to spend the gala evening waiting on table? Shouldn't they be sitting together in the dining room, cool and relaxed, in their prettiest dresses, the honored guests of the evening?

This happy state of affairs can be achieved at the church banquet, just as well as at a hotel; and the banquet is just as easy to give.

HERE'S HOW—Caterers are hired to cook the meal, for which an experienced church member does the necessary marketing. The choice of a menu rests, to a large extent, on the price of the tickets—in this particular case, $1.50 for adults, $1.25 for children.

The church's dads serve the meal. They wear white chef hats and barbecue aprons.

The choirs, senior and junior, provide the program. The after-meal dish-washing and cleaning up of the church kitchen is done by two cleaning women, who are thrilled by the generous amount of left-overs they are allowed to take home to their families.

A few members from each women's circle meet in the church dining room on the morning of the banquet, to put up the tables and set them.

They know how many tickets have been sold, so can arrange the needed chairs around the tables, being sure that enough elbow room is allowed and giving special attention to the speaker's table.

One woman folds the paper napkins which tie in with the gay nineties theme; another places the glasses; another stacks the plates in piles of twenty on a side table in the kitchen. It is too early to put sugar and cream on the tables, so another helper arranges all the small cream pitchers and sugar bowls on trays near the kitchen door, ready for the men waiters.

That has taken less than two hours. The members of the table committee go home. Nobody is tired.

THE DECORATING COMMITTEE—An artistic member of the senior choir is in charge. Since she is a working girl, she has only the noon hour in which to decorate the basement dining hall with touches that recall the gay nineties. Most of these decorations she has prepared at home, using her evenings.

The hall has stretches of bare cement walls. She relieves the monotony by giving them a row of daintily-draped "windows." The lovely effect is gained by the simple method of hanging drapes of pale pink crepe paper, just as it comes from the fold. Each drape is festooned back by a little bunch of crepe paper roses, the stems of which have been pushed through a lace paper doily to resemble an old-fashioned nosegay.

She has a dozen of gay nineties portraits, all ready to tape up between the improvised windows, and on the bare, unattractive pillar supports. They are hilarious chalk drawings of characters of the gay nineties era, each mounted on an oval-shaped background, cut from composition board. They are guaranteed to send mothers and daughters into gales of laughter at first sight of them, with daughter giggling, "Oh, mother, look at the crazy way the women wore their hair in those days." Whereupon mother will inform her, "That was called a pompadour. It was very stylish in those days. But do look at that haughty young man's funny little mustache. And, oh, my land! Just see what went for a hat in the gay nineties!"

TABLE DECORATIONS—The idea is to keep the table decorations to the "easy-does-it" plan, too. No hours on end, the chairman rules on making intricate little do-dads, to be filled with this or that. Something simple, please.

The clever member of the senior choir decides on floral chains, making them at home in spare moments. They consist of pink crepe paper roses in bunches of three, scotch-taped together, at regular intervals along the length of a thin, twisted rope of green crepe paper.

It takes just a few minutes to stretch one of these floral chains down the middle of each long table, with little sprays of asparagus fern pushed in here and there as finishing touches.

A florist has sent gift baskets of flowers. These are placed on the speaker's table. The gift bouquets or corsages to be awarded to lucky mothers have been ordered days in advance and will be delivered, fresh and fragrant, in time for presentation.

There are no favors to make. A local business man has donated adorable little folding fans, with the advertising in very fine print, along one wooden edge.

THE SOUVENIR PROGRAMS—The programs have been mimeographed in the church office. The cover of colored construction paper reads:

MOTHER-DAUGHTER
BANQUET

(Church) .... (Date)

recalling
THE GAY NINETIES

The above cover is decorated with corner sketches of a mother and daughter in costumes of the gay nineties day, and of a high-wheel bicycle which was so popular in those less-speedy years.

The first inside page repeats what is on the cover, showing another sketch of an old-style bicycle, below which is the following menu:

Menu

Baked Ham		Raisin Sauce
Scalloped Potatoes		Green Beans
Coleslaw		Rolls
Radishes	Celery	Carrot Sticks
Coffee		Milk
Ice Cream		Cake

The second page of the souvenir program gives a poem, a tribute to mothers, also a table prayer, original words, sung to the tune of the doxology. The words are:

Thank God for blessings from above,
Thank Him tonight for mothers' love:
Thank Him for daughters, good and true,
Let's thank Him by the things we do!

The third page reads:

Program

Toastmistress	Name
Table Prayer	Sung by All
Welcome Speech	Name of President
Mother-Daughter Response	Name of Mother and Daughter
Group Singing	Led by........name of Song Leader
Presentation to Mothers	Name of President
"In the Good Old Summertime"	
"My Mother was a Lady"	
"Mother"	
Junior Choir, led by	name of Choir Director
Group Singing	Led by ....name of Song Leader
Talk	Name of Speaker
Hymn	Sung by All
Family Prayer	All

Many organizations give the proceeds of a Mother's Day banquet to some project dear to a woman's heart. Thus, some churches give the profit to their mission field in "Mother India" or to some other cause in which they are interested, such as local orphanages, children's wards in hospitals, or to an old ladies' home.

For this reason, a place on the program has been given for a good speaker to give a short, enlightening or inspiring talk on whatever special project is being promoted.

The hymn or song that follows the talk should tie in closely with the project.

The family prayer is printed on the last page of the souvenir program. The words of the closing hymn or song are also printed. The rest of the space is given to the words of the songs to be sung by all, many of them appropriate parodies, such as the following, sung to the tune of "Farmer in the Dell."

Daughters:
> My mother's here tonight,
> It gives me great delight;
> I brought her here to meet you, dear,
> My mother's here tonight.

Mothers:
> My daughter's here tonight,
> It gives me great delight;
> She brought me here to meet you, dear,
> My daughter's here tonight.

Everyone:
> We're glad to see you here,
> It gives us joy and cheer,
> Sure, it is true, we say to you,
> We're glad to see you here!

WELCOME SPEECH—The speech is given by the president of the women's organization. After the welcome to guests, there come the introductions and then thanks to the various committees for their work.

MOTHER AND DAUGHTER RESPONSE—The mothers' and daughters' reply comes after the main course. The mother gives as her tribute to daughters, Alan Beck's delightful, heart-touching essay, "What Is a Girl?" (See the note at the end of this banquet number.)

What Is A Girl?

Little girls are the nicest things that happen to people. They are born with a little bit of angel-shine about them and though it wears thin sometimes, there is always enough left to lasso your heart—even when they are sitting in the mud, or crying temperamental tears, or parading up the street in mother's best clothes.

A little girl is sweeter (and badder) oftener than anyone else in the world. She can jitter around, and stomp, and make funny noises that frazzle your nerves, yet just when you open your mouth, she stands there demure with that special look in her eyes. A girl is Innocence playing in the mud, Beauty standing on its head, and Motherhood dragging a doll by the foot.

Girls are available in five colors—black, white, red, yellow, or brown, yet Mother Nature always manages to select your favorite color when you place your order. They disprove the law of supply and demand; there are millions of little girls, but each is as precious as rubies.

God borrows from many creatures to make a little girl. He uses the song of the bird, the squeal of a pig, the stubbornness of a mule, the antics of a monkey, the spryness of a grasshopper, the curiosity of a cat, the speed of a gazelle, the slyness of a fox, the softness of a kitten, and to top it all, He adds the mysterious mind of a woman.

A little girl likes new shoes, party dresses, small animals, first grade, noisemakers, the girl next door, dolls, make-believe, dancing lessons, ice cream, kitchens, coloring books, make-up, cans of water, going visiting, tea parties, and one boy. She doesn't care so much for visitors, boys in general, large dogs, hand-me-downs, straight chairs, vegetables, snow suits, or staying in the front yard. She is the loudest when you are thinking, the prettiest when she has provoked you, the busiest at bedtime, the quietest when you want to show her off, and the most flirtatious when she absolutely must not get the best of you again.

Who else can cause you more grief, joy, irritation, satisfaction, embarrassment, and genuine delight than this combination of Eve, Salome, and Florence Nightingale? She can muss up your home, your hair, and your dignity, spend your money, your time, and your temper, then just when your patience is ready to crack, her sunshine peeks through, and you're lost again.

Yes, she is a nerve-racking nuisance, just a noisy bundle of mischief. But when your dreams tumble down and the world is a mess —when it seems you are pretty much of a fool after all—she can make you a king when she climbs on your knee and whispers, "I love you best of all!"

PRESENTATION TO MOTHERS—Absorbed in the program, guests have not noticed that corsages have been slipped from the piano top to the speaker's table.

Now the president rises and asks, "Who is the youngest mother in the room?" Then, "Who is the oldest?" After a good deal of comparison of ages, then birthdays, two happy women come forward, each to receive a lovely corsage.

Next, "Who is the mother of the most children?" Several of them have an equal number. What to do? Finally it is agreed that the corsage shall go to the mother of the oldest daughter.

GROUP OF OLD SONGS—During the presentation of the corsages, the little girls of the junior choir and their peppy director have slipped out of the room to don their Gay Nineties bonnets for the singing of their group of songs.

Now they reappear, their director in such an absurd, old-time costume that the little choir girls can hardly keep their faces straight. Each of the girls looks quaintly sweet in a little poke bonnet made of a paper pie plate, laced here and there with florist's ribbon, and then tied demurely under the chin.

GROUP SINGING—The song leader has worked and played with Cubs and Girl Scouts, and introduces several of their stunt songs to the audience. All join in singing, "One Finger, One Thumb, Keep Moving;" then, "Jacob's Ladder," and "Poor Old Slave," with great delight and many mistakes.

DADS TAKES A BOW—After the speech of the evening, the President thanks all who have helped to make the evening such a success.

The caterer and the "dads" who served as waiters are called from the kitchen to take a bow.

Then all join in the singing of the special hymn or song, followed by repeating together the family prayer. Thus, a most successful mother-and-daughter banquet, cooked and served at the church, is over.

"So easy to give!" reports the chairman, "With nobody worn or worked to a frazzle."

GAY NINETIES PHOTOGRAPHS—As the guests leave the dining hall, a pretty teen-ager asks them if they wouldn't like to have their pictures taken, as a memento of the occasion.

This is a side attraction, put on by an enterprising daughter, to make money for the young people's society.

Her studio is the church hall. In it are two posters, done in pastel chalks by the same artistic girl who has done the portraits in the banquet hall.

One poster shows a gay nineties mother, with the last word in the amazing hair-do and costume of that day. The other shows a daughter of the same era—a girl with long yellow curls, wearing a straight straw hat, with one flower standing bolt upright in the middle.

Where the faces on the posters should be, a round hole has been cut in the cardboard. Customers who yearn for those romantic old styles can have a photograph of themselves so clad, by putting their faces through the hole in the pictured gay nineties beauty. At fifty cents a "take," this stunt is an easy money-maker. Also a wealth of wholesome fun is enjoyed, not only by the girl with the cameras, but also by the customer, not to mention the crowd that gathers to see that justice is done to the photographed one, and to josh and jeer!

NOTE—The reading, "What Is a Girl?" is reprinted by special permission of the New England Mutual Life Insurance Company of Boston. Copyright, 1950.

A FAN-CIFUL BANQUET

Why wilt with your collar? When the temperature hovers around ninety in the shade, it's time to go fancy! With Japanese and electric fans; palm leaf and folding fans; radio, movie and television fans; baseball, knitting, or puzzle fans —in short, any old fan you fancy!

INVITATIONS—Invitations are written on fan-shaped cards, captioned "A Fan-ciful Banquet," followed by the breezy jingle:

> Oh, radio fans and movie fans,
>   And golf and tennis, too,
> And camera fans and baseball fans—
>   What kind of fans are you?
>
> We're giving a fan-ciful affair,
>   Come, fan awhile and chat;
> The breeziest place in town is where
>   The fans are. Fan-cy that!

The day, date, time, and place of the banquet should be added.

FAN POSTERS—Posters advertising the banquet should be displayed at least two weeks before the banquet, and could show head and shoulders of a pretty girl flirting from behind an open fan of the folding type. It could be an original sketch, done in pastel water colors or a picture of a beauty from a magazine cover, with the fan cut from colored cardboard and pasted in place. On the fan, in either case, is printed in bold letters, "A Fan-ciful Banquet."

FANCY WORK—Banquet decorations are just that,—fans, fans, and still more fans! The gayest paper ones, in assorted sizes, can be bought for a few cents each. Or the decorating committee can make its own from showy wallpaper, or from crepe paper in some of the more oriental colors—violet, cerise, jade, silver, gold. Huge display "flat" fans, with confetti floral designs and serpentine ribbons and rosettes, are easily made.

FANCY FREE—If the banquet is to be given in church social room, clubhouse or hall, it should overflow on to porch and grounds, which are decorated with strings of pink, yellow, and green Japanese lanterns, each over an electric light.

If the banquet is to be given in a private home, a rambling old porch may be used or a bit of the garden, or both, where guests may relax or saunter in the cool of the evening.

Here and there, in the shrubbery, cosy groups of wicker or bamboo chairs and tables may be arranged with a rosy Japanese lantern to give glamor to the scene, and on each table an incense burner to bring romance nearer—and, perhaps, drive the mosquitoes away!

A FANCY HALL—The hall should have an oriental atmosphere. The prosaic furniture should be moved out and straw mats put on the floor. Japanese furnishings may be borrowed for the occasion, such as screens, dragon wall-panels, Japanese prints and paintings, paper fans, parasols, kimonos, bamboo novelties, jade-colored vases containing a few chrysanthemums arranged in Japanese style, inlaid tables and chests, a willow-ware set on a handsome Japanese lacquer tray, a display of oriental curios, etc.

Even though the Japanese may prefer to sit on cushions on the floor, a few bamboo or reed chairs are permissible.

A FANCY WELCOME—The banquet hall and porch should be made a cool delight. Even though air-conditioned, some fancy way should be devised whereby every guest not only feels, but sees the breeze. A fan-ciful fountain does just that. To make one, an electric fan, face toward the ceiling should be placed under an upturned wire wastebasket, the sides of which are decorated with green paper and branches of paper plum or cherry blossoms. Narrow crepe paper ribbons or balloons on strings should be tied to the top— actually the bottom—of the wastebasket. The fan is connected with a floor socket, and then the "fountain of color" can be made to play at will.

A fan blowing across a chunk of ice in a dishpan is a good, old-fashioned air-conditioner, guaranteed to keep the mercury down and lift the spirits from their annual midsummer slump. Dark green branches overhead and the frosty tinkle of Japanese wind bells say in their own way, "Keep cool!"

FANCY HOSTESSES—Guests are greeted as they arrive by pretty girls in Japanese dress, who bow deeply and say, "Komban wa!" which is Japanese for "good evening."

FREE FANS—Each new arrival is given a paper fan, with the warning, "Keep fanning—or else!" Fresh-air fanatics are on guard to arrest all found violating this "be breezy" ordinance. Later on in the evening, these offenders are brought before "The Phan-tom"—an assistant, made up and dressed to resemble a fierce-looking Japanese official who pronounces sentence in the form of "fan-tastic" forfeits, all having to do with fans.

FANCY BANQUET TABLE—The table is first covered with a white tablecloth as a foundation. To decorate it, two strips of crepe paper streamer of silver or any oriental color are run down the middle of table, about five inches apart. The ends, at head and foot of table, are boxed with another strip. A "ruffle" of paper about ten inches wide is pinned, pasted, or thumbtacked all along the edge of table.

Fan-shaped place mats are cut to match or contrast with the color of central strips and ruffle. Arranged on the white cloth, they are very attractive.

The centerpiece is formed of two lacy fans, set up, like bookends, with the length of the table and placed several inches apart, so that, if wished, a box may be set between them to hold favors for the guests. The favors may be small boxes of preserved ginger or any other Japanese sweetmeat; or tiny fans, each favor tied to a length of narrow silver ribbon, the other end of which fans out to one of the guest's plates.

The double centerpiece fans are made like folding fans, and either of colored lacy crepe paper or of large lace paper doilies. Each open fan is fitted into a base, so that it can stand upright on the table. An empty cleaning tissue carton for instance, the base of each fan being inserted into the slit of the box. Weights can be placed in the box to steady it. The box may be glamorized to tie in with the color scheme, and baby chrysanthemums, or cherry blossoms made of paper may be arranged on top and around the sides.

Tall pink candles flank the centerpiece. They rise from

holders, trimmed with flowers to match the base of the centerpiece fans, and each holder is placed on a lacy paper frill or mat to match the lace of the fans.

FANCY PROGRAM—The cover shows a lovely, almond-eyed Japanese girl peeping around a flirtatious fan, and the words, "A Fan-ciful Banquet," with date and place are added.

The inside pages carry the menu and the program, and if space allows, the words of songs or parodies to be sung to well-known tunes.

FANCY TOASTMASTER AND TOASTS—The toastmaster, his real name "orientalized" on the program, is dressed in costume. He uses a Japanese dinner gong to get attention. This gong may be used all evening instead of the usual leader's whistle.

Toasts could be built around the three Japanese lucky monkeys—one who sees no evil, one who hears no evil, and one who speaks no evil.

For a musical number, a selection from the opera, "Madam Butterfly," would be suitable, such as the ever-popular "Some Fine Day." For a surprise comedy number, Sing Lee may give a much-advertised lecture on Japan. He appears in native dress, with a manuscript as thick as a mail-order catalogue in his hand. It is evidently a masterpiece of impassioned oratory, but although the lecturer speaks English, it is all Greek to his audience. For Sing Lee reads page after page backwards, a la Japan!

Attractive favors are wee Japanese dolls, such as can be bought at dime stores, or tiny boxes of Japanese water flowers.

FANCY ENTERTAINMENT—The stage can be a charming Japanese scene, with Japanese girls, their raven locks piled high and adorned with tiny fans, flitting with bird-like little steps hither and yon, their arms full of boughs of cherry and plum blossoms.

A good storyteller, dressed in costume, could tell the story of the opera, "Madam Butterfly," with musicians playing soft background music from the score.

Books giving the stories of operas may be found in most libraries. It is best to read the story, then write it in one's

own words and memorize it; then practice telling it, so that
the charm comes through.

There are places in the story where a good soloist can
sing selections from the opera. The singer can do so, if
wished, from behind a Japanese screen on the stage.

A group of little girls, dressed in gay Japanese costumes,
could give a drill with paper parasols. Sometimes a dancing-
school teacher is pleased to have her small pupils dance
before a kindly, uncritical audience.

If this banquet is given by a church which has a mission
field in Japan, an interesting talk, perhaps illustrated by
colored slides, might be given by the pastor or the missionary
chairman, about this work and its needs and dreams.

GAMES—Fan-ciful games may be preferred, instead of the
rehearsed platform performance. Here are some that are
fun:

1. On each guest's back is pinned the name of a different
fan, as auto, baseball, camping, diet, etc. In ten minutes,
each must find out what sort of a fan he is by asking other
players questions that can be answered by "Yes," "No," or
"I don't know."

2. Players draw little fans from a box. On each is written
the name of some movie or television star with characteristic
speech or mannerism.

On the word, "Camera!" each star, in turn, "emotes" or
gives his distinguishing line or lines until guessed correctly
by the audience, which shows by volume of applause which
impersonation is the most life-like.

3. The plumpest, jolliest guest is asked to give an impromptu lecture on "How to Eat and Grow Thin."

4. The men are seated in a close circle. The girls parade
outside the circle until, at the signal from the gong, they
halt, each behind a man's chair. Then from the center of the
circle, the leader says, "Tom, Phyllis is behind your chair.
Without a backward glance, describe to the company here
assembled, the dress she is wearing. Company, fan him!"

The seated company solemnly fan in unison, while he gets
warmer every minute—also Phyllis!—as he flounders, "with
little rag-ends, sort of, around the neck—"

5. In this fanning contest, each contestant is given a toy balloon and a palm-leaf fan. At the sound of the gong, each player must bat his balloon up in the air and keep it there until it has reached the finish line at the other end of the room. Should a balloon fall to the ground, its owner must pick it up with his fan. Contestants may not roll the balloons along the floor.

FANCY FOOD—To be really Jappy, perhaps the refreshments should be live fish or cooked birds' nests! But probably guests would prefer the following fan-ciful menu:

Shrimp Cocktail

Chicken Chow Mein		Fried Noodles
	Soya Sauce	
Rice Cakes		Japanese Preserves
	Cherry Ice	
Tea		Preserved Ginger

A wee Japanese flag may be stuck in each guest's cherry ice. Tea is unsweetened and flavored with cloves, lemon, or orange.

Recipes

CHICKEN CHOW MEIN

Remove the meat from two uncooked four-pound chickens. Cut it in one inch strips. Cook in a frying pan five minutes with four tablespoons of fat. Add two cups of stock made from chicken bones mixed with two teaspoons full of cornstarch. Simmer three minutes or until the meat is tender.

In another frying pan put four tablespoons full of fat. Add two onions cut lengthwise in very fine pieces. Cook three minutes. Add two bunches of celery cut in very fine strips, two inches long, and one-half pound of dried mushrooms soaked two hours in cold water, drained and cut into thin slices. Cook three minutes, stirring constantly.

Combine the mixtures, add two cans chop suey vegetables, two teaspoons full of salt, one-half a teaspoon full of pepper, and a few grains of cayenne. When the mixture is thoroughly heated, pour over the fried noodles. Boiled rice may be served with chow mein. With chow mein serve soya sauce. This recipe serves sixteen.

FRIED NOODLES

Beat two eggs slightly, add on teaspoon salt and flour enough to make a very stiff dough. Kneed, toss on a floured cloth or board, roll as thin as possible, sprinkle with flour, fold in layers about two inches wide, slice very thin, shake strips apart, and fry a few at a time until delicately brown in one pint of salad oil. Drain on soft paper.

JAPANESE RICE CAKES

4 egg whites   ½ cup softened butter
4 tablespoons sugar   1 teaspoon vanilla

1 cup rice flour

Beat the egg whites stiff. Add the sugar and rice flour, beating in lightly. Stir in the softened butter and vanilla. Grease a cooky sheet slightly and drop the batter by spoonfuls, spreading out very thin. Bake in a moderate oven (325 F.) until crisp.

JAPANESE PRESERVES

2 pounds rhubarb stalks, cut   1 pound pulled figs
  in pieces   1 cup boiling water
4 cups sugar   2 teaspoons lemon juice

Remove stringy portions from the rhubarb and cut the stalks in inch pieces. Cover with sugar and let stand several hours or over night. Remove the stems from the figs and wash thoroughly. Cut into small pieces and add boiling water. Combine figs, water, rhubarb, and sugar. Add lemon juice and bring to the boiling point. Simmer until thick like any preserve.

This preserve is especially good to serve with cold meats.

A WORLD-OF-FUN BANQUET

Calling the clan to take a world's-eye view of things and go gaily cosmopolitan! The theme is suitable for all the year, but is especially so when vacations are in the air, as travelers prepare to take off on a vacation or have just returned from one. It can be adapted in a dozen different ways.

POSTERS AND INVITATIONS—Often the art teacher in the local school will help by having her classes make the posters. If prizes are offered for the best they stimulate competition.

Posters show the world—a pale blue globe, complete with faintly-traced meridians, equator, tropics, arctic circles, and a rough outline of the continents, as shown in a school geography book.

Something not in the book should be added—a heavily-marked little doorway, with the one word, "Fun," on the door. Under the sketch of the globe, the following stanza is printed:

> The business world, the world of art,
>   The world of fashion, too,
> The world of science, underworld,
>   To mention just a few.
> So many worlds within our one!
> Our banquet's just a world of fun.

All necessary information is added.

If invitations are to be sent, they can be globe-shaped, cut from pale blue correspondence cards with lines and continents sketched in lightly, but sufficiently enough so that guests recognize them as worlds rather than blue balloons! The invitation verse can be written on the back.

WORLDLY DECORATIONS—Globe-trotters, upon arrival, find that the usual entrance has gone worldly, too. For placed before it is a huge replica of the globe, as shown on the posters advertising the banquet, even to a swinging door, marked "FUN," which is on hinges, and through which they enter.

A special "men of the world" committee of do-it-yourself enthusiasts has cut this globe-shaped entrance from cardboard or plywood and painted it pale blue, after putting in the necessary global lines, circles, and continents.

This great, flat cutout of the globe can be set against any entrance—street, lobby, banquet hall—through which all guests must pass.

Murals of as many of the different worlds as wished adorn the walls, with the best creation over the speaker's table. These can be bold pictures, done with colored chalk or tempera paints on lengths of wrapping paper.

Some of the worlds to be so gaudily depicted could be: The World of Fashion; The World of Music; The World of Art; The Scientific World; The World of Business; The Social World; The World of Amusement; The Political World; The World of Outer Space; The World of Sport; The Racing World; The World of Travel; The Ancient World; The Prehistoric World; The Underworld; The Prison World, etc.

WORLDLY TABLE DECORATIONS—For the speaker's table, the centerpiece could be a really fine illuminated globe of the world. Sometimes a local office supply shop will lend such a globe—or several—for the publicity it gives the firm.

If there are several tables for guests, each table could take a different world for its decorative motif.

THE WORLD OF ART—The art table could have as its centerpiece a doll artist, complete with beret, smock, and easel, busily at work on a half-finished painting of yet another world. Souvenir favors could be palettes cut from construction paper, daubed with different smears of paint, or just a box of school crayons or chalks.

THE WORLD OF MUSIC TABLE—The music table could have a toy piano as its centerpiece or a set of the quaint little imported pottery figures of orchestra musicians, with music notes cut from black cardboard scattered on top of the table.

Favors could be tiny musical instruments from the dime store, or miniature music sheets, hand-done, of the old popular song, "The Music Goes Round and Round."

THE WORLD OF FASHION TABLE—The fashion table could stage a style show as its centerpiece, with clothespin or lollipop models, dressed in long, full crepe paper dresses that hold them erect. Favors could be wee, stylish hats, made on a nut cup foundation.

THE PRISON WORLD TABLE—This table could have as its centerpiece a courtyard (the bottom of a cardboard suit box)
with a miniature penitentiary tower set in the middle of it,
with toy soldiers guarding it on all sides. The tower is made
of a tall, oblong box, neatly covered with stone wall crepe
paper, with a double tier of barred windows marked on. A
roof, cut in turrets, is added to the tower, with more tin soldiers stationed there.

Favors could be handcuffs, made of 20-inch lengths of
brass picture chain from the dime store, looped at each end
to make bracelets.

WORLDLY BANQUET PROGRAM—The cover design, cut round
like a globe, could show, map-fashion, the western hemisphere on the front cover and the eastern hemisphere on
the back. The inside pages carry the menu and the program
of table entertainment. A sample menu follows:

Mexican Cocktail
English Roast Beef

French String Beans   Irish Potatoes
Swiss Rolls   Italian Olives   Spanish Pickles
German Apple Pie with American Ice Cream
Brazil Coffee   Ice Russian Tea

Of course, this menu may be changed at will. The main
dish could be Swiss steak, chili con carne, macaroni a l'Ital-
ienne, Hungarian goulash, etc., in which case the rolls may
be named Dutch, Danish, or Norwegian.

The entertainment program follows:

Citizen of the World .... (Name of Toastmaster)
The Light of the World .... (Invocation)
The World of Song
The Political World
The World of Fashion
The World of Art
The World of Amusement
The Scientific World
The World of Music

THE WORLD OF SONG—The song director leads the guests in
singing songs of other lands. He has been notified some
weeks in advance, and the words of the songs he has select-

ed may be printed on the program or mimeographed on separate song sheets. Some song directors arrange to have pre-banquet meetings for rehearsing the songs, inviting those they know have good voices—glee club and choir members —so that they can "spark" the rest on the night of the banquet.

Of course, only a few songs will be needed—one for three or four countries probably. The list of song titles below gives a choice. Most of the old songs may be found in any inexpensive collection.

Travel plans—Far Away Places; Dream Train.

Bon Voyage—Rocked in the Cradle of the Deep; A Capital Ship.

England—Oh, Dear! What Can the Matter Be?; Drink to Me Only With Thine Eyes; John Peel; Westminster Chimes.

Scotland—The Bluebells of Scotland; Loch Lommond; Comin' Through the Rye; Annie Laurie.

Wales—All Through the Night.

Ireland—Sweet Rosie O'Grady; When Irish Eyes Are Smiling; Where the River Shannon Flows; Believe Me, If All Those Endearing Young Charms.

France—La Marseillaise; Mademoiselle.

Spain—The Spanish Cavalier.

Italy—Isle of Capri; Yes, We Have No Bananas.

Germany—The Watch on the Rhine.

Japan—Poor Butterfly (Soloist).

West Indies—Begin the Beguine.

Hawaii—Tahitian Paradise.

The end of the singing tour can be announced any time by the pianist playing a few bars of "Home, Sweet Home," followed, if wished, by a medley of our own songs about states, or sections of America, such as "Home on the Range," "Chattanooga Choo-Choo," "Carolina Moon," "The Trail of the Lonesome Pine," "Old Folks at Home," "Carry Me Back to Old Virginny," "My Old Kentucky Home," "Beautiful Ohio," "Maryland! My Maryland," "Back Home Again in Indiana," "The Sidewalks of New York," "Old Man River," a Negro spiritual such as "Nobody Knows the Trouble I've Seen," closing the medley with a few stirring bars of "America, the Beautiful."

THE POLITICAL WORLD—There may be time for this stunt before and while the cocktail is being served. Two soap boxes are placed in a roped-off circle, and two rival young "politicians" are chosen by the emcee who announces that there is to be an election to pick the funniest globe-trotter in the World of Fun, or the most-traveled, wittiest, most worldly-wise, etc., and that these two are the candidates, and each is to make a stump speech for himself, telling why any intelligent, fair-minded voter would vote for him.

At the signal, "Spiel!" both must throw themselves into their self-eulogies, both speaking together and both remembering that points will be given for vehement action and rousing eloquence.

At the signal to stop, both must do so, even if in the middle of an impassioned sentence. Then two ballot sheets, with the candidates' names on them, will be passed, one along each side of the table. These are for the guests' secret ballot. The prize can be any globe-shaped trifle, as a popcorn ball, or a round ball of perfumed soap labeled, "Soft Soap for Aspiring Politicians."

THE FASHION WORLD—Madam Ima Stylist directs this contest between rival "Parisian Dress Designers." They work in teams of two—the head designer and his assistant. If there is a World of Fashion table, both teams are drawn from this. If not, the rival teams can be chosen from two different tables, or one from each side of a long banquet table.

"We have with us tonight," announces Madam, "two Paris dress designers of international fame, each with his trained assistant. Before our eyes, these two great artists will fashion two unique creations, for which the best-dressed women of America will pay a small fortune."

Two card tables are brought in. On each table are assembled a large sheet of wrapping paper, a box containing two dozen patches of mixed dress materials—gay cottons, velvet, silk, lace—no patch being larger than two inches square; one button; a paper of common pins; a pair of scissors; and a box of crayons.

Madam tells the chief designer of each team that he is to draw a picture of his manikin on the paper, then dress her by pinning on her shape patches of the material, any of which he may cut if he wishes. He must not forget the button, but he is not allowed to use chewing gum to stick it in place!

His assistant hands him the pins and patches, cuts them as his chief directs, and makes himself generally useful.

When the time is up, each designer is required to display his new model and describe it in a glowing sales talk. For example: "This is a wedding dress. You will notice the sleeves of this elegant creation reach half way to the knees . . ."

The prize creation is judged by the volume of jeers, and, as a reward, the winning table or side might be allowed to parade once around the losing team, singing the well-known tune:

> They say—the know-nothings!—we ain't got no style,
>   Got style all the while, got style all the while.
> They say—the know-nothings!—we ain't got no style,
>   Got style all the while,
>   All the while, all the while!

THE WORLD OF ART—Cards and pencils are passed. Guests are asked to draw anyone present, sitting on top of the world. Prizes go, not to the best drawing, but to the artist whose world-sitter is most easily identified.

The first prize may be a small toy globe, with a tiny baby doll in a cardboard cradle glued to the top of it, with a card reading, "The hand that rocks the cradle rules the world."

THE WORLD OF AMUSEMENT—This world may be represented by any platform stunt. The Topsy-Turvy World is an old one, but always fun.

A sheet is stretched across the platform high enough to hide all but the necks and heads of the singers, who stand behind it. These can be a row of mixed singers or a quartet.

They can wear comedy hats or not, as wished. The property shoes should be selected to get a laugh.

The Topsy-Turvy Quartet members sing a verse, then disappear behind the sheet. Soon a row of assorted, wriggling, inverted shoes appears over the top of the sheet, while the song goes on, never missing a note.

To the audience, it appears as if the singers were standing on their foolish heads. Of course, when they dropped from view behind the sheet, they put on their hands the pair of shoes that were there, awaiting the moment.

They could sing any song popular with the audience or a foolish parody to some well-known tune. One of the latter type that has convulsed audiences may be sung by a group of what appears to be completely exhausted shoppers. They wear their bashed-in hats askew, while one has her veil in ribbons, and they give the impression of being badly bargain-beaten.

They sing to the tune of "The Farmer in the Dell":

> My feet are hurting so,
> My feet are hurting so,
> Oh, me! Oh, weary me!
> My feet are hurting so.

> You see, I shopped all day,
> You see, I shopped all day,
> Oh, me! Oh, weary me!
> It made 'em ache this way.

> My corns and bunions, too,
> My corns and bunions, too,
> Oh, me! Oh, weary me!
> I'll tell you what I'll do.

> I'll use my head, instead,
> I'll use my head, instead,
> Oh, me! Oh, weary me!
> I'll stand upon my head.

> The weight is off my feet,
> The weight is off my feet,
> Oh, me! Oh, weary me!
> I'm grateful for this sheet!

> I'm glad it hides from you,
> I'm glad it hides from you,
> Oh, me! Oh, weary me!
> This topsy-turvy view!

THE SCIENTIFIC WORLD—Professor C. Outerspace calls for two young men of scientific minds to help him test out a new principle of balance. This is just the old stunt in which each contestant sits on a large, round jar or crock strong enough to hold his weight, which is placed on its rolling side, on the floor.

Crossing his feet and lifting them from the floor, each contestant, on the word, "Go," is supposed to thread a large-eyed needle with thread, or, still more difficult, reach to one side for a matchbox, light a match, and then blow it out, without losing his balance.

THE UNDERWORLD—Should the banquet come near Hallow-een, this stunt may be the usual hair-raising "Chamber of Horrors."

A WAIST-WHITTLING BANQUET

This is a strictly social banquet, suitable for any women's organization—church, club, or civic organization. Do the ladies want to be as seductive as an hourglass? With the rich food holidays over, do they now solemnly resolve to whittle down that waist to a stylish wasp size, to suit the new silhouette? Then, here's your banquet!

INVITATIONS—Waist-whittling posters or invitations are illustrated with carbon sketches or cutouts of any shapely lady getting that way—doing her daily dozens, touching her toes, or, flat on her back, pedaling for dear life. Under the sketch is written the following:

> Do you want to take off a couple of chins?
> Or a couple of midriffish pounds?
> Then come to our waist-whittling banquet,
> And lose 'em by leaps and bounds!

P.S. Bring a photo or snap of yourself, taken at your slimmest, to hang in our pin-up girl gallery.

The day, time, and address of the banquet hall, renamed for the occasion, "The Reducery," are added.

The third line of the invitation may be changed to suit any other occasion, as "Come to our New Year's banquet" or Spring-Slimming, Fall Style, etc.

WAIST-WHITTLING REDUCERY—The hall should look as much like a "waist-away" gymnasium as possible. The comfort and charm are cleared out and "the works" are brought in—the dumb-bells, the punching bag, the scales.

Family albums may be ransacked for photographs of women gowned in quaint old styles—the thirties, the twenties and beyond. These photos are numbered and displayed on walls or a table for a date-guessing contest.

Old fashion books, showing colored illustrations of the styles of the gay nineties may be consulted and a few poster-size copies of the most amazing and amusing may be made, showing enormous leg-o'-mutton sleeves and an eighteen-inch midriff.

Is there a Gibson girl hiding her whittled waist in the attic? She may be dusted off for the Reducery walls. Illustrations showing Hollywood lovelies glamorously exercising to preserve that gold-edged figure may be cut from magazines and tacked up for inspiration.

Posters giving ideal weights and measurements; correct weight for women of certain height and years; the measurements of the "perfect thirty-six" and of Cleopatra, Venus, de Milo, the local beauty queen, etc. are all good "atmosphere," also a few enlarged calorie charts of various articles of food.

WEIGH IN—Signs reading "Weigh In" are displayed at the entrance of the banquet hall, which is now plainly marked "The Reducery." Upon entering, guests find the entrance flanked on each side by a couple of bathroom scales, each discreetly hidden behind a screen, marked "Private."

Two receptionists in professional white uniforms weigh each guest and record her correct weight "for the files," warning her to keep her weight a secret. As she weighs in, she is handed a membership card, on which is typed:

> Do you long to be a whiff,
>   Streamlined, willowly, and slim?
> You can whiffle in a jiff
>   With twenty lessons in our gym!

WAIST-WHITTLING HELPS—Abashed first-comers are rushed to these helps and told to get busy and memorize as many as they can, as a prize will be awarded to the one who repeats them with the most expression at the banquet table.

The helps are a set of well-printed jingles, made poster size, illustrated with appropriate picture cutouts, pasted on. If guests assemble in a room to await a summons to the banquet hall, the jingles should hang on the walls of this room; otherwise, in the hall itself.

The committee may whip up their own figure-reforming ditties. Here are two samples:

COUNT YOUR MANY CALORIES
> Do not eat that mayonnaise,
>   Or that gravy, sugar, fat!
> They will boost your calories;
>   Oh, be very sure of that!

ADAM'S SPARE RIB
> To achieve that "spare rib" look,
> Don't dine out and never cook;
> Eat dry lettuce, toast, and stuff,
> And never, never eat enough!

WAIST-WHITTLING TABLE DECORATIONS—Vases are milk bottles, plainly labeled "skim milk," in each of which is one skimpy blossom of the tall, thin kind. Between them, stand books on dieting, some the real thing, others novels, given gay jackets for the occasion, and new titles, as "Eat and Grow Thin," or "Outlaw That Rich Dessert! Take a Slice of Lemon." Samples of well-known health or diet foods make suitable favors; or fancy tape measures, to measure the inches lost where guests can best spare them.

A WAIST-WHITTLING PROGRAM—A copy of the program is at each place. The cover has the name of the banquet lettered across the top, with the date and time at the bottom. In the space between is a sketch of a slim beauty in a brief bathing suit, and the words:

REDUCING CHART

Take it off by the inch;
It's a cinch!
Take it off by the yard;
It's not hard!
Take it off by the mile;
Be in style!

The inside pages of the program carry the program and the trick menu. The real menu that follows is a surprise one, rich in dishes forbidden to dieters!

Program

Madam Whittler (Toastmistress) .... (Name)
Reach for the Stars .... (Blessing)
Roll Call, by weight
Calorie Count
Get Your Iron
Pep Talk
Waist-whittling exercises

If a serious note is to be sounded, the pep talk may be given by a speaker who is an authority on food or dieting, giving it a title that fits the theme, as "You Are What You Eat." But a definite time limit should be set for the speech.

If a light tone is to be maintained, the speaker may tell jokes, all concerning food.

The menu follows:

Slimmer's Fruit Cocktail
(25 calories)

Beanpole Soup   **Rash Main Course**
(25 calories)   (25 calories)

No-Starch Pratie
(No calories)

Slender Vegetable   **Waist-whittling Dessert**
(2 calories)   (25 calories)

How-Dry-I-Am-er   **Slimmer's Solace**
(25 calories)   (No calories)

(Total calories, 127)

The slimmers' cocktail is one stewed prune; beanpole soup, a small cup of bouillon; rash main course, one small slice of crisp bacon; no-starch pratie, a picture of an Irish potato; slenderite, one string bean; waist-whittling dessert, six grapes; how-dry-I-am-er, one ry-krisp; and slimmer's solace, a cup of coffee, straight, with no cream or sugar.

Of course this menu may be changed to anything that is sparse to vanishing point and too light to spoil the real banquet that follows.

At the right moment, as guests look disconsolately at their waist-whittling plates, Madame Whittler arises to announce, "No starches, please!" Then sternly continues:

> Keep those starches in their places,
> Lest you snap your corset laces!
> You will suffer fallen arches,
> If you do not shun those starches!

FALLING OFF THE DIET—A cute little waitress now appears from the kitchen, and, slyly mimicking Madam, says:

> Falling off a diet—
> Did you ever try it?
> Nothing really to it;
> This is how you do it!

This recital introduces the first course of the actual banquet, the menu of which can be anything richly guaranteed to "run to waist."

ROLL CALL—After the banquet Madam Whittler asks each guest to rise in turn and give her name and present weight and what she weighed when eighteen years old.

CALORIE COUNT—Madam Whittler asks how many memorized the figure-reforming ditties. Those who raise their hands are given a chance to prove it. Contestants are rated high for expression. The prize can be an hourglass. "It has such a tiny waist!"

GET YOUR IRON—So important in a reducing diet! If there is an equal number of guests on each side of the table, all may take part. If not, an equal number from each side is taken to form rival teams and stand well away from the table, so that the rest have a good view of them.

They form two lines, facing each other. Each player is given a toothpick. Player One of each line—the leader—is given a saucer to hold in her left hand. In it is one raisin for each player on her team.

On the word "Eat!" the leader spikes a raisin on her toothpick and feeds it to player Two, then hands the saucer of raisins to her. Player Two spikes a raisin and feeds it to Player Three, then hands her the saucer. This procedure continues until the last player of one team eats the last raisin from the saucer, holds it aloft, shouting, "All gone!" and so wins the contest.

The game may be complicated further by allowing each dieter two raisins, and ruling that the saucer containing them must come back down the line of players, each being fed another raisin, until it reaches the leader. If played this way, each player receives two toothpicks, and must hold the first one in her mouth after eating her first raisin, until she has safely spiked the second. For every dropped raisin, three are put in the saucer as a penalty.

Waist-whittling Games

Madam Whittler refrains from making her guests do any strenuous exercises directly after a rich meal, so gives them sitting-down games.

WHAT SIZE, LADY?—Madam Whittler hands out pencils and slips of paper. On the top of each slip, she has previously written the name of a guest, one name to a slip, folded it over at the top to hide the name, and pinned the fold securely down.

"Now," she says briskly, "let's size up your figure, so that we can trim it down. All information will be confidential. Please write the supposed weight of the one whose name you think is hidden on your paper, fold it over, then pass it to the guesser on your right."

Next, players are asked to write down the supposed age of the unknown one, fold it down, and pass the slip on to the player on the right; then the supposed measure of her bust, waist, and hips; then the size she takes in dresses, girdles, and shoes.

To complete the record, players are requested to write down the subject's daily calorie intake; her disposition, for what she is noted, and finally, what she may be doing ten years from now.

When these records are finished, Madam collects case histories, hands them to an assistant for "filing" and, later, the most amusing are read aloud, while each receives her own hit-and-miss estimation of her proportions, as a souvenir, for home consumption.

HIDDEN HUNGERS—Madam Whittler now wishes to probe for unsuspected causes of their last-year figures.

"Overweight," she announces, "is sometimes the result of frustration. There is a hidden hunger, a suppressed desire, so we eat too much, instead of taking to drink! I will now call on each one of you, in turn, to act out her suppressed desire to be somebody else."

If their respective desires are too deeply buried to be dug up at such short notice, Madam has a few handy, each written on a slip of paper, which guests draw from a box. They read: actress, author, opera singer, orator, poet, artist, boxer, jockey, taxi driver, etc.

If there is a good singer in the group, and she can keep a secret, it adds to the fun to have her come prepared to give some highfaluting grand opera—a parody of the real thing, using foods as the words she flings to the rafters, such as: "Ice cream, rutabagio, potatio, macaroni, spaghetti, ripe tomatios, succotashio, fricasse," etc.

WAIST-WHITTLING EXERCISES — After banquet rest time is over. Madam arranges her class in rows, in drill formation, with plenty of room between players.

"Now," she says brightly, "how about a spot of exercise for the midriff?"

Guests recognize the old game of "Simon says, thumbs up!", with new directions, and get set.

"Fashion says, 'Touch stars!' " barks Madam, s-t-r-e-t-c-h-i-n-g up, up, up with both hands towards the ceiling.

The class stretches. "Fashion says, 'Touch toes!' " barks Madam, neatly touching her own. The class struggles to obey. Orders are barked in rapid succession. The catch comes when Madam gives the order without the authoritative "Fashion says."

"Touch stars!" she shouts, reaching up with her own hands. The unwary are caught reaching up with theirs.

"Follow only Fashion's edict," she scolds. "If the command is not preceded by 'Fashion says,' do nothing. Anyone who fails to obey a 'Fashion says' command instantly, or anyone who obeys a command not prefaced by 'Fashion says' is out and must sit down and watch the rest reduce. Now we'll begin again. Your attention, please!"

The whittling goes merrily on, with Madam snapping out her orders with bewildering speed. As she makes it more confusing by going through the action herself each time, regardless of whether fashion says it or not, muddled whittlers, reduced to not knowing stars from toes, fall into the nearest chair and gasp, "Out!"

DEEP BREATHING—"I notice some of you are a little out of breath," says Madam. "Line up for some deep breathing exercises. Take a deep breath; count five. Then let your breath out in a whistle; count seven. Ready? Begin! In! Out! Fine! Repeat! Now, rise on your toes to inhale, coming down with the whistling exhale. Ready? Begin! Up! Down! Relax,"

POSTURE DRILL—Madam calls for class formation for more whittling. She asks the class to repeat after her:

> Lift up thy head;
>   Hold high thy chin;
> Keep thy shoulders back,
>   And thy stomach in.

She pleads with them to draw up slim through the midriff. "There! Hold it! What a superb effort! Now march, ladies, holding it in! Left, right, march!"

Madam is not satisfied with the result. She halts them. Perhaps, she suggests, they might find it easier to walk with more restrained elegance if they would move to rhythm. All right!

She says, "Does everyone know the tune to 'The Farmer in the Dell'? Then sing these words to it:"

> Oh, hold that tummy in!
> Oh, hold that tummy in!
>   **Un—laced!** The hourglass waist!
> Oh, hold that tummy in!

As the class "shapes up," while they are still in the line of march Madam may introduce new waist-whittling exercises by demonstrating them, as she marches ahead as their leader, now singing to the same tune:

> The Battle of the Bulge!
> The Battle of the Bulge!
>   We'll win! Of course we'll win
> The Battle of the Bulge!

Additional waist-whittling exercises could be: bending from the waist, first to the right, then to the left; then twisting sharply at the waist, first to the right, then to the left, all in time to the music.

Madam halts the waist-whittlers at intervals, so that they may catch their breath, and she may lecture, as follows:

"Are your ankles alluring? Let's march tiptoe, to make them so. Please sing to the same tune, as you march:"

> The ankles should be slim!
> The ankles should be slim!
>   Tiptoe! To make them so;
> The ankles should be slim!

"This is good fun, but strenuous. Short session, please!

RECESS—Guests are given a respite in which to inspect the pin-up girl gallery and guess who's who; and to view the exhibit of old fashion plates and try to date them, etc.

WAIST-WHITTLERS' RESOLUTIONS—Madam calls all to a rest-at-ease circle and repeats:

> "Resolutions are in order;
> Now before it is too late,
> Will each lady kindly tell me
> How she will reduce her weight?"

She then calls on a few guests who, she knows, can be relied on to give some funny methods, and then on some slim one to tell how she ever did it.

A FUNNY-BONE BANQUET

Here is a Halloween Frolic for the young crowd, with the emphasis on merriment rather than on an elaborate menu.

Without doubt, the real backbone of Halloween society is the very ribsy Skeleton family, whose ancestry dates back half a million years or more, and whose family crest, the skull and cross-bones, elevates any bottle of poison showing on its label to a lofty position—usually the topmost shelf of the medicine cabinet!

FUNNY-BONE POSTERS OR INVITATIONS—The invitations show in bold letters, "A Funny-Bone Banquet," the carbon sketch or cutout of any funny bone—ham, chicken, fish—and the words:

> It's just a funny-bone affair,
>   To cut expenses to the bone!
> 'Twill save a lot of wear and tear
>   If you will kindly bring your own.
> 'Most any kind of bone will do,
>   From stays to soup, from fish to fowl,
> Just bring it to the Skullery,
>   And join the skeletons and prowl.

All necessary information is added, together with the postscript: "Come looking as bony as possible. Prizes given for the boniest costume, for the funniest bone brought, and for the funniest story told about your bone."

FUNNY-BONE DECORATIONS—The decorations meet the guests more than halfway. On the garden gate, entrance to the grounds, garage door, parking space, and along the driveway or garden path to the porch, scary cards are tacked up. Each is attached to a real bone—the sort Fido buries under the dog house—and is lighted by a single blue bulb or a skull lantern from the five-and-ten. It shows a skeletonized hand, like an X-ray photograph, pointing a bony finger, "To the Skullery."

FUNNY-BONE SCARES—The scares may be printed, if wished, below the bony directing hand. As, for instance, on the first and largest card, fastened to gate or entrance:

> Where lie the bones of Skinny Joe,
> > Dissected by his gangster nieces?
> Although it happened years ago,
> > His longing for revenge increases.
> He cannot rest in peace, you know,
> > So hangs about the place in pieces.

Each "piece" that hangs in its bare boniness about the place inspires the Halloween poet to new riming atrocities. Thus a string of large beads that might or might not be Skinny's backbone, is inscribed:

> Hist! Old Skinny flops around,
> Searching for his spinal cord.

To a collection of badly-mixed bones hangs a skeleton-ized- hand sign, reading:

> Hark! Just hear how Skinny groans
> Over all his muddled bones!

To any other display of used, reconditioned bones:

> He's aroused! Alas! Alack!
> Hear his bones go click-a-clack!

To some toothsome "piece," such as the jawbone of a horse:

> Here—both top and underneath—
> Are old Skinny's handsome teeth.

To sprawling rib remains:

> Skinny's ribs! Please, everyone,
> Do not feed the skel-e-ton!

PICK-A-BONE VILLA—This is the grisly name under which the home or hall masquerades. It can be spelled out in letters, the straight parts of which are formed of single bones. Whitened pieces of worn-out garden hose can form the curves.

The porch is lighted with gaily gruesome skull lanterns, all lit up like a Christmas tree, with a tiny colored electric bulb from the Christmas tree lights shining through the empty eye sockets and toothy grin of each skull.

A BONY WELCOME—On the threshold, or placed where every guest must step over it or stay outside, is a long, coffin-like box from which spill bones, real or cut from cardboard. A blue-shaded electric flashlight burning inside the box makes it a still more jittery threshold to cross.

The front door has a sirloin bone for a knocker and bears a sign which is the last link in the chain of cards which have led from gate to porch. Instead of the skeleton hand, there is the skull and cross-bones crest, below which is printed:

> Skinny says it gives him fits
> Thus to find himself in bits.
> Hear his gloating, hissing whine,
> "Ah! Revenge at last is mine!"
> Enter singly, each alone,
> Handing him your funny bone!

Behind the door, members of the Skelegant family are stationed to handle the sound effects. The door is opened to admit one guest at a time, and as it closes upon that shrinking form, shrieks, howls, moans, and hisses are heard to a background of rattles. Bones used by the endmen at that last minstrel show make perfect rattlers, but two pieces of wood or bone of the right length and thickness, flipped between the fingers, make good substitutes.

WANTED—OLD BONES!—In many an attic, gathering dust, are motley assortments of used skulls, both lantern and cardboard, and full-sized cardboard skeletones left over from other Halloween capers. They may be reconditioned by tacking each skull to the shoulders of a wooden dress-hanger, draped with a vapor of black cheesecloth. A wisp of black tarlatan shrouding the face hides the ravages of time. Full-sized cardboard skeletons can be placed in dim corners, guarding choice heaps of old bones.

A FUNNY-BONE EXHIBIT—This exhibit pretends to feature a collection of the skeletons of prehistoric monsters. Barrel hoops, chopped into half circles, whitewashed and nailed to a lath "backbone," will pass as outsized ribs. The remains are tagged with some absurd label, such as, "Only existing remains of the prehistoric Tin Lizzieard, Crank-It-Don't-Get-Sore-Us."

A "big bones" committee, given time to work out some of their own ideas on this, can make it not only a big fun feature of the banquet, but a natural for advance publicity. Prizes can be offered for the best prehistoric skeleton, made in the home garage and brought to the stage for exhibit before the opening hour of the banquet.

WHAT THE BEST-DRESSED SKELETON IS WEARING—This outfit seems to vary very little from year to year. The approved funny-bone costume for host, hostess, and helpers is a white skeleton mask; a long black garment, surplice-style or slacks, with the "bones" boldly outlined in white tape or chalk; and a pair of white gloves. An individual note may be struck by make-up and the accessories—a little touch of phosphorus around eye sockets, nose, and molting teeth; six-inch claw nails of lissom whalebone glued to the fingers of the gloves, etc.

BONE CALL—The roundup of bones is made by the Secretary Skeleton, who collects all the funny bones brought by the guests before allowing them to remove their wraps. He slips each one into a brown paper sack on which he writes the initials of the owner, and then puts the sack into a bushel basket where repose a few extras for any guests who fail to bring their own. These home-bagged bones are surprising specimens—a piece of ancient, well-boned corset, a row of bone buttons, a bone knitting needle, a toy trombone, and a pair of dice.

FUNNY-BONE SIGNATURES—If the banquet is being held in a home, the secretary skeleton's assistant ushers the guests, as they arrive, to the right desk or table. If the banquet is in a hall, a hollow-voiced "spirit" can announce on the loud speaker, "Kindly register. Each guest is asked to sign the Funny-Bone Book."

FUNNY-BONE BOOK—This book is made up of separate loose leaves, and beside it on the table is a bottle of black ink, and pens to suit all comers. Since a heavy, inky signature gives the best skeletonized result, pens with old-fashioned steel pen nibs are best, or a fountain pen with a broad nib.

As the name is signed, the secretary skeleton hands it to a helper, who carefully folds the paper lengthwise, while the ink is still wet, folding it right through the name. This makes a weird-looking "blotograph," all ribs and spine.

With the addition of a few sketchy lines to the framework of the skeleton—a monocle, a pair of donkey ears, roller skates, sprouting wings, etc.—each blotograph can be made a slyly telling caricature, to be used later, if wished, as a place card.

If there is a budding cartoonist on the guest list, he is asked to come prepared to do a professional job of retouching the blotographs.

THE SKULLERY—The Skullery is the main room, if the affair is being given in the social rooms of a church, or in a club hall. If it is being held in a private home, then the basement, attic, laundry, garage, or barn makes an ideal place.

In any case, the Skullery should resemble a crumbling vault, cave, or dungeon where any skeleton would feel at home. Strands of mournful crepe paper moss are dangled along the top, with a few bleached bones hanging on black threads. Peering around the doorway, grinning a sardonic welcome, a skull-headed member of the Skelegant family is placed, with his cardboard face shining bonily through an ominous cloud of black tarlatan.

Near the entrance is arranged a display of hideous teeth —a set of old false ones, or a complete upper and lower, cut from orange peel. Above them is posted the notice, "No chattering allowed. This rule also applies to teeth."

FUNNY-BONE DECORATIONS — The decorations are done in black and white, with here and there a desolate waste of gaunt gray, inhabited by bony beings, intact or in pieces. Mile-a-minute skeletons can be turned out by the score. White cardboard skulls are tacked to coat-hanger shoulders, over which cape-like shrouds of fringed black paper are draped. A bony arm and a claw-like hand, stark white against black, protrude from the fringe. Hung on a nail, these "remains" relieve the monotony of any dark spot.

BONIEST DRESS PARADE—Judging this parade is more fun if done to music. The contestants line up and march by the reviewing stand, singing to the tune of "John Brown's Body" the following words:

> A prehistoric cave man went a-digging skel-e-tons,
> A prehistoric cave man went a-digging skel-e-tons,
> A prehistoric cave man went a-digging skel-e-tons,
>   But he didn't get a (clap twice) bone!

CHORUS:

All he got was tonsilitis,
All he got was tonsilitis,
All he got was tonsilitis,
But he didn't get a (clap twice) bone!

He dug up all the real estate in prehistoric booms,
He dug up all the real estate in prehistoric booms,
He dug up all the real estate in prehistoric booms,
But he didn't get a (clap twice) bone!

Substitutions may be made in the chorus. For example: "All he got was stomach ulcers, halitosis, falling dandruff, etc." Or any article or animal of amusing significance to the present company may be mentioned, such as Peter's car keys, Sally's tortoise, Mary's goldfish, Richard's front tooth, etc.

If the judges announce that each contestant's singing ability will add points to those won by his costume, the noise will increase.

Prizes could be any trifle made of bone or ivory or a skull souvenir paper weight.

FUNNY-BONE CONTEST — The basket of picked bones is brought in, and each guest claims his own. There is a bare table ready for the exhibit, and each proud contestant is given five minutes in which to display his entry to the best advantage.

Three solemn judges compare and confer, at last announcing that it would be easier to arrive at a decision if the story of each bone could be known.

FUNNY-BONE STORIES—Guests are told they can pair up, if they wish, and collaborate on a joint story, featuring both bones. This helps the shy ones, who often have more original ideas than the brash ones.

They are given ten minutes to plot their tall tales. Then they are seated before the literary guild—the same three judges, but now wearing horn glasses to give them an intellectual air—and stories are called for in turns, after it has been announced that applause is not allowed, only groans and hisses.

THE JOINT—The name, in big white letters on a black card, tops a black-draped booth which is decorated with a huge white skull and crossbones. On the table-top of the booth is an empty punch bowl, labeled "Bone Dry." On the floor in one corner is a witch's cauldron, marked for the occasion, "Soup's on! Scoop out a bone!" The cauldron, in charge of a member of the Skelegant family, is filled with sawdust, sand, bran, or what have you? In the filling are bones for all—those for men tied with one color, those for girls with another. Bits of raw macaroni or pretzels make neat little bones. Sometimes a local hotel will save wishbones for favored patrons. In which case, the best specimens may be saved for gilded table favors, and the rest used in the joint soup cauldron.

To each bone is tied a fortune, like the one following:

> A sardine bone will be your finish.
> Abstain from fish and order spinach.

> A rolling stone who's rolling bones—
>   It sounds so odd and funny!
> But if that fellow telephones,
>   He'll bone you for some money.

> What you feel in your bones—gee whiz!—
> Is nothing but rheumatiz!

FUNNY-BONE TABLE DECORATIONS—The centerpiece could show a black-covered shoe box, in which a startled skeleton sits upright. If the table is long, there could be smaller boxes at intervals, each with its aroused skeleton.

Another idea is to have a big skull standing on a black-draped box, with a family of small skeletons cavorting around it. These can be homemade, the bony frame made of white pipe cleaners, the head of a marshmallow, with features marked in with a toothpick dipped in melted chocolate. Or, easier still, each head can be made of two Halloween skull stickers, stuck back to back, with the pipe cleaner spinal cord caught between them.

The blotograph signatures, used as place cards, make suitable souvenirs if mounted on a narrow bookmark cut from black cardboard.

Wishbones can be used as favors, either gilded or colored, or made into odd little saucer men, their bowed legs thrust into any base that will hold them erect—a big, black, round gumdrop, mint, or apple—and the head being anything handy, from a wad of cotton batting held in place by a crepe paper cowl, to a marshmallow or a linen button.

FUNNY-BONE MENU—The main course of the refreshments is fried chicken, with the big platter of golden-brown dissected pieces labeled, "A Bone to Pick with You."

Chocolate ice cream can be shaped into neat little grave mounds, with a wreath of colored gumdrops on each. A tombstone can be added by icing slab-shaped cookies with white frosting, and printing the initials on in chocolate letters.

THE SKELETON IN THE CLOSET—If a skeleton is placed in the closet where the company's wraps hang, it will certainly speed the parting guest!

A MANY-THANKS BANQUET

This banquet is planned for a neighborhood affair, but it could easily be adapted to the family clan for entertaining aunts, uncles, nephews and nieces, cousins, and in-laws. Food and fun for thankful folks are mixed in equal quantities, and the menu is planned so that one day of shopping and preparation is all the ahead-of-time fixing required. That is certainly something for which to be thankful!

INVITATIONS—Invitations should be sent out early. Posters for the banquet may show a picture of a Puritan man and maid. These may be cut from colored pictures on magazine covers or may be heads done in bold crayon. For invitations, either a carbon sketch may be made or a correspondence card may be decorated with a Puritan sticker. Beneath is printed or written the following:

> Many thanks! Many thanks!
>   Come and help us count
> All the things we're thankful for—
>   Such a great amount!
>
> There'll be food, lots of food,
>   Fellowship and fun!
> Come and count your blessings, folks,
>   Yes, count them, one by one!

All necessary information is added.

DECORATIONS—The decorations are supplied by woods and fields. Shocks of wheat stand on the stage and in the corners of the banquet hall. Branches of gay autumn leaves may be used in the home. Seed pods and rose berries, bittersweet, pine cones, and sweet-smelling herbs are lovely.

TABLE DECORATIONS—Since food is featured at all Thanksgiving celebrations, the table decorations should receive special attention. Fruit, grain, and vegetables take the place of flowers on this occasion. A most attractive centerpiece can be built around a verdant base, made by covering an upturned pan with parsley or any green tops of vegetables. A pineapple may be set on this base, and vegetables and fruits arranged in a pattern around the mold.

PILGRIMS SERVE—Pilgrim maids, with demure white caps, kerchiefs, and cuffs, should wait on table. If the boys help, too, they may wear round collars and cuffs of white on their dark coats, with knee breeches and buckled shoes. Collars and cuffs are easily cut from paper, and the sterling silver buckles can be tinfoil-wrapped cardboard.

BANQUET PROGRAM—A master of ceremonies, three judges, and typed song sheets insure a smooth banquet program. The emcee, with a watch and typed program before him, keeps things moving. It might be better to fortify him with a little turkey before he starts.

The first "thanks," of course, is the grace, which can be sung by the Puritan waitresses or by all, after which guests are seated, and the emcee arises to announce that they are to be served fun with their food. He divides the group into two competing sides, Indians and Pilgrims. Blackboards are set where all can see, and after each event, the judges confer and mark up the score to the winners.

The emcee begins the fun by saying that he thinks there is time to sing the first verse of Song Number One on the song sheets, while the waitresses are serving the first course. The song is to be sung to the chorus of the well-known song, "Hail! Hail! The Gang's All Here." The words are:

> Thank you! We'll take some soup!
> Oyster, bean, potato,
> Chicken, beef, tomato,
> Thank you! We'll take some soup!
> Any sort of soup will do.
> What's that? The soup's all gone?
> What'll be the next course?
> What'll be the next course?
> What's that? The soup's all gone?
> What'll be the next course, now?

Other verses, sung while courses are being served or cleared give thanks for all the main dishes on the menu. A ready jingler on the entertainment committee can write his own, but here are samples:

Thank you! We'll take some meat!
 Turkey, duck, or what luck,
 Ham or hash or potluck,
Thank you! We'll take some meat!
 Any sort of meat will do.

What's that? The meat all gone? Etc.

Thank you! We'll take some pie!
 Pumpkin, mince, or cherry,
 Peach or huckleberry,
Thank you! We'll take some pie!
 Any sort of pie will do.

What's that? The pie all gone? Etc.

Thank you! We'll take ice cream!
 Choc-o-late, vanilla,
 Plain, with cherry filler,
Thank you! We'll take ice cream!
 Any sort of cream will do.

What's that? Ice cream all gone? Etc.

FREE-HAND TURKEY—The guests should do justice to the turkey while it is hot, so instead of having a talking or singing contest, the judges put down before each plate twenty grains of corn. The emcee then asks each guest to outline a turkey on the tablecloth with the grains, doing it whenever he can spare the time. Toward the end of the course, the judges examine the turkeys to see which side scores.

CRANBERRY NECKLACES—Between meat and dessert, there is time to pass things from hand to hand without hindering the waitresses too much. The judges give each of the top two guests at the sides of the table a dish of cranberries, and the last two guests at the bottom, a threaded needle. On the emcee's word to start, the head players pass their cranberries, one at a time, down the lines to the end players, who hurriedly thread them. When the last dish of dessert has been served, time is up, and the necklaces are collected by judges who count the cranberries and mark up the scores.

THANKFUL SPEECHES—With dessert over, the more formal part of the program begins. If, in the community, there is a war veteran who spent a Thanksgiving Day in the trenches, behind barbed wire, or among the wounded he may be asked to come prepared to give a simple, short talk about it. In any church, club, or neighborhood, there is some handicapped person—blind, crippled, or paralyzed—who is sunshine itself. For a real bracer, one of these brave souls may be asked to talk on what they have to be thankful for. How they will come through!

THANKSGIVING GAMES—After a big meal, adult guests are in favor of inactive games. A souvenir booklet for each guest, should be prepared in advance, the cover showing the Puritan motif, with the date of the banquet on cap or kerchief. On the inside pages are typed or printed, "Six Things————————Should Be Thankful For." The blank is filled in with the written name of a different guest.

After the banquet, pencils should be handed out to all, and a booklet given to each. Care should be taken that nobody gets his own, and that those inscribed with the names of the oldest guests and any others the committee especially wishes to honor should fall into the hands of somebody who will "do them proud."

It should then be announced that each is to set down, in his best handwriting, the six things for which he thinks the person whose name is inscribed in his booklet, should be grateful.

This is a surprising and heartening game. It is moralebooster, for instance, for a somewhat discouraged pastor or church organist who flushes with pleasure at the list of fine attributes some discerning church member thinks he should be grateful to possess; or for a weary hostess, who learns for the first time, that she should be grateful for:

1. Being the best all-round cook in the world.
2. Keeping her schoolgirl complexion.
3. Raising such well-mannered children.
4. Having a husband who publicly admits that he has a better wife than he deserves.
5. Knowing how to grow African violets.
6. The way her Sunday school class adores her.

Guests should have plenty of time to give a thoughtful list. After all, who wants to hurry after a turkey dinner, with all the trimmings? Then the booklets may be collected, and, if desired, someone may read aloud those about the ones the committee especially wishes to remind how very much they are appreciated.

PURITAN FAVORS—Thanksgiving favors are kitchen-made, since they are made of food: raisin turtles with tail and feet of cloves; little nut men, with features of black gummed paper; puffed what-nots, glued together with cooked sugar syrup—the kind used for popcorn balls; vegetable animals; decorated candy bars; or lifesaver rolls.

Adorable Puritan doll favors are easily made of six marshmallows, toothpicks, and a few cloves for features and buttons. (See Fig. 1.) One marshmallow forms the head, another the body, and one each for chubby legs and arms. Dressed each in a wide crepe paper cape, with a big chin bow, and a Puritan tall hat, complete with shining buckle, they look too charming to eat!

Fig. 1

MENUS—Turkey is an aboriginal American, and it is especially fitting that he be given the honor place on the banquet menu of the original American feast day. But if supply and prices will not permit, a pair of ducks or baked fresh ham with onion dressing may be substituted. Two sample menus follow:

Menu No. 1

Cream of Tomato Soup
Small Hot Crackers
Roast Turkey
with Chestnut or Oyster Dressing

Potato Puff   Giblet Gravy
Glazed Carrots   Baked Spanish Onions
Celery   Salted Peanuts   Green Olives
Cloverleaf Biscuits   Cranberry Relish
Lettuce Salad with Russian Dressing
Pumpkin Pie   Cider Apple Pie
Coffee   Mints

Menu No. 2

Fruit Cocktail or Oyster Soup
Baked Fresh Ham with Onion Dressing
Mashed Sweet Potatoes
Buttered Cabbage
Celery   Crabapple Jelly
Graham Muffins
Jellied Cranberry Salad
Baked Indian Pudding
with Whipped Cream
or
Thanksgiving Fruit Pudding
Coffee   Nuts

Recipes

(For the unusual dishes given in the menus.)

POTATO PUFF

2 cups mashed potatoes   2 tablespoons butter
2 eggs, separated   1 cup hot milk

Mash the potatoes and season well with salt, pepper and
butter. Beat the egg yolks until light, add to the hot milk,
and stir the mixture into the potatoes. Then fold in egg

whites stiffly beaten. Turn into a buttered baking dish and bake from twenty to thirty minutes in a moderate oven. The proportions of seasonings and milk can be varied to taste. Bake in a large dripping pan, or several, when preparing for a crowd.

CRANBERRY RELISH

1 package quick-setting orange gelatin
1 cup boiling water
¼ cup sugar
1 cup cold water
1½ cups cooked cranberries

Dissolve the quick-setting orange gelatin, in boiling water. Add the sugar and cold water. Put the cranberries through a food chopper. Add them to the gelatin mixture and chill. When the relish starts to thicken, stir and pour into molds. Chill until firm. This recipe makes twelve generous servings. When making in quantity, mold in 9-by-12-inch pans and cut into squares.

CIDER APPLE PIE

1 package gelatin dessert (lemon flavor)
1½ cups cider
2 cups apple sauce
A few grains of salt
1 baked pastry shell

Dissolve the quick-setting gelatin in cider, which has been heated to boiling. Add the apple sauce and salt. Chill until it begins to thicken, then pour into the pastry shell. Chill until firm. Garnish the top with meringue or whipped cream. This recipe makes one large pie.

ONION DRESSING

1¼ pounds onions
½ cup butter
1 egg
3 cups soft stale bread crumbs
15 sage leaves

Fry the onions until a light brown. Season with salt, pepper, sage leaves, and butter. Mix the onions with bread crumbs and the egg, slightly beaten. This makes enough dressing for one ham.

GLAZED CARROTS

8 medium-sized carrots   1 cup brown sugar
½ cup butter

Wash, scrape, and cut medium-sized carrots into strips, about eight strips to a carrot. Cook in boiling, salted water fifteen minutes and drain. Cook slowly until soft and glazed in the butter and brown sugar. Allow one or one and one half carrots to a portion, depending on size.

CRANBERRY SALAD

4 level tablespoons gelatin	3 cups celery, diced
6 cups cold water	2 cups chopped nut meats
4 cups sugar	2 teaspoons salt

2 quarts cranberries

Cook the cranberries in the water for twenty minutes. Stir in the sugar and cook for five minutes more. Add the gelatin which has been soaked for ten minutes in two cups of cold water. Stir until dissolved, then strain. When the mixture begins to thicken, stir in the celery. Turn the mixture into shallow pans and chill. When firm, cut in squares and place a whole nut meat on each square. Serve on lettuce and garnish with mayonnaise and chopped nuts. This recipe serves twenty five guests.

THANKSGIVING FRUIT PUDDING

½ pound prunes	¼ to ½ cup brown sugar
1 inch stick cinnamon	¾ cup orange juice
6 whole cloves	2 tablespoons lemon juice
1 package quick-setting lemon gelatin	½ cup sliced figs
	½ cup seeded raisins
1 cup hot prune juice	¼ cup sliced citron

¼ cup shredded almonds

Soak the prunes in enough water to cover. Add the cinnamon and cloves and cook slowly in the same water until soft. Remove the prune pits and chop the prunes. Measure a cup of prune juice and heat to boiling. Dissolve the quick-setting gelatin in the prune juice. Add the sugar and orange and lemon juice. Chill until the mixture begins to thicken, then add the chopped prunes and the remaining ingredients. Chill in a pudding mold until firm.

A BOXY BANQUET

Although this banquet is especially suitable for a pre-Christmas affair, the theme is an all-year-round one and can be used, with slight changes, whenever the purpose is "the lift of loving gifts." It is easily adapted to fit a pay-as-you-enter dinner, to sponsor a special cause, such as the collection of gifts for a mission; toys for an orphanage, children's hospital, or an empty stocking drive, with the admission being one suitable gift, nicely boxed.

It has been used as a social to collect gifts for an old people's home; also to collect luxury foods for a lonely shut-in, who otherwise might have been overlooked at the box-happy time of Christmas.

It has served as the cover for the presentation of an unexpected boxed gift to a hard-working church janitor—and was he surprised! The recipient could have been the pastor, Sunday school superintendent, choir director—anyone the church, club, or society wished so to honor.

Moreover, the repast served need not be an elaborate banquet. It can be a simple dinner, a still simpler supper, serve-self or snack, or even light party refreshments.

Finally, a Boxy Banquet can be given as just that, its sole purpose being the truly worthy one of providing food, fun, and fellowship for others.

Boxy Posters or Invitations—The invitations can be cut from double construction paper and shaped like a box. A carbon sketch of a box may be drawn on cardboard and cut out as a pattern. Then the pattern is laid on the uncut fold of the construction paper, its outline is drawn in pencil and then cut out. Thus the invitation will be double. The outside cover is decorated with gummed holiday seals, and on the lid of the box is printed "A Boxy Banquet," or whatever it is—dinner, supper, social, etc.

Inside, a folder of white paper carries the invitation verse.

Boxy posters show boxes of all shapes and sizes, tissue-wrapped and be-ribboned, or just plain brown paper ones, coming by mail, freight, or express, from local friends and from the very ends of the earth.

Under the boxes or on the inside page of the invitation the following is printed or typed:

> This is the season for boxes,
>   Boxes of holiday glee;
> Boxes of gifts from old Santa,
>   Boxes for you and for me.
> Boxes delivered by mailman,
>   Boxes for ev'ry last one;
> So let's have a gay boxy banquet,
>   With boxes and boxes of fun!

The day, date, time, and place of banquet are added.

BOXY DECORATIONS—The plan for decorating assembly hall and banquet hall is simple. It goes something like this:

> Boxes to the right of you,
> Boxes to the left of you,
> Boxes to the front of you,
>   Boxes unnumbered!

BOX SEATS—Community tradesmen may be asked for permission to rummage in their rear premises for empty wooden boxes, or box-shaped crates, big and strong enough for guests to sit on. Gay-patterned wallpaper is pasted on them, and they are tied with green and red Christmas rope, or ribbons of red tissue paper. They will look like giant Christmas boxes.

Big cartons used for transporting mattresses, scooters, and merchandise of all sorts pile up during the hectic weeks before Christmas and are willingly donated by businessmen, who are glad to have them carted away.

The biggest box may be placed across the doorway of the banquet room, so that guests must pass through it to enter. The lid opens like a door, with a baggage tag serving as the handle; or, if the door is a big one, a round face powder box is attached to serve as the knob. If the lid needs reinforced hinges, they can be made of strips of cloth or oilcloth.

Homes may be searched for empty gift boxes, the prettier, the better—candy boxes, gay-lidded boxes that have contained greeting cards, stationery, etc. But the plainest box quickly becomes a thing of beauty by simply covering it with the holly paper sold in almost every store at Christmas time.

Most women have little hoards of Yule wrapping paper, saved because it is too pretty to throw away, too small or too full of holiday stickers to use. Now is the time to bring them out. Empty match boxes, with a bit of gilt paper pasted on their utilitarian sides and lid, look glamorous enough to be jewel boxes. Old shoe boxes, tea and cereal boxes, even pill boxes, can be made to look fresh and festive in a few seconds with a little paste and a bit of Christmas wrapping paper.

It is a good idea to box as many of the room's furnishings as possible. A box with one end knocked out can frame the clock. Or an imitation clock face can be marked on the bottom of a round hat box, and so masquerade as the wall timepiece. A vase of flowers can be placed in a box high enough to hide the vase. Tiny boxes can dangle on tinsel strings or spool ribbons from chandeliers and doorways. Each lump of loaf sugar can be wrapped separately in gift wrapping paper, tied with a wisp of cord, given a wee label, and hung, as a fringe, in some cool spot.

COUNT THE BOXES—As soon as the guests arrive they are to count the boxes in the room. Each is given a pencil and a luggage label on which to jot down and initial the count.

It should be explained that nothing must be moved, as only boxes in plain view are to be counted. Of course, a previous count has been carefully made, and a few small boxes placed in not easily discovered—but not concealed—spots. As, for instance, one box might be clipped to the stalk of a house plant, or a book-shaped one tucked between books on a shelf. No prize is offered unless all guests start the count together.

BOXY CONVERSATION—When all guests have arrived, it is announced that a little boxy conversation is now in order. Guests are arranged in two concentric circles which march around in opposite directions, to music. At the sound of the whistle, players halt, and each shakes hands with the partner nearest to him and starts talking on whatever topic of conversation is announced by the leader.

After a moment of—we hope!—animated talk, the music starts again, everyone says, "Good-box!" to his partner, and

the two circles again march around in the opposite directions, until stopped by the whistle, whereupon each player,
as before, takes the partner nearest to him for a new topic.
    These topics could be as follows:

1. Have you ever eaten a box oyster? How? When? Where?
   And why?
2. How much should a boxing glove weigh? Why?
3. What is a box pleat? How is it made?
4. Can you box the compass? Let's hear you.
5. What's a newspaper box? What would you put in it?
6. Describe a box spring, with actions.
7. What do you like best about a box office?
8. What do you like least about a theater box?
9. Ever see a box border? Where?
10. What's the best thing you ever saw in the pitcher's box?
    Show his style.

BOXY TABLE DECORATIONS—If guests are to receive inexpensive, individual gifts as favors, then the box forest centerpiece would be a good choice. If the gifts are bought already
boxed, such as candy, they need not be boxed and wrapped;
and if they are all alike, they need not be tagged with the
names of guests.

    Now for the forest. Wired to each box is a small, bushy
twig of box, or any other evergreen shrub, that stands upright like a tiny tree. When all the gift boxes are piled in
the center of table, to form a natural-looking hill, these little
twigs stick up and make a forest. The boxes are covered with
crushed white paper, which in turn is covered with cotton
batting to resemble snow and sprinkled with sparkling
"frost," making when completed, a miniature snowy forest.
Each guest is invited to pull up his own little tree, and find
his box at its root.

    If there are several tables, a smaller box forest could be
the centerpiece of each.

    There is another boxy centerpiece more amusing than
the box forest one, but it requires more time, trouble, and
talent to make. It shows Mr. and Mrs. M. T. Boxes in the
act of having a spirited boxing bout, with "the missus"
getting the best of it. (See page 124.) The two peppy little
figures are made entirely of small boxes of various sizes and

shapes, connected by spirals made by winding wire around a lead pencil. They stand on a platform—the ring—which is a flat, thin box of the type in which fancy handkerchiefs or gift blouses are packed.

Fig. 2

Each head is a box connected to the box body by a spiral neck. Expressive features are inked on each face—long-lashed eyes and a pouting little red mouth for Mrs. Boxes; an aristocratic mustache and monocle for her husband. Their hefty shoes are boxes, and they have boxes for hands at the ends of their spiral arms.

Flower boxes could bloom, at intervals, down the length of a long banquet table, being simply flowers in a low bowl placed in a pretty box, with the stalks set in wet sand.

BOXY FAVORS—If the favors are not in boxes under the box forest centerpiece, they can be small boxes of raisins, such as can be bought in grocery stores, placed at each guest's plate. They are given "as is," or may be decorated to harmonize with the color scheme.

Boxy Banquet Program—The cover is shaped like a Jack-in-the-box, opened, with the words "Boxy Banquet" and the date printed on Jack's peppy chest.

Inside the cover, the menu and program of table entertainment are printed on colored pages, and the whole is tied with Christmas cord or ribbon. If wished, a small colored pencil may be taped or tied on, to be used by autograph-collectors, and for playing the paper games.

Boxy Menu—The menu may be served with the main course in individual boxes, as for a box luncheon. The extras are brought in on box lids, used as trays, with nuts and mints on the table in boxes.

Any good, seasonal menu can be selected, with the table decorations and program left to carry the theme.

An edible Christmas box dessert may be served. Each box being a small square sponge cake with the center scooped out, and iced all over. The lid is an iced cracker and lifts on and off. Inside is a scoop of ice cream or some cute little favor in a jeweler's box.

Program Schedule—The program follows:

Chief Boxer .... Toastmaster
Boxy Songs .... Group Singing
What Rimes With Box? .... Paper and Pencil Game
Boxed Noses ....
Box Wrappers ....
                                                             Stunts by Guests
Jack-in-the-Box Surprise .... Musical Stunt on Stage
How Old Is the Christmas Box? .... Speech

Boxy Songs—There may be time to sing the following stunt-song before the fruit cocktail is served. Since it requires vigorous action, it cannot be used while waiters are placing dishes.

The emcee explains that the singers are to sing "My Boxes Lie over the Ocean" to the old tune of "My Bonnie," with the following actions:

At the word, "My," they point to self.
At the word, "Boxes," outline a square box in the air, using the first finger of both hands.

At the word, "lie," rest cheek on folded hands.

At the word, "over," point widely ahead.

At the word, "ocean," make big waves in the air, using both hands. (Up, down, up, down.)

At the word, "sea," the same.

At the word, "bring," beckon with one hand.

At the word, "back," give own back a resounding whack.

At the word, "to," show two fingers of right hand.

At the word, "me," point to self.

The chorus is especially rugged, with all its back-thumping and almost every word required a quick action.

"What sort of a box am I?" is another song that requires less action and concentration. The guests on opposite sides of the table make two singing teams. Each team chooses a leader who decides what sort of a box is to be dramatized. The members of the team sing to the tune of "We Won't Go Home Till Morning:"

> We hope you counted the boxes,
> We hope you counted the boxes,
> We hope you counted the boxes;
> What sort of box are we?

Then the singers act out the kind of box they are. When the other team thinks it knows, it sings its answer to the same tune. For example:

> We think, perhaps, you're a toolbox,
> We think, perhaps, you're a toolbox,
> We think, perhaps, you're a toolbox,
> What sort of a box are we?

If these singers guessed right, it is their turn to choose a box and dramatize it.

Box names easily acted out are: hat, jewel, paint, egg, theater, sentry, candy, shoe, match, cigar, mail, money, music, pencil, sewing, pitcher's, box car.

WHAT RIMES WITH BOX?—When the main course is served, eating is in order, but there may be time to jot down on a box-decorated card, or baggage label, all the words that come to mind that rime with the word, "box."

BOXED NOSES—Competing teams are called forward to see which can first pass a matchbox lid down the line, from nose to nose. No hand may be used. One player must "jockey" the lid from the tip of his nose to the tip of the nose of the next player in line. It adds to the difficulty of the nosey ones—and to the hilarity of the audience!—if a tall man is placed next to a short girl.

BOXED WRAPPERS—Two couples compete. Their equipment is identical—the same size of box, the same number of sheets of wrapping paper, the same length of fancy cord, and, above all, the same number of fancy stickers. Oh, the heated arguments over a miscount!

On the table at which the parcel-wrapping is done, each box is stood on its wrapping paper. To add to the wrapping difficulties, the cord and stickers are placed inside the box.

Each couple must lock inside arms. They must wrap and tie the box and decorate it with every last sticker, while handicapped by being allowed to use only outside hands.

JACK-IN-THE-BOX SURPRISE—A huge jack-in-the-box is on the stage, placed directly before an ornamental screen, presumably there as part of the stage setting.

The top of the box springs open and out pops a comedy musician, with a fiddle made from a cigar box. He makes a great commotion about tuning his crazy instrument.

Then, to everyone's amazement, he plays a beautiful violin selection. At its conclusion, there is a volume of applause, which he acknowledges with deep bows.

He grants an encore, but during an impassioned bar, his fiddle falls into the jack-in-the-box. The tune continues. He tries in vain to rescue his instrument. The tune still continues. Finally, in his frantic struggles to shake it out of the box, he knocks down the screen, revealing the real violinist seated behind it.

There are a dozen variations of this stunt. The fake violinist may be taken by an unbearable itch in the small of his back, which he finally scratches with his bow, or he may be seized by a violent sneezing spell; or he may announce his encore, only to have the real violinist play something else, whereupon he loses his temper and berates the man behind the screen, then pulls it aside, thus disclosing the hoax.

Speech, "How Old Is the Christmas Box?"

That question has even the antiquarians guessing! Perhaps, they say, it goes back to the days of early sailing vessels. Before such a vessel set sail on a long voyage, a priest set a box aboard, and into this box the sailors dropped money and valuables during the voyage. The harder the gales blew, the faster the coins clinked in, for those rough fellows knew that back home the good priest was on his knees praying for the safety of his souls at sea.

When the sailing ship returned to port, the savings box—had it not saved the ship?—was returned to the priest to be opened at Christmas time and its contents spent for the benefit of the poor and the sick.

Centuries later, the Christmas box was an earthenware one, in which the English apprentice boy saved his few pennies. Since he received no wages, his master permitted him at yuletide to collect what tips were his due from household, workshop, or customers. All through Christmas Day he could shake his box, but not beg. It must speak for him, saying,

Christmas box!
No keys, no locks!
Bring yuletide joy
To 'prentice boy!

The day after Christmas, still "Boxing Day" throughout England, he "bruk his box," since there was no other way to get his money out.

Or, the antiquarians suggest, the crusaders of old may have brought home from their travels, along with other outlandish wonders, the Arabic word, "Backsheesh," meaning "gratuity." Spoken fast, the word sounds like "box." And box it most certainly was to that picturesque army of later centuries, lamplighters, waits, turncoats, dustmen, beadles, and town criers, who marched abroad at Christmas time, rattling their boxes on doorstep of cottage and castle alike, not begging, just giving people a chance to show their good will and spread joy.

Or, a third guess, the Christmas box may have started from the church's doorstep. The humble alms box, the contents of which were distributed the day after Christmas, may have been the ancestor of them all.

In any case, the giving of Christmas boxes is a good old yuletide custom, and we are all for it!

PARTIES, SOCIALS, SUPPERS, PICNICS, and TEAS

A TIME'S-UP SOCIAL FOR THE NEW YEAR

Planned for a big crowd of young people in a hall or a gymnasium, this social takes them all around the year, with a game for each month.

TIMELY POSTERS—Pictured on the posters are two watches, side by side. Printed across the dial of one is, "Be on Time!" and across the dial of the other, "Be on the Watch!" Then, in larger letters, is printed the announcement, "A Time's-Up Social."

Below is printed:

> Be on time! Be on time, to the minute!
> For a Times-Up Social, you know,
> Like the times, may exceed the speed limit,
> But can never, never be slow!
>
> You must be on the watch every minute;
> Not an instant to lose or to spare!
> For your time by a stop watch is reckoned
> At this up-to-the-minute affair.

The date, place, and address are added, with the name of the organization giving the social.

TIMELY WARNINGS—These warnings are placed in prominent and well-illuminated positions on the way to the hall. One, for example, may be placed at the entrance of the grounds, another halfway to the porch, another on the front porch, with others in the hall, at the foot and head of the stairs, etc.

The warnings are such well-timed notices as:

> Time and tide wait for no man!
> No speed limit. Time's up!
> To keep up with the times, try our gasoline!
> Anyone found beating or killing time will be prosecuted!
> Visitors are warned against punching the time clock!
> Our clocks are dangerous—they strike!
> Remember the watchword: It's "Tick-Tock!"

TIMELY DECORATIONS—These decorations may feature anything used to tell time. An improvised sundial is on the stage, a grandfather clock in one corner, a huge cardboard hourglass in another, a cuckoo clock in another; and in the best corner, three big cardboard clock faces with movable hands. These are easily cut out, with a big round tray used as a pattern, and the cardboard hands attached by paper fasteners.

Real clocks of all sizes and descriptions may be borrowed for the occasion, and toy watches strung everywhere. A metronome, set to tick loudly, adds to the timely and relentless "Time marches on!" atmosphere.

FATHER TIME—Arrayed in a sheet, a wig and a white, flowing beard, and carrying a cardboard scythe and a stop watch, Father Time meets guests at the door and keeps things moving rapidly throughout the evening. He is assisted by the four seasons, attractive girls dressed to represent spring, summer, autumn, and winter.

Everything is done to make guests feel rushed. There are no leisurely greetings at the door. Instead, newcomers are briskly told to get out of their wraps and step lively, please! One of the seasons hustles them to the dressing rooms, telling them they are holding up the entire calendar; so they'd better snap into it! Before the girls have time to dab a little powder on their party make-up, they hear a loud, hurried thudding at the door. It is Father Time.

"Time's up!" he snaps. "We're going all around the year tonight. Get a move on!"

The men get a similar order. With the air fairly crackling with a brittle briskness, the guests are moved to the social hall with the precision of a fire drill.

THE PAST, PRESENT, AND FUTURE—These are well-timed divisions into which to separate the guests. The first game of the evening is planned to accomplish this end.

"We are starting the year with the month of March," announces Father Time, "and don't ask me why. I allow only fifteen minutes to a game, and none at all for questions. So play 'em fast!"

MAD MARCH—Coming in like a lion, March starts the guests in their mad career around the year. Three men are selected as team captains. Father Time explains that when he strikes the gong, each captain is to rush up to a girl and seize her by the hand; then, hand in hand, they are to race to a man, whose hand the newly-acquired girl grabs, and so on, alternating men and girls as much as possible, until every guest is in one of the three teams' lines. This, Father Time warns them, is no time to protest that they do not want to run on fast time, for when the gong sounds again, a count will be taken, and the captain whose line is longest will have his team clocked as the winner of the first event.

The lines keep growing at a frantic rate until the last guest has been grabbed. Then Father Time bangs the gong, shouting, "Time's up!" and thus bringing some order out of chaos.

There will be an unequal number of players in the three lines. The seasons quickly remedy this, arranging it so that the lines are equal in count, if not in talent. Each line now becomes a team and takes up a position in a different corner of the room, as directed. Father Time and the seasons occupy the corner where the gong stands, and the three big cardboard clock-faces with the movable hands.

The hands of the three clocks all point to twelve o'clock. Father Time is the official timekeeper, and clocks the winners of the March stampede by advancing the hand of that team's clock one hour. After that, at the end of each month's event, he marks the success of the winning team by advancing the time on its particular clock one hour.

APRIL FOOLISHNESS—This is supposed to be a restful game for all but the performers. The winning point goes to the team whose representative tells the best joke on himself. Father Time makes the announcement, giving the teams just one minute to choose their humorist, and the funny man just one minute to think of that lay-'em-in-the-aisles joke.

At the signal, "Time's up!" the men come forward and seat themselves at the speakers' table. The painful difficulty they find in expressing themselves is not entirely due to diffidence. For each, before rising, is handed a large, sticky molasses kiss, divested of its paper, and told that the piece of cloying sweetness must be put in the mouth entire and chewed throughout the telling of the joke. The sight of Father Time standing before them, stop watch in hand, does not tend to add to their poise or fluency.

MAY'S MELODY—This stunt is usually anything but! Father Time makes the rashly optimistic statement that everybody knows Mendelssohn's "Spring Song." The winning point, he announces, will go to the team which gives the most sympathetic rendering of this classic. Every member of the team must contribute something to the melody. It may be whistled, hummed, laughed, or even coughed, he tells them, and while each team's choir provides this musical background, ten young men (or fewer, according to the number in each team), chosen from the group by the captain, are to dance around an imaginary Maypole.

When the gong strikes for "Time's up!" the Maypole dancers are to pose motionless in whatever position they were at the time it struck.

The judges—Father Time and the four seasons—decide quickly which team is the winner, allowing not a second for argument; and then Times marches on!

JUNE BUGS—This buzzing relay race is for the girls. Each team enters an equal number of players. The rival teams line up, each behind its leader who, black crayon in hand, toes the starting line. Tacked to the wall at the end of the hall and on a line with the three columns of players are three large squares of white cardboard.

On the sound of the gong, the first girl of each column races to the board and writes the name of some bug on it, then tears back and hands the crayon to Player Two who, in turn, rushes forward and writes on the board the name of a different bug.

Players must buzz constantly from the minute they grasp the crayon until they hand it to the next in line. The seasons hover near to see that they do! The winning point goes to the team which has most bugs buzzily listed when the gong strikes for "Time's up!"

JULY PICNIC—A Fourth of July snack picnic is an event for the men. As in the previous contests, each team enters an equal number of players, the rival groups lining up in column formation, each behind its own leader. At the far end of the hall, in a line with the columns, are three picnic spreads. These spreads are paper tablecloths laid on the floor, on each of which is laid an identical assortment of food. The spreads can be almost anything so long as the menu is varied enough, as, for instance, a cooky, a pickle, a shelled hard-boiled egg, a cracker, a few potato chips, a wiener, half a banana, a spoonful of raisins twisted up in wax paper, a licorice stick, and a caramel.

At the sound of the gong, the first boy of each column runs to his team's picnic spread and, without the slightest thought of counting his calories, selects an article to eat. This he gobbles down, while a season stands near him to see that every particle is swallowed before he runs home to touch off Player Two. Player Two then dashes up to get a quick lunch; and so it goes until all the appetizers have been bolted, the contest being won by the team whose last player is the first to choke down his final mouthful and race home.

Father Time quickly advances the movable hands one hour on the winning team's clock, and announces, "August!"

AUGUST HAY FEVER—The winning point, Father Time announces, will go to the team which gives the most gigantic sneeze. There must be no one who is immune to hay fever.

No matter how atrociously unfair the judges' decision seems to the two losing teams, Father Time makes it clear that there is positively no time for discussion.

SEPTEMBER SCHOOL—Father Time thinks it is about time the rival teams have an original yell. He gives them two minutes to make and rehearse it. At the call, "Time's Up!" whether they are ready or not, silence is demanded. Then, team by team, they come forward and perform, the winning point going to the group whose racket sounds most like a regular school yell.

OCTOBER FORTUNES—This game gives the poor players a

chance to leave the noisy present and ponder about the silent future.

Father Time gives the captain of each team six correspondence cards, with the request that he write on the top of each the name of a member of his team. Two cards in every set of six are marked J. All the cards are then collected and redistributed, so that each team gets cards on which are written the names of players on a rival team.

Father Time then tells them that when the gong strikes, every player holding a card must immediately write a clever or horrible fortune for the person whose name it bears.

The cards marked with a J carry a jinx—the jinx being that the holder must write the fortune in verse!

When the gong strikes for "Time's Up," the cards and pencils are collected by the seasons, the cards being marked to denote which team is to be held responsible for the horrible fates so gleefully foretold.

The winning point goes to the team with the best rimed fortune.

At refreshment time, Father Time reads aloud the name on each card, then the fortune, giving special publicity to the winning rimed fortune and the runner-up.

NOVEMBER ELECTION—This is a game after a politician's heart. Father Time gives the teams just one minute to elect a candidate for the office of dogcatcher. Then all three are seated before the audience and, one at a time, each makes a two-minute speech on his own apparent fitness for this office. The winning point goes to the team whose speaker works hardest for election, not only by his speech but, in addition, gives the best imitation of a dog barking his protest at being caught and popped into the wagon.

DECEMBER'S SANTA—Each team is given a basket containing pieces of crepe paper of several widths and shades. These are rolled up and a rubber band snapped around each roll. A pair of scissors, needles and thread, and a paper of pins are placed on top of the basket.

Father Time announces that there is a demand for more Christmas toys, especially dolls. Therefore when the gong strikes as a signal to start, all the girls, with the help of the crepe paper ribbons and their own make-up kit, are to make the men resemble dolls as much as possible.

This must be done with lightning rapidity, as only five minutes will be allowed for the transformation. When the gong sounds for "Time's up!" the men must step forward into the spotlight to be reviewed.

To aid in picking the winners, a member from each team may be asked to perform, to say, "mama" and "papa" when pressed, to close and open eyes in clockwork jerks, to smile sweetly, or to cry bitterly. The winning point goes to the team which has the cutest doll babies.

JANUARY'S RESOLUTIONS—This is a contest for all the players in each team. Father Time tells them that they are to think of a good resolution for the new year—not the usual individual resolution, but one for the whole team as a group. Then each team, in turn, is to pantomime its resolution.

A season may have on hand three resolutions, each written on a separate slip, to hand to despairing captains who can think of nothing to resolve, in the face of Father Time's thought-paralyzing stopwatch. For instance, "I resolve to attend church regularly," or "I resolve to pay my bills," or "I resolve to quit smoking."

The winning point goes to the most dramatic portrayal.

FEBRUARY'S HEARTINESS—Father Time demands that the losers of the January contest give the winners three hearty cheers; next, that the winners return the compliment. Then how about a little hearty applause? And now a hearty laugh? Fine!

Now all that is left is to give the winning point to the team which showed the heartiest all-around enthusiasm. Then hearty congratulations are in order, and then hearty refreshments.

The all-winning team is awarded a round, white hatbox, on the lid of which the face of a clock has been marked. As Father Time presents it, he says, "A man, like a watch, is known by his works. This watch resembles the team."

When the lid is removed, "the works" are found to be nothing more than a lot of assorted noisemakers.

"Just like the winning team!" comments Father Time.

Then with a brisk "Time's up!" he hurries the guests to a snappy serve-self luncheon, presided over by the four seasons, Spring serving the chicken salad; Summer, the peach shortcake; Autumn, the salted nuts; and Winter, the snow-topped (marshmallow) chocolate drink.

If simpler refreshments are preferred, they may serve sandwiches, coffee, olives, celery, ice cream, and small, round cupcakes, iced in white, with clock faces painted on the top with melted chocolate.

As midnight approaches, Father Time slips away, returning just a second before twelve to stand in the open doorway. He is dressed in outdoor garments and carries a suitcase. He strides through the hall to get his cardboard scythe and hourglass. "Time's up!" he shouts for the last time and slams through the door just as the bells and sirens usher in the New Year.

GET-YOUR-MAN PARTY FOR LEAP YEAR

At long last, it is the girls' turn! No longer need they look and languish. Now they may look—and leap! If that new perfume has failed to lure the current heart-throb from his state of single cussedness, now is the chance to stun and seize him!

NECK-OR-NOTHING INVITATIONS—The invitations are sent only to the girls, each of whom not only invites her unsuspecting victim, but sees that he gets there, by fair means or foul.

They are illustrated with cutouts or carbon sketches of persuasive aids to leap year wooing, from the good old kitchen poker to a rolling-pin, lasso, or revolver. This arsenal frames the following fighting words:

Get Your Man!

To arms! Again it's leap year,
When any lady can—
Because tradition gives permission—
Go out and get her man.

Attend my leap year party;
Escort your leap year hope.
Yes, when you've licked him, bring your victim
At gun's point or by rope!

The time, day, date, and place are added, and if the hostess is the one deciding who brings whom to woo, she adds the postscript: "Please call for .... and bring him with you. Conduct yourself as a gentleman. This will induce him—we hope!—to be a perfect lady at the party."

If, on the other hand, the hostess is leaving the choice of the young man to her guest, she substitutes, "Please call for your date," etc.

LEAP YEAR ETIQUETTE—This is the title of the tiny red-covered book enclosed with each invitation. It lists the conduct rules of the evening. They are the usual good manners, but hilariously topsy-turvy, because it is the girls who are expected to behave, in every instance, like perfect gentlemen! Proper conduct requires them to spring to open the car door and help the abashed young man to alight; to guide him gently across roads, up curbs and steps, and so on.

After arrival, leap year etiquette requires a girl to rise when a man enters the room; to smother the escorted one with attentions, such as fanning him, should he seem to be getting a little hot under the collar; bringing him ice water; stuffing cushions behind his rebellious head; hastening to pick up anything he drops; fussily serving him at refreshment time; asking him if the excitement has given him a headache, etc.

The rules of conduct in the little red book are numbered as follows:

1. Help the gentleman don and doff coat and rubbers.
2. Pull out the gentleman's chair at table.

This helps Emily Roast to keep an accurate record of those who transgress during the evening and enables her forfeit committee to make the punishment fit the crime.

Upon arrival, each man is presented with a handmade fan to be coy behind; and if the hostess wishes to help him to be a perfect lady, she directs his attention to a big placard on which are crayoned some special rules of etiquette for him. For example:

1. Do not cross the knees.
2. Do not straighten the tie or finger the collar or smooth the hair in public.
3. Avoid loudness of speech.
4. Use no slang.
5. Acknowledge graciously any small attention a lady pays you.

The hostess who knows what's done and what isn't in her particular crowd, can add her own ribbing rules to the conduct code. At the foot of the mind-your-manners poster is the request: "If you see an instance of any man showing bad leap year manners, report same instantly to Emily Roast."

LEAP YEAR DECORATIONS—The decorations show the girls mean business. There are two poster-size valentines, lacy with shelf paper. One carries the verse:

> Sisters, let's be up and doing!
> Let us leap to meet our fate!
> Here's where women do the wooing,
> While the men—confound 'em!—wait!

The other shows in its center a heart, covered with snap-shots and portraits of the local lads on whom the female of the species has designs. Its motto is a terse, "Get Your man!"

Suggestions for getting him are part of the decorative scheme, from fish hooks to lassos. Cupid's golden arrows are flanked by more modern weapons: toy revolvers, rolling-pins, knock-out perfumes. There is a clothesline plainly tagged, "Rope and tie him!" Also a pair of handcuffs labeled "wedding rings;" an improvised ball and chain tagged "hold him!" and toy reins marked "matrimonial harness."

PIN-UP BOYS—Pictures of handsome young men, from a royal prince to the latest collar-ad profile, can be found in magazines: stalwart athletic stars, each garbed for his sport; movie, stage, and radio favorites; fashion celebrities in for-mal attire—any presentable young man will do for framing!

If there is one super-eligible in the crowd—football cap-tain, for instance—for whom every girl pines and primps, the hostess gets his latest photograph by hook or by crook, and displays it prominently, marked, "Prize Matrimonial Ex-hibit."

THE LEAPING LENA LINE—There is a vividly-colored poster in the hall, reading:

For a Thrilling Trip, Take the Rocky Route to Matrimony on the Lovers' Special, over the Leaping Lena Line.

Bigger Thrills! Bigger Chills!! Bigger Bills!!!

The ticket booth, a card table, is in charge of Slim, a sister or friend of the busy hostess. She wears a conductor's cap, punches the tickets, and serves as emcee on the train.

The tickets are long strips of paper, which will take pen-cil writing. They are arranged somewhat like dance pro-grams, with the stations listed, and space left for a different partner's name to be written against each. The gate is any homemade affair. An old-fashioned clothes horse, a low screen with folding panels, or a big carton, with one side cut loose to form a door, would serve beautifully.

GREET AND GUSH!—This game is a merry mixer, where pas-sengers mill around in the hall, meeting one another before boarding the train. Slim hands to each a paper bag which contains ten peanuts. She announces that on her signal, "Greet and Gush," everyone is to shake the hand of some-one else of the opposite sex, and that the person who pre-sents his or her hand first has the right to claim one peanut from the slower greeter. But—and this is important!—with each handclasp must go a gushing greeting, as, "Gee! My one-and-only!" or, "Bill, you great, big, boo'ful brute!"

No repeats are allowed. Helen can't dash from one lad to another, calling each a great, big boo'ful brute; nor can Bill breeze along telling every girl she is his one-and-only.

The gushing greeter who collects the greatest number of peanuts in five minutes is given a card entitled, "An Etiquette Pointer, by Emily Roast." It reads, "Do not be noisy in public places."

"All aboard!" yells Slim. "Get your tickets at the booth before passing through the gate!"

No passenger is allowed to go through the gate until leap year requirements are met. These are that each girl must state in ten words why she would make a good wife. Her partner—presumably dragged to the party—must tell in ten words why she wouldn't. It's no time for fellow pas-sengers to be convulsed with laughter. Their turn is coming.

THE LOVERS' SPECIAL—This is a train of chairs arranged in rows, with a wide aisle down the middle. The conductor blows her whistle. All rush to get a seat. There aren't enough to go around, and passengers standing in the aisle are re-quired to produce the proper sound effects to create the right atmosphere. They must "choo-choo" and puff and steam, hoot warnings at imaginary crossings, etc. Since there are frequent stopovers at stations for new games and stunts, the standees can soon grab seats, crowding out others to do the choo-chooing.

Girls are given five frantic minutes in which to date a different man for each station listed on her ticket. As each victor nails her victim, she jots down his name on her ticket and her initials on his.

The stations are as follows:
1. Greater Palm Beach
2. Whispering Pines

3. Moonlight Memories
   (Intermission)
4. Fairfax View
5. Lovers' Leap
6. Honeymoon Lane
   (Intermission)
7. Feed 'Em Junction

The conductor calls each station with great gusto, and has the big pockets of her coat filled with all the smaller requisites for the games.

She sees to it that no man conveniently loses his souvenir fan, picking it up and restoring it to him from every slick hiding place.

GREATER PALM BEACH—At the conductor's whistle, each girl grabs her partner's hefty hand and starts to read his palm, giving special attention to the heart line. The watchful conductor has a few palmistry charts in her pocket and hands them to floundering females.

WHISPERING PINES—At the whistle signal, each girl tells her new partner what she pines for in a husband. She must tell it to him in a loud whisper, for he is seated three feet away from her, the distance measured by the conductor's yardstick. Nor can her partner turn a deaf ear, for he must write down her "pines" on the card with which the conductor supplies him.

Packages of lemon life-savers are passed around to the girls, after their whispering frenzy.

MOONLIGHT MEMORIES—Each girl hunts up her new partner, links her arm in his, and goes strolling in the moonlight, openly courting him, while he hides his coy blushes behind his fan.

The synthetic moonlight comes from the property moon —a bulb in a round cardboard box, such as a hatbox— from which both lid and bottom have been removed, and the openings then covered with double layers of yellow paper. A smiling face is sketched on the side and when all the other lights are turned off, the soft, dim glow in the box should mellow the heart of the most confirmed bachelor.

Topic? The girls are to tell about their first sweethearts. The lads tell nothing.

INTERMISSION—There are two intermissions on the ticket. They provide a chance for the girls to stop their ardent "twosing" and play together as a group. Get-together stunts are in order, such as group singing of the latest hits in popular love songs, the paying-off of forfeits by the men who have broken leap year rules of etiquette, or seeing which one can tell the best love joke. For example, the following: A lovelorn sailor, one payday, decided to celebrate it by sending a wireless message to his girl in Grand Rapids. He sat there, chewing on a pencil for several uninspired minutes, then finally turned in a cable, reading, "I love you, I love you, I love you. Jack."

The clerk in the cable office read it over, counted the words, and said, "You're allowed to add a tenth word for the same price."

More pencil-chewing, more pondering. Then the lovelorn sailor added the tenth word. It was "Regards."

LEAP YEAR FORFEITS—Any of the following would do as a forfeit:

1. Shake hands with ten different girls, saying to each, in turn, "You are my only love," without laughing.
2. Impersonate a man disappointed in love.
3. Hold the hand of a girl and say the alphabet backwards, leaving out the letters that spell the word, "love."
4. Say, "I adore you!" in six different tones of voice, to the same girl.
5. Sing any love song soundlessly, until someone guesses what it is by the shaping of your mouth.
6. Give a rule for all mothers-in-law in less than ten words. Sing it up and down the scale.

FAIRFAX VIEW—"All aboard!" yells the conductor, and when all are in place, she hands round a box containing a number of little envelopes. In each is a letter telling of a heart problem, either one cut from an Advice to the Lovelorn column, or written by the hostess. No tragic problems should be presented, only foolish, absurd, or fantastic ones.

The conductor's box contains problems suitable for the girls to read aloud with a sob; also some suitable for the lads to present with a jeer. The hostess has marked the little envelopes with a G if they contain girls' heartaches, and with a B if they contain the boys' problems. The conductor distributes them accordingly.

First, a girl calls on someone in the group to help her solve her heart problem. She reads it, pulling out all the emotional stops. She wants—boohoo!—advice.

She gets it! Then, in turn, her advisers get it, since listeners feel called upon to challenge such preposterous solutions! When the din has died down, a lad bares his breaking heart and calls on some girls to tell him if there is any way out but suicide. Thus it goes, until all have had a chance to prove that true love never runs smooth.

LOVERS' LEAP—This station is the peak of the evening, the jumping-off place, where each girl proposes to every man she can grab, starting with the one whose name she wrote on her ticket, against this momentous event.

As for the pursued young men, they go into hiding, aided and abetted by the husband, brother, or son of the hostess, or any other male ally who believes that all men should stick together during leap year—or else!

The conductor has all the girls go to a far corner of the house, where they lie in wait, while the men hide in closets, basement, porch, or attic.

Before the chase begins, each girl is handed a pencil and the cutout of a rolling pin, on which she is to write the name of her Lovers' Leap partner—already on her ticket—and after that the name of every other man to whom she succeeds in proposing.

She must capture her partner before she can hunt another man—which is an exasperating delay!—and she must propose to him when she catches him. After that, she can play the field.

After a given time, the conductor blows her whistle, and the husband hunt is over. The girl who captures the most men and proposes to each receives as her prize a book entitled, "Cooking for Two."

If any man succeeds fairly—he may not sit it out in his parked car, or on the fire-escape!—in escaping his pursuers, he is given a sewing kit, so that he can sew on his own buttons.

HONEYMOON LANE—This station is the lull after the storm. Each couple collaborate on writing an essay of one hundred words—count 'em, ladies!—telling where the honeymoon should be spent and why. Authors are encouraged to illustrate their masterpieces with pencil sketches of the scenery.

MATRIMONIAL MARKET—A good stunt for the second intermission is the matrimonial market, at which the men are auctioned off to the highest bidder. Each girl selects a "money bag"—her marriage "dot," which she may not open until all the men have been auctioned off. The bidding starts at a nickel, and a dollar is the limit. "For," says the girl auctioneer, "no man is worth more than that!"

One by one, the men are brought forward to stand on the block, while merciless auctioneer puts him through his paces. "He has such a shy smile," she announces. "John, smile for the ladies! Aw, come, come, Jackie! You can do better than that. I'm trying to get a fifty-cent bid for you. This is bigger-and-better smile week! Ladies, he has a merry laugh. John, laugh merrily a moment. Will you? And such manly feet! John, just lift your foot up, so that the customers can see the huge size you wear in shoes. Higher, John! Thank you! That brings in another dime. And just see how cute his hair grows at the nape of his neck!" If he blushes, his healthy color is stressed by his tormenter.

Finally, the last bargain is knocked down to some girl, and they are told to come forward, pay for their prizes and take them away. Each lad is ticketed with the price he fetched and the name of the owner.

Great is the dismay of the shoppers when each girl opens her money bag only to find that she can't afford her man. He comes too high! Nobody has more than ten jelly beans— a dime!

FEED 'EM JUNCTION—"Lunch is served in the dining car!" announces the conductor, and the passengers whoop into the dining room where card tables, seating four, are arranged along the walls.

The girls escort their men to any table, seat them with elaborate courtesy, and hand them the leap year menu. This resembles the real thing. It carries a dainty black-and-white illustration at the top, picturing an old-fashioned valentine, but in place of the romantic motto is printed, "Feed the Brute"

The menu reads:

Lovers' Leap Special
Big Four Plate
(Four assorted heart-shaped sandwiches)
Neckin' Nectar
(Iced punch or hot chocolate)
Fortune Cake   Candy Kisses
Raspberry Gelatin
(Cut heart-shaped, served with whipped cream)

Leap Year Fortune cake should be rich in the traditional treasures of thimble, dime, ring, etc. Each girl serves a slice to her partner, with the gleeful hope that it contains the old maid's thimble, since most of the evening he has been handing her the mitten.

LAST MINUTE FUN—Leap year fun is served with the food. The best honeymoon essays are read aloud. The winner of the whispering pine game is asked to stand with his star piner while he reads aloud his written record of her "pines."

If there are any forfeits still unpaid for, the scores can be settled all at one fell swoop. The hostess announces that the following men, having shown themselves sadly lacking in a taste for domestic life, are now asked to dramatize various domestic utensils. Will the audience identify them, please?

The men draw from a box slips of paper on which have been written the names of such articles as lawn mower, washing machine, fly swatter, egg beater, rolling pin, self-wringing mop, electric iron, etc., and proceed to demonstrate in turn.

As the girls take leave of their partners, they say, "Happy Leap Year! Watch your step!"

A TWELFTH NIGHT REVEL

The sixth of January or Twelfth Night is, by right of centuries of tradition, the time for the jolliest of parties. It is the wind-up of twelve days of celebration, the grand finale of the yuletide festivities, when all the joys of the season, big and little, appear on the stage together, to make their bow before the curtain falls for another year.

TWELFTH NIGHT POSTERS—The posters show an old-time herald or quaint town crier making the announcement which is printed below the sketch:

Hear All! Hear All! Twelfth Night Revels will be held on ye sixth of january, at ye ...., at ye hour of .... Ye Lord of Misrule will be King of Yule for ye night.

TWELFTH NIGHT DECORATIONS—The decorations are all the usual Christmas evergreens—which, with the tree, are burnt as the last event of the evening—candles, stars, and one sample, at least, of all the old-time joys of Christmas. The sample may be a plum pudding, a huge mince pie, a Yule log, a wassail bowl filled with spiced fruit juice, or an imitation boar's head.

Also the traditional Twelfth Night Christmas tree, which is the old tree hung with nothing but gaily-wrapped edibles of the cake and cooky kind, such as tiny individual squares of tinfoil-wrapped fruit cake; cookies cut as stars, camels, palms and Christmas trees; gingerbread bells; or doughnuts in green and red cellophane bags.

TWELFTH NIGHT SUPPER—The supper starts the evening. To be really consistent with tradition it should be served on bare boards laid on trestles and lit by tapers standing in old brass, pewter, or iron candlesticks, evergreens being the only table decorations.

The meal can consist of a hot meat dish, hearty rather than dainty, and for dessert, a slice of the edible centerpiece, the Twelfth Night cake, a must for this sort of a celebration.

Or, if a more elaborate meal is preferred, it can be served as individual box lunches in "yule logs," made of crepe-

covered corrugated cardboard, rolled with the ridges outside to resemble bark. The menu follows:

Chicken Dinner Pies

Potato Salad

Toasted Celery Crackers

Olives   Cracked Nuts

Fortune Cake (Elizabethan Orange Loaf)

Coffee

The recipes for chicken dinner pie and fortune cake are
given at the end of the chapter.

ORDER OF PROGRAM—A Twelfth Night program, however informal, usually follows the same pattern. The order is:
supper; cutting of the cake (which determines who is the
King, Queen, and Knave or, in this case, the Court Jester);
coronation; allegiance; acclaim. The last is any form of jubi-
lation in which the crowd can take part, such as a rollicking
song, a folk dance, a singing game, or a stunt march.

THE REIGN OF MERRY DISPORTS—After supper, with its crowning ceremony of cutting the cake, the Lord of Misrule and
his lady are immediately dressed in their royal robes and
regalia, all of which have been prepared beforehand, also the
makings of the throne. The foolish crowns can be made of
anything handy—a red Christmas wreath, a man's linen collar, or a saucepan lid. The scepters are equally absurd—a
candy stick, a toasting fork, golf club, or garden rake. A
royal throne is easily improvised from armchairs, gilt paper,
plush drapes, ornate shawls, old velvet finery, and cushions
on which subjects may kneel.

THE COURT JESTER—The Court Jester is dressed in traditional
cap and bells, and when not sitting at the King's feet, is dart-
ing here, there, and everywhere, taking the royal orders to
leaders—or, rather, mistaking them, for it is his mischievous
job to turn the world topsy-turvy for this one mad night.

MERRY ALLEGIANCE—Guests come in couples to kneel on the
cushions before the throne. The King says solemnly, "It takes
a wise man to be a fool. Arise, wise ones, and be merrily
foolish!" As he says this, he hands the man a paper hat, or a

popping cracker containing one, while the Queen hands the girl one. The Court Jester gives each a balloon or a paper "teaser" of some sort.

If the crowd is a large one, the allegiance ceremony can be performed en masse. In which case, the subjects form in two columns, girls in one, men in the other, all facing the throne. The King rises and with much dignity proclaims, "It takes a wise man to be a fool. Away, wise ones, and be merrily foolish!"

The columns then march toward the throne to receive their paper hats and favors, then separate to march in single file around the hall, meeting at the center rear, where a leader awaits them to give the royal order for the next event.

TWELFTH NIGHT PROGRAM—Now the evening is formally launched, and the program that follows is up to the director, who arranges it to suit the number there, the ages of the guests, the floor space, the available talent, and the time limit. He reserves a reasonable amount of time for the final ceremony of the burning of the Christmas tree and evergreens, then fills the rest of the program to suit his particular plans.

ROYAL SPORTS—Games for all can be interspersed with performers' numbers, the King announcing such frolics with the royal edict, "Let the people play!" Whereupon any of the old-fashioned games are in order, such as blind man's buff, musical chairs, or spin the platter. In most groups there are gymnasium graduates who know some of the old English folk dances from student days—such as rufty-tufty, gathering peascods, and sweet Kate—who will enjoy romping through them. The Virginia Reel, and its more simple cousin, A-hunting We Will Go, are gay country dances that adults like. Leaders may come prepared to start some of the old favorite singing games that were once played on the village green, such as London bridge is falling down, Oranges and lemons, here we come gathering nuts in May, there was a jolly miller, etc.

COURT ETIQUETTE—Here is a way of drafting local talent to contribute to the program, and for filling out an evening's entertainment with stunts that look impromptu but are not.

It is announced that after the crowning ceremony, the royal couple must be treated with all due deference. Therefore, any subject turning his back on them while they are sitting in state will be penalized by a royal guard and made to pay a heavy fine. However, when the King and Queen join their subjects in games or dances, they travel incognito, and no forfeits can be collected. By unexpectedly and frequently mounting the throne, singly or together, their Royal Highnesses find that the court etiquette of even their most loyal subjects is sadly at fault. By the end of the evening few escape paying a penalty.

A FORFEITS CHAIRMAN—The forfeits chairman has been appointed previously to find amusing and fitting forfeits, then write them on cards of two colors, red for the men and green for the girls. The cards are sorted and placed in two "jewel caskets"—shoe boxes covered with gold paper. The Queen holds the casket of men's tickets, and the King, the girls'. The first offending man steps up to the Queen's throne. She takes up a card, apparently at random, and reads aloud the sentence that is written there, whereupon the culprit serves his sentence before an unsympathetic audience. Then the first lady offender approaches the King's throne to hear her doom, which his majesty reads from the card he picks from the casket. She gets her sentence over as quickly as possible. So it goes until justice has been done.

SPECIAL TALENT STUNTS—The forfeit chairman has prepared for the special talent stunts by writing the names of such performers each on a white card, with whatever is their specialty, such as, song, skit, dance, stunt, mouth organ, impersonations.

The talent is also prepared, for all performers have been warned that they will be called upon to exhibit their chief talent at forfeit-paying time. There may be two comics among those invited. The forfeit chairman asks them to work up a funny skit that they can do as a team. Then when one of the talented culprits comes before the King, the white ticket with his name on is drawn from the casket. The King orders him to find his partner in crime and serve their joint sentence.

THE GATHERING OF THE GREENS—Near the end of the evening, a lively march, such as "Jingle Bells," is played, while the King's loyal subjects parade around the room. When the music stops, marchers rush to gather the Christmas evergreens that have been used to decorate the hall. When the music starts again, they rush back into line, carrying their evergreens, and go on marching.

As they pass the throne they throw their collected greenery at the King's feet, so that when the music again stops suddenly, their hands will be free to collect more. The heap grows bigger as the room, by degrees, is stripped of all its evergreens. Not a leaf must be left.

There is time out now for guests to don their wraps; for the ceremonial burning of the big Christmas tree and evergreens is an outdoor rite. Carols are played or sung to preserve the continuity.

TWELFTH NIGHT TREE PROCESSION—The King's nobles take the tree and lead the procession, the King and Queen following. Then come the evergreen carriers, bearing their load, followed by the rest of the company. The Court Jester, true to character, brings up the rear with the sweeping of a few leaves and holly berries in a dustpan. The procession moves to the outdoors, where the official fire-makers and tenders—boy scouts in medieval costumes—have all in readiness for a sure, swift, and safe blaze.

Recipes for Twelfth Night Supper

The pies are to be eaten in the hand, sandwich fashion.

CHICKEN DINNER PIES

2 cups canned chicken or other canned meats	Minced parsley or celery
	White sauce
½ cup canned peas	Seasoning

Pie Pastry

Flake the meat and add the peas. Season with salt, pepper, some parsley, celery, or any other seasoning preferred. Moisten with a small amount of medium white sauce. Roll the pastry out and cut in rounds about the size of a saucer. Place some of the meat mixture in the center of each pie, bring the edges together, and bake in a hot oven until a warm brown. Cool before packing in waxed paper.

POTATO SALAD

Potato salad should be packed in waxed paper cups, the one quarter pint size which have tight-fitting covers. A jellied vegetable salad would go well with the chicken pie. A paper fork should go with each serving.

CELERY CRACKERS

These appetizer crackers come in a tin. They have a delicious butter-toasted taste and are unusual, being embedded with poppy seed and celery salt and caraway seed. They should be oven-heated before packing into the yule log boxes. With the crackers as a salad accompaniment, and the chicken wearing a pastry overcoat, no bread need be included.

Any little knickknacks—cracked nuts, a few candy sticks, or a tiny popcorn ball would be suitable to add a little fillup to the box.

ELIZABETHAN ORANGE LOAF

However simple, no Twelfth Night celebration is complete without a fortune cake. As well have Easter without eggs! Here is a new variation of the traditional loaf cake. The orange flavor mixed in the batter itself lends an indescribably good tang and fragrance. Boiled icing with cream of tartar added gives the crowning effect of snowy whiteness. The recipe follows:

1 cup butter	3 teaspoons baking powder
2 cups sugar	½ teaspoon salt
5 egg yolks	½ cup orange juice
3½ cups cake flour	½ cup milk

3 egg whites

Cream the butter, add the sugar gradually, and cream until light and fluffy. Add the egg yolks one at a time, beating well after each addition. Sift the flour and measure; sift again twice with baking powder and salt, and add to the first mixture alternately with orange juice and milk. Fold in stiffly beaten egg whites. Pour into a greased and floured 10-inch tube pan and bake in a moderate oven, 350 degrees, for sixty minutes. When it is cool and before frosting, push a bean and a clove into one side of the cake and a pea into the other. Mark, so that the hostess will know which side contains the pea and which the bean and the clove. Then frost with the following frosting:

FROSTING

2 egg whites	¼ teaspoon salt
1 cup sugar	3 tablespoons cold water
½ teaspoon cream of tartar	1 teaspoon vanilla

Put all ingredients in the top of the double boiler. Place over boiling water and beat with a rotary beater for seven minutes, until the mixture holds its shape. Cool slightly before spreading on the cake. The approximate places where the pea, bean, and clove are imbedded can again be marked in the frosting by a sliver of candied peel, cherry, or a silver candy.

Decorate around the edge of the cake with a wreath of angelica leaves and red cherries and place in the center a tiny Christmas tree, and the little figures of the king, queen, and knight (or knave) from a chess set.

When the time comes to cut the cake, the slices for the men come from that side of the cake where the lucky bean and the clove are embedded; the slices for the girls, from the other side where the pea is hidden.

The finder of the bean is crowned King of the Revels, while the girl whose slice of cake contains the pea is his Queen.

Since the Court Jester is expected to be the life of the party, the hostess can deftly handle the plates so that the clove falls to the natural cutup of the crowd. A bell-trimmed fools' cap is put on his head, which is his license to clown as soon, as often, and as long as he wishes.

A YOU'LL-REMEMBER PARTY

This is a quiet little home party for Twelfth Night, to which one's relatives are invited or just a few intimate friends or neighbors. It is best suited for the hostess whose home has a fireplace in its living room.

INVITATIONS—The invitations are written on cards shaped like a yule log and lettered, "A You'll-Remember Party." Below is written the invitation verse:

> Do come and tell us
>   By yule log and ember,
> The happiest Christmas
>   You can remember,

All other necessary information—day, date, time, name, and address of the hostess—is added wherever it seems to fit best.

DECORATIONS—These are kept as simple and easy as possible. Since Twelfth Night commemorates to many the supposed arrival of the Three Wise Men in Bethlehem, any fine Christmas cards showing them crossing the desert or worshiping at the manger can be placed on the mantel shelf.

A long panel or frieze picturing the Wise Men is a real addition. Some firms at Christmas time sell a tracing of a Wise Men project which can be cut from black mat stock. Camels, palm trees, Bethlehem, and the star are in silhouette and stand alone. When placed on a tray of sand, with a light so arranged that the shadows of the scene are cast on the miniature desert, this scriptural cutout is most effective. Silver stars can be fastened each to a silver cord and hung from the chandeliers or festooned across the room. Care should be taken that none is tied to the evergreens; for no star must be burned, when at the end of the evening the tree is burned in a bonfire.

ILLUMINATION—Atmosphere is important for this type of party. Since candles and the yule log are so closely related, the electric lamps are turned off. Soft candlelight, a blazing log fire, and a few well-chosen phonograph records, and the setting is complete.

THE YOU'LL-REMEMBER TREE—Many a loyal American citizen will have nostalgic memories of the beautiful Twelfth Night tree of her European girlhood. There are no toys on it, no tinsel, but holiday goodies galore in the form of cakes and cookies in fancy shapes and fancy wrappings. "Snowballs"—balls of cake, roughly iced and tied with red ribbon —are always a favorite with the children, and a whole Noah's Ark can be made of animals cut from cooky dough, and when baked, colored with boiled icing to match their real colors.

The hostess can hang the tree with a tagged and packaged food treat for each guest.

YOU'LL-REMEMBER GAMES—It is fun to do some of the foolish stunts they did in the old-time celebrations of Twelfth Night. Marching from "threshold to roof-tree," for instance, following the tallest guest, who parades from cellar to attic, carrying on a high-held tray a loaf of bread, so that no one under that roof shall want for bread that year. Each guest may put on the magic tray a scrap of what he most craves —for the charm always works!

Then can come the mummers, or their twentieth century descendant, which is charades.

A Cake Quiz is an easy contest for a cozy fireside group. Each guest is handed a pencil, and a card which is decorated with the colored illustration of a very fancy cake, cut from the advertising pages of a magazine. The card reads:

What cake or confection would you bake for the following?   Answers

1. Advertiser .... Cream puffs
2. Banker .... Doughnuts
3. Champion Trackman .... Cupcake
4. Colonial Lady .... Martha Washington
5. Englishwoman .... Tea cake
6. A Titled Aristocrat .... Lady Baltimore
7. Gossip .... Spice cake
8. His Satanic Majesty .... Devil's food
9. Heaven .... Angel food
10. Idler .... Loaf cake
11. Milliner .... Ribbon cake

12. Monkey .... Coconut
13. Old Soak .... Sponge
14. Politician .... Plum
15. Pugilist .... Pound cake
16. Quaker .... Oatmeal cookies
17. Redhead .... Ginger
18. Society Hostess .... Reception
19. Engaged Girl .... Bride's cake

If there are in this list cakes of which the hostess feels her guests, in these package-cake days, have never heard, she can omit them from the list.

BEFANA—Befana can be the surprise of the evening. Dressed as an old Italian peasant, she tells the guests she is on her way to visit the little children of Italy, and has too much in her load of gifts for them, so would like to give a Twelfth Night remembrance to each guest. Her basket is filled with the cake gifts snipped quickly from the tree by helpers, while the other guests are absorbed in some game. It is all done so smoothly that few notice it, and it clears the tree for the burning ceremony, and distributes the gifts with little sacrifice of time.

If wished, Befana can tell the legend about her, so beloved of European children. A simple version can be found in most libraries. Sometimes it is possible to get a real Italian, who speaks English brokenly, to take the part and tell the story. It is most effective when given with the slow earnestness of the foreigner speaking a new tongue, and especially if it is followed by the singing of a carol in her own language.

YULE LOG STORIES—An old-time minstrel man is in charge of a big holly-decorated log which lies near the fireplace as if awaiting its time to be thrown on the fire. From time to time he sallies forth and lassoes a guest with a rope of ivy. Drawing him to the log he makes him spin a yarn about the happiest Christmas he can remember, while the rest listen.

FIRESIDE SUPPER—Sometimes the hostess who has a fireplace would like a menu of "finger foods," with her guests sitting around the hearth, enjoying the fun of cooking their own meal. The following is that sort of menu. It requires no plates or cutlery.

Cheese Toasts

Pig and Onion Bobs

Olives   Pickles   Celery

Nuts to Crack   Marshmallows to Toast

Fortune Cake

Coffee

CHEESE TOASTS—For these toasts, American cheese and thin sliced bacon, each slice halved, are cut in one-inch squares. A half slice of bacon is wrapped around a square of cheese, then is stuck on a long-handled fork and broiled over the coals. When the bacon is crisply sizzling and the cheese is melting, it is popped into a bun which has been warming by the blaze.

Guests are asked to make their own cheese toasts, one after another, eating as they go.

PIG AND ONION BOBS—These bobs are an honest-to-goodness delight. Three small sausages are alternated on a skewer with quarter-inch slices of onion, then broiled. They are, of course, to be eaten in buns.

If plenty of olives, both stuffed and ripe, also celery and pickles are provided, a salad will not be necessary.

BURNING THE CHRISTMAS TREE—Just before midnight, all the evergreens and the Christmas tree are gathered into a heap in the back yard and solemnly burned; for no Christmas tree should suffer the indignity of being thrown out like rubbish.

There is something mystic in any dying fire, and no crowd, however gay, can watch the Christmas tree go to ashes without being sobered in spirit, so that a religious close—hymn, prayer, or benediction—seems to be the only fitting end. "Blest Be the Tie That Binds" is especially comforting as a reminder of lasting things in a world where even Christmas is gone in twelve days.

A SNOW BALL

Looking for something seasonal for that midwinter dance? Then why not throw a Snow Ball, all white and silver, with King Winter and the Snow Queen sitting in state on a snowbound throne and worrying, not about how they shall break the ice, but for fear a thaw will set in? For Old Man Thaw, in mud-splashed yellow slicker and rubber boots, is the villain of the party, always waiting for a chance to get in his dirty work!

SNOWBALL POSTERS—A poster guaranteed to start the ball rolling has a background of midnight blue, with the lettering a frosty white. In the foreground is a huge snowball made of crushed white crepe paper and pasted in place. A winter landscape of snow-covered trees and houses can be cut from decorated crepe paper of such design or from snowy scenery pictured on magazine covers, and then pasted on the poster at each side of the giant snowball.

In the midnight blue of the poster above the snowy scene is printed in white lettering:

> We're gonna throw a Snow Ball;
> C'mon and join our play;
> 'Twill be the biggest Snow Ball
> That ever came your way.

On the strip of midnight blue cardboard below the pictured snow scene is the necessary information, also in white lettering. For example: Guild Hall   Jan. 10   Tickets $1.00

DECORATIONS—That first impression — the importance of which let no decorating committee under-estimate—should be so convincing that the guests' first thought will be, "Snowed in, b'gosh! And who's going to dig us out?" No effect is so thrilling to produce or so breath-taking in its white and silver loveliness.

The plan of decoration will depend largely upon where the dance is to be held. The small home dance can be given a beautiful setting by the clever hostess in a few hours.

But the decorations for the larger dance, sponsored by club or school, and given in a hall or gymnasium, will need careful planning by a capable committee. In the latter case, efforts probably will center upon working out an effective and original treatment for stage, lights, and orchestra.

The decorating committee will find ordinary chicken wire an invaluable first aid to the stranded. For instance, a too-high ceiling that defies any other treatment can be hidden from view by a false ceiling made by running lengths of chicken wire, edge to edge, below and parallel with the real one. Pine twigs woven into the mesh make a Christmasy evergreen roof, which is a wonderful foil for the white and silver color scheme. The wire can also be used as a fence around the front edge of the stage and transformed into a sturdy-looking hedge by twining in pine twigs. All the boughs are generously sprinkled with cotton batting snow, glittering with mica dust.

A DECORATIVE SNOW STORM—Guests find a decorative snow storm awaiting them. Countless fleecy flakes, all made of specks of cotton batting tied to threads of varying lengths, are suspended from the overhead wires. Not only is the air full of snow, but all around are evidences that it has been snowing for weeks! The glittering Christmas trees and shrubs stand in deep drifts of it. It covers the window sills, the platform, the piano, the refreshment booth. It is everywhere! White icicles—the crepe paper kind that can be bought ready cut in strips ten feet long—hang all around the room from the top of the walls, the balcony, the stage, and from doorways and arches. Yes, one of those old-fashioned winters when Christmas was Christmas!

WHEN WINTER COMES—What is needed to make winter come to the Snow Ball? Plenty of white crepe paper, cotton batting and sparkling artificial snow dust; some tinsel and white and silver balloons; a little paste, time, and ingenuity. That's all.

If snow underfoot is wished for on the stage, a few old sheets or pieces of tarpaulin, sparkling under thickly scattered mica snow, will get the effect.

Sometimes hall windows present difficulties to the decorating committee. They can be realistically frosted by smearing them with Bon Ami.

A quick way to produce a snowy foliage background is to spray branches and weeds with white paint, and while they are still wet, sprinkle them with metallics or colored crystals.

Another way to make winter shrubbery is by smearing bare branches with paste and then thrusting them into a pan of white confetti and dusting them with mica snow.

When a large, snow-covered area is required, white crepe paper may be crushed in the hands until it is softly fluffy. Then it is splashed here and there with library paste, which is sprinkled well with Christmas snow dust before it dries.

If colored posts in the hall need to be camouflaged, they may be wound with strips of white crepe paper and splashed with silver paint.

SNOW MEN—A few of the posts or pillars in the hall can have a jolly old snow man, sparkling with good humor and mica, built around each. The body and head are made of crushed white crepe paper and the snow man's features and coat buttons are cut from black mat stock. The hat he wears is made, silhouette-fashion, out of cardboard and his big paper tie is of flaming and brilliant red.

To form a natural and picturesque setting for the snow man, strands of white crepe paper moss are hung overhead from branches wired to the post.

A snow man that can be moved around at will is made by sewing cheesecloth over a couple of bushel baskets and covering them with crushed crepe paper. A round head is added and the features are marked. A broomstick, a pipe, and an old slouch hat complete the costume.

Two of these snow men can be made the pillars of an original snow arch. A flexible bamboo pole or strong wire forms the curve of the arch, each end apparently held in the broomstick hand of a snow man. When wrapped in white cotton batting and hung with alternating tinfoil icicles and cotton snowballs, these arches make attractive markers for any entrance, refreshment booth, etc.

SNOWBALL LIGHTS—Nothing lends so much glamor to decorations as the right kind of illumination. The committee may experiment with blue, green, and violet lights to determine which will add the right Arctic touch, avoiding the slightest suggestion of glare. A few blue lights, with one strong spotlight over the stage, may do the trick.

One lovely way of making hanging clusters of glaring white lights cast a storybook spell over the snowy scene is as follows: Green, blue, and violet bulbs are used, and pale blue sparkle floss is fastened to the rim of a wooden hoop to form a brilliant and glittering covering for the lights. Cotton snowballs, splashed with mica, are fastened on strands of silver tinsel cut in uneven lengths. These strands are tied to the hoop so that they shower down at intervals among the sparkle floss fringe. Finally, narrow white paper streamers are draped up from the hoop to form a peak several feet above it.

SNOWBALL TREES—In each corner of the hall could stand a Christmas tree, decorated entirely in white and silver. It is hung with cotton snowballs—small, medium, and big. If wished, these can be shaped around some inexpensive little favor, and during one of the novelty dances they can be cut from the tree by the Snowflake Twins and then thrown to the dancers, as souvenirs, one to a guest. The favors for the men could be in snowballs that are tied to the tree with silver cord; those suitable for the girls, in snowballs tied with white cord. A huge tree could stand in the center of the hall, or in the entrance or lobby, hung with white balloons.

KING WINTER, THE SNOW QUEEN AND SNOWFLAKE TWINS— Their Royal Highnesses could watch the snow frolic from a throne draped in white cheesecloth and ermine trim of cotton batting. Behind the throne is an aurora borealis background, simply made by hanging lengths of cheesecloth in brilliant sunset colors behind a veil of thin white cheesecloth, painted with silver.

Two blond girls, dressed in fluffy white, with snowflakes sparkling in their hair, could impersonate the Snowflake Twins, helping to distribute the favor snowballs and also any other favors needed for the novelty dances on the program.

At a holiday dance such as this, every other dance could be a novelty dance or one in which partners are left to chance by some device as matching snowballs, snow men, etc., or property fitting together snow scenes cut into two jigsaw halves.

OLD MAN THAW—Old Man Thaw doesn't deserve it, but he has been the hit of the evening. His appearance may be timed to fit in with other events on the program, or he may come in whenever the spirit moves him. In any case, he may be depended upon to create excitement with each appearance.

For whenever he slouches on to the platform, the Snow Queen, King Winter, and the Snowflake Twins begin to wilt visibly. Whereupon the Master of Ceremonies or some other hero rushes to the rescue, and with a frosty tinsel rope drags the villain, protesting loudly, off the scene. Then the Royal Snow family resume their frozen reign, and all is well with their snowbound subjects.

During the last dance, Old Man Thaw makes his final appearance, defies the royal house, stops the orchestra, and warns the crowd of dancers to get ready to melt away.

"A snowball," he announces loudly, "has as much chance with Old Man Thaw as a snowball has in—Well!"

SNOWBALL PARTNER FINDERS—The men find that at a snow ball it literally snows partners. Two sets of snowflakes are cut from white paper and numbered in duplicate. One set is arranged to form a snowdrift, from which each girl takes a flake.

A sheet has been stretched across a convenient corner, behind which is concealed a stepladder. Someone mounts the ladder, carrying a box containing the other set of flakes. The men take up positions near the other side of the sheet, so that they can be conveniently snowed on. Partners are found by matching the numbers on the flakes.

A jingle-bell novelty number might follow, danced to the tune of "Jingle Bells." The dancers are told to sing the song as they dance, omitting the words, "jingle bells" and "jingle" whenever they occur and substituting for them a vigorous ringing of their sleigh bells. The dance can start slowly, getting faster and faster, until it is such a quickstep that there is more jingling than singing.

SNOW WONDER SINGERS—During intermission, a few vocal numbers could be introduced, if wished. Irving Berlin's "I'm Dreaming of a White Christmas" would be a perfect choice.

Other suitable numbers would be "Winter Wonderland" and "I've Got Your Love to Keep Me Warm."

A big, jolly fellow, dressed as a small boy, and carrying ice skates, could sing "All I Want For Christmas Is My Two Front Teeth."

An elimination dance is always fun. A Snowflake Twin could throw a soft, white, wooly ball at the dancers. The couple she strikes with the snowball must leave the floor. This procedure continues until all but one couple are eliminated. The last couple left can be asked to give an exhibition dance and receive a small prize, such as a couple of white popcorn balls, decorated with holiday ribbon.

Just before the last dance, confetti can be distributed in the form of snowballs, the outside cover being of white tissue paper. Thus the dance can have a gala finish.

SNOW BALL REFRESHMENTS—The refreshments can be served at the "North Pole," which rises from a mound of artificial snow. Toy teddy bears climb the pole. If sandwiches are served, they should be as white as possible—chicken, for instance, or cream cheese. Ice cream can be served in snowball shape, accompanied by snowball cakes. The cakes are round cupcakes covered with white frosting and coconut.

A SOUVENIR SPOON PARTY

A grand mixer, a spoon! This is a Valentine Day frolic for young people, featuring spoons instead of the usual hearts and darts. Why? Because Cupid loves to find a match for a good cook!

SPOONY INVITATIONS—These can be written with silver ink on a red correspondence card—or with red ink on a white one—and decorated with a Cupid sticker. A large spoon cut from contrasting colored paper can be pasted on the card, or a tiny doll-size toy spoon can be thrust through a double slit cut in one corner of the card. The following lines explain the spoon:

> Dan's speeding this hearty
> Invitation to spoon
> At a Valentine party
> That's coming off soon.

The time, date and place are added and the envelope is sealed with a winged Dan Cupid sticker and the cutout of a tiny silver spoon.

SPOONY DECORATIONS—Any Valentine trimmings will do, with the addition of spoons of all sorts and sizes. The spoons may be the real thing, as well as scores of spoons cut from aluminum foil and silver paper.

Mammoth souvenir spoons can be cut from cardboard, their bowls inscribed with some such sentiment as "Lover's Spoonshine," or "A Gift from Kiss Korner." If a guest has a collection of silver souvenir spoons, antique spoons, or the old country apostle spoons, given in times past at the baptism of babies, these can be borrowed for the occasion and given a safe place of honor.

Two huge valentines, each a yard wide, can be made of lacy shelf paper and doilies, the corners trimmed with double red hearts, each pair pierced with a spoon instead of the usual arrow. The verse is bordered with a frame of spoons, entwined with true lover's knots of paper ribbon. On one valentine is printed some fond sentiment, such as:

> Oh, sweetheart, let us sit and spoon
> Beneath electric light or moon,
> Beneath the sun or in the dark,
> Or by the notice, "Do Not Park."

The other valentine may be used for a bright line contest, to give the first-comers something to do until the others arrive and the regular program can start. The early bird is given card and pencil and asked to supply the second valentine with a bright last line. Any foolish verse will do, for example:

> Oh, sweetheart mine, I wish to say,
> I'm thinking of you all the day,
> I'm thinking of you all the night,
> _____

Poets are asked to fill in the blank line and sign their efforts before turning them in for grading. At refreshment time, the cleverest, the funniest, and the most awful are read aloud. The best could win a spoon-decorated telephone pad containing the telephone numbers of all present and tagged, "We like your line!" The writer of the most hilarious example of atrocious poetry could be awarded a candy-filled glass toy telephone to which is tied a card reading, "Line out of order!"

SPOONY TABLE TRIM AND CENTERPIECE—Any Valentine setting —festive paper cloth, napkins and plates, silver tarletan spread over red, fluted double panels of red and white crepe paper—can be given the right spoony touch with a little ingenuity and a spot of humor.

The spoony centerpiece could be a kewpie doll cupid, gone nudist except for a brief gingham apron. In one hand he holds a spoon; in the other, a toy saucepan. The size of both spoon and pan will be governed by the size of the doll.

Before Chef Cupid on a toy deal table is a fat little cookbook, entitled, "Two Can Live as Cheaply as One," and two small kitchen canisters, one labeled "Sugar" and the other, "Spice."

SPOONY FAVORS—A paper-spoon lady is easy to make. A doll face is sketched with India ink on the rounded back of the paper spoon's bowl, the cheeks and lips tinted, and a darning-silk fringe glued on. A coal-scuttle bonnet hides the absence of head at the back.

If her full crinoline dress of crepe paper is made double, the lady will stand. Beneath her ample skirts there is room to hide any small favor, such as cigarettes, candy, powder puffs, colored matches, chiffon handkerchiefs, tiny bottles of perfume, lucky spoons, or heart charms.

SMALL SPOONY TABLES—A simple but attractive decoration for card tables, seating four, is a setting made of large, square lace paper doilies arranged to form a cross. At each of the four uncovered corners a winged heart cutout is placed, silver paper spoons or toy spoons being substituted for the outstretched wings.

MEETING PAST SPOONERS—This stunt is a good way to get guests merrily mixed up. A pair of famous lovers is chosen for each couple invited. The famous—or infamous!—ladies' names are written on little white paper spoons, a different siren on each. A pin is run in each spoon handle and all are placed in a white box.

The names of their masculine mates are written on red paper spoons, pinned and put into a red box. Such names as Romeo and Juliet, Mark Antony and Cleopatra, the Prince and Cinderella, King Arthur and Guinevere, Dante and Beatrice, Sir Walter Raleigh and Good Queen Bess, Robert Burns and Annie Laurie, John Alden and Priscilla, and Launcelot and Elaine may be used. Comic strip lovers will do just as well.

On the party night, a red spoon is pinned on each man's back and a white one on each girl's, while cards and pencils are distributed with instructions to find out who's who in Spoonland. The object of each player is to read the celebrated name on the back of each guest and write it on his own card against the wearer's name, while at the same time concealing his own glamorous self in any manner except standing with his back pressed against a wall. This game may be played for about ten minutes.

The game is made more difficult by substituting a dash for every vowel in the name, and funnier by adding a sentimental or satirical description to the name pinned on each back. For example, after Cinderella, "Iccle Tootsy-Wootsies;" or after Henry VIII—any one of his many wives can be paired with him—"Old Faithful."

SPOONERS' PROMENADE—In the previous game, each famous lover has discovered his mate. Guests all line up, properly mated for the promenade.

It is fun to rig up a moon to give the right romantic atmosphere for this event. This can be made of a round box, the lid and bottom of which have been removed and replaced by two or more thicknesses of fireproof yellow crepe paper, on which the features of the man in the moon have been marked in crayon. A small electric light bulb is inserted in the box, and the box hung high on the wall in a conspicuous place, and during the promenade all other lights are turned off, leaving only the one in the moon.

The couples are told to link arms and go strolling in the moonlight. Each man is to try to propose to his lady before the clashing of a spoon against a saucepan lid signals him to leave her and link arms with another, to whom he must try to propose.

The girl is not to co-operate. She is to use every effort to prevent her partner from completing his proposal—every fair effort, that is. Of course, she may not choke him! She can keep up a continuous chatter, so that he cannot get in a word for himself, or she can outwit him by distracting his attention at the critical moment, or she can drop a few articles to induce him to waste precious moments in picking them up.

There are restraining rules for the man. He may not yell, "Marry me!" the instant the signal sounds. He must lead up to the proposal by at least two tactful, conversational sentences about the moon.

The man who succeeds in completing most proposals, with his lady agreeing that he did it fairly, receives a silver jam spoon. But the handsomest prize goes to the girl who stops, by quick sparring or ruses, the most declarations.

CROONING SPOONERS—For this game, couples may remain the same, as in the previous promenade, or partners may be shuffled by some simple pairing-off game, as, for instance, spoons may be cut in duplicate, of different colors and sizes, the mates separated in two boxes. Men choose from one box; girls, from another, then match spoons for partners.

Couples separate, the men going into the adjoining room, with an open doorway between. Each man decides on five love songs to sing, classic or popular. He writes the list on a card which he hands to the radio station conductor. When all lists are in, the conductor compares them all, and if there are duplications, he asks the performer to make another choice.

He explains to his "talent" that each performer's public consists of one fan—his girl, in the other room, who sits breathlessly listening, trying her utmost to recognize and name the song he is singing to her, which is not so easy. For at a signal from the station conductor, all radio singers must start to sing together, each his chosen song. And, what is more important, they must stop together. No hang-over notes to provide a clue to a listening lady!

Each fan is provided with a pencil, and a card on which she is to jot down the name of each song she thinks her hero is singing. When the concert is over, each performer rushes to his "public," only to learn the worst. He gave his best to "Sweet Genevieve," and she thought he was singing "A Frog, He would a-Wooing Go" — of all the crushing blows!

LITERALLY SPOONING—After the previous game, a quiet game will be welcome. This one is an amusing adaptation of the old blindfold spoon-and-water stunt. A team consists of a man and a girl, both blindfolded. They sit on newspapers spread on the floor. Each is given a spoon and dish of crisp potato chips. On the word to start, each attempts to feed the other by means of the spoon. If several spoon at the same time, it adds to the fun—and the debris!

The prize is awarded, not to the one who first empties his dish, but to the one who deposits its contents in the right place. Contestants may not speak, but a player may help a bewildered partner who has lost all sense of direction, by a little judicious humming of any love song.

STRINGED SPOONERS—Couples compete to see which pair can first eat a large dish of ice cream. The difficulty is that the right wrists of man and girl in each couple are joined by a cord twenty inches long, which prevents putting spoons into their mouths at the same time. Sooner or later, one couple discovers that the only way to empty the dish is for one to dip while the other eats. This trick learned, the two become synchronized spooners and race to victory.

SPOONY REFRESHMENTS—Guests find their table silverware consists only of spoons. All items on the menu are such as can be eaten by hand or with spoons.

A simple menu that can be eaten this way is: minced ham sandwiches; potato salad, decorated with pimento hearts; cherry ice and white cake.

A more elaborate menu is:

Four Ways Plate
(Four assorted heart-shaped sandwiches)

St. Valentine's Nectar
(Iced Punch or Hot Chocolate)

Fortune Cakes   Candy Kisses

Raspberry Gelatin
(Cut heart-shaped, served with Whipped Cream or
Vanilla Ice Cream)

The sandwiches, which may contain any chosen mixture, are served on a heart-and-spoon decorated lace doily on a paper plate. They seem more festive if made of different kinds of bread, one of rye bread, another of whole wheat, a third of whole wheat, a fourth of raisin bread, and one on white. The tops may be garnished with tiny hearts and spoons cut from pimento, green pepper, or thin, sliced cheese.

Minced ham with chopped mustard pickle is a good combination that the men will like. Other tasty combinations are: pimento butter sandwiches, chopped maraschino cherries and cream cheese, marmalade and peanut butter, minced chicken with pineapple, and pecan nuts moistened with mayonnaise.

Other refreshment suggestions are Waldorf salad served in rosy apples, and layer cake with a ring, button, and penny wrapped in pieces of waxed paper and placed between the layers.

Sometimes a simple dinner is in order. In which case, the following menu would be suitable:

Chicken a la King

Glazed Apples   Cranberries

Creamed Potatoes

Hot Rolls

Lime Sherbet   Cake

Tea or Coffee

A ST. PATRICK'S DAY TEA

There comes a time when every woman's club is looking for something that will be successful both socially and financially, yet will not be too great a burden on the busy president or on some overworked committee.

A competitive community tea may be the answer. It can be planned for any holiday season or red-letter day that lends itself to pretty table decorations. But a St. Patrick's Day "tay" seems to be the favorite.

THE DATE AND PLACE—As soon as the date for the tea is decided, the place should be secured for it. Since this is a special day, the committee should speak at least a month in advance for the club house or church hall for the afternoon of March seventeenth.

TABLES AND HOSTESSES—The president appoints her hostesses, each to have charge of a table and choose her own helper. Twelve tables make a fine display.

PRIZES—The president announces that prizes will be awarded for the most beautiful, the most original, and the most amusing table. Excitement mounts. There is nothing like competition to add zest to effort.

ADVERTISING THE TEA—Advance notices of the tea are inserted in the town papers. If there is a local community paper, the cooperation of the society editor is asked. Stories are submitted to her, telling of the unusual features of the competitive tea, with mysterious hints to arouse the interest of readers and make them want to come and see the tables.

Amusing imaginary incidents of the chitchat sort can be sent in, telling how Mrs. So-and-So, a well-known leader in the community and a hostess for the tea, was overheard in the local pet shop asking where she could procure a green parrot that could be taught to say, "Begorra."

A COMMUNITY AFFAIR—The idea is to get people in the community to attend the tea, as well as members of the club and church. So tickets are sold from door to door. They cost so little—just fifty cents—and each one entitles the owner to entrance, tea at any table, and a chance to hear whatever entertainment may be offered.

This advance selling of tickets is good in several ways. It advertises the tea in a very personal way. A charming lady at the door, full of enthusiasm about the coming attraction, has more magnetic pull than the printed advertisement. Then, too, should it rain, snow, or hail, the ticket money is safely in. Also the fact that the tickets already have been paid for insures a certain attendance, regardless of the weather.

STARTING EVEN—No aspiring contestant may bring her own fancy table, and so get an edge on the others. Only folding card tables are used, and since they are small, two are put close together and set as one. This makes for uniformity, and, when all are decorated, achieves a general loveliness.

But from then on, each hostess is on her own, the only requirement being that she keeps to the traditional green color scheme. Hostesses and their assistants may dress in Irish costumes or wear dainty little aprons and kerchiefs to match their table decorations.

WELCOMING TEA DRINKERS—Standing at the door to greet all arrivals are four charming official greeters. These members of the club or church have been especially chosen for this important duty because of the genuine warmth of their personalities, their graciousness, and their popularity. Should a stranger appear shy or diffident, one of these greeters escorts her to one of the tables and introduces her to the hostess.

THE SERVICE TABLE—A long, beautifully decorated table is placed at one side of the hall. On it stand candelabra, choice flowers, and two steaming Russian samovars, or whatever modern equivalent is available.

Each hostess has her individual teapot filled here. Then, seated at her own table, she pours tea and chats while her helper serves and replenishes the sandwiches. The hostess and her helper take turns at pouring.

Tea House—The tea house is a Japanese booth, selling home-baked cakes, cookies, and pies. Each hostess, in the course of conversation, mentions this booth to the visiting house-wives at her table, many of whom will welcome this chance of taking home some delicacy for the family's supper dessert.

Tea-wagon—A pretty colleen in costume wheels a tea wagon among the tables. On it are boxes of homemade candy, priced according to size and contents.

Tea Ball—The tea ball is the entertainment provided for floor or stage. It can be a wandering fiddler playing Irish airs, a good quartet giving a medley of Irish songs, or a row of little girls in costume dancing an Irish jig.

Table Prizes—Three judges are appointed to make the difficult decision. All the tables are so attractive, they say, that they only wish there were twelve prizes instead of three. The prizes are big St. Patrick cakes, iced in green. After all the guests have departed, the winners cut the cakes and share them with the other hostesses, their helpers, and the judges. Then all sit down happily to a cozy cup of tea.

A NEW SPUD SHINDIG

Other St. Patrick's Day parties may give festive place to pipes, pigs, and plug hats, jokes and blarney, shamrocks and snakes, and all the other gay and goofy things associated with Pat and Mike; but this party features his prized "praties."

New Spud Invitations—The invitations can be written on gay correspondence cards, all "pratied up" with sketches of big potatoes. Or a picture of one can be cut from a seed catalogue and pasted in place. The potatoes' most promising eyes are selected and long inked eyelashes and roguish, come-hither pupils are added to them. Below the picture is written or printed: "Looking for you at the potato party!"

The day, date, time, and place of party are added, with the postscript, "Admission, one potato;" also, if wished, "Prizes will be given for the smallest, the largest, and the queerest-shaped potato."

New Spud Decorations—Flower vases and candle holders may be made from Irish potatoes. For the candlesticks, in one end of the potato a hole is cut large enough to hold the candle. Then a piece from the other end of the potato is cut out so that the candle will stand up firmly, and this end is mounted on a shamrock cut from heavy green cardboard.

The flower vases are made the same way, a cone or cup of heavy oiled paper being inserted in the top of the potato to hold water into which the flowers, such as green carnations, are put.

A mirth-provoking "house plant" can be prominently displayed, labeled, "Rare species of pratie plant. Please do not eat the flowers." Its leaves and petals are potato chips, glued on a leafless branch.

New Spud Exhibit—An Emerald Isle booth, decorated with trailing Irish moss cut from green crepe paper, has before it a table on which to display the potatoes brought to the party by the guests, as entries in the contests. A pretty girl, dressed in Irish costume, is there with pencil, pins, and slips of paper. She writes the name of the guest bringing the potato on a slip, then pins it on the potato, in this way preventing any later Irish brawl over which is whose.

POTATO PORTRAITS—First arrivals are immediately enrolled in the Potato Art Class. Artists' palettes have been cut from white cardboard, and on each has been pasted a large potato, cut from light brown paper that will take ink without blotting. In the interest of fairness, all potatoes are cut from the same pattern. No eyes are marked on the potato. It is the mere outline. Guests are to add whatever is needed to make each potato into a person, persuasively or pugnaciously Irish.

On a table in the art corner are crayons, pen and ink, pencils, gummed circles, water colors, and lipstick. There are also a few clever samples of amusing little "potato people," made by adding to the potato-shaped cutout pasted on the palette, expressive features, active little inked-in legs and arms, and suitable — or unsuitable! — costumes and accessories.

The artists are asked to sign their names on the back of their completed masterpieces. When finished, the sketches are collected, given a distinguishing number on the front, and then thumb-tacked in the Potato Art Gallery.

While other games are in progress, a committee of three "potato experts" judge the potato portraits, and hang first, second, and third prize ribbons on the winners. All ribbons are green.

POTATO QUIZ—When all guests have arrived, potato-decorated cards are distributed and pencils. On the signal to start, each guest tries to interview as many of the other guests as possible in a given time. The question is, "How do you prefer your cooked potatoes?" It means baked, boiled, roasted, mashed, escalloped, fried, potato cakes, chips, French fries, potato salad, etc.

Quizzers are asked to write on their cards the name of each person interviewed and his choice in cooked potatoes.

At the signal to stop quizzing, the cards are collected, and, at refreshment time, a prize is awarded the quizzer who was able to interview most potato-eaters and list their true preference. Quizzers are not allowed to speed things up for themselves by jotting down any old way of cooking potatoes against the name of some slow guest who is giving the great question deliberate and analytical consideration.

Prizes could be a package of instant mashed potatoes or potato chips.

POTATO SNATCH—This is a good game to play while everyone is full of pep. The guests form a circle, ready to march at a signal. Potatoes, one less than the number of players, are piled in the center of the circle. The guests, as they march, should be several feet away from the potatoes, to make the "snatch" exciting.

The starter stands outside the circle, whistle in hand. He should be someone with a good Irish singing voice, to keep the players at concert pitch.

"Remember!" he warns them, "this is not only snatch. It's sing, too! If I see anyone not singing when he should, begorra, I'll see that he pays a forfeit later!"

To the tune of "My Father and Mother Were Irish," the guests march around in a circle, singing:

> The Irishman loves his potatoes,
> The Irishman loves his potatoes,
> The Irishman loves his potatoes,
> Begorra! I love' em, too!

> CHORUS
> Begorra! I love' em, too!
> Begorra! I love' em, too!
> The Irishman loves his potatoes,
> The Irishman loves his potatoes,
> The Irishman loves his potatoes,
> Begorra! I love' em, too!

When the whistle blows, guests all dash into the middle of the circle and snatch up a potato; that is, all but one! He drops out. Then all the potatoes, save one, are set back in the center of the circle again, and the marching and singing is resumed until the stop-and-snatch signal again eliminates a player. The leader continues to take out one potato each time until the last one is snatched up by the winner.

POTATO-PARING CONTEST—It is well to follow every active game with a quiet one. This paring contest can be used to pay off forfeits from the previous game. The starter can see to it that two men and two girls are accused of not singing, or not singing loudly enough, or too loudly—anything to make them culprits.

A sheet is spread in the middle of the floor, to protect it. Each girl is given a potato, and each man a paring knife. The hostess should make sure that all potatoes are exactly the same size.

Says the starter, "The lady holds the spud, and the gentleman pares it, and each couple races to see which gets through first. Bandages on request!"

The prize could be a box of candy potatoes.

IRISH STEW—This is a lively game of the fruit basket type, so strenuous that it should not be played long. Players sit in a circle and number off, "One, two, three, four." The leader then explains that all the ones are potatoes; all the twos are cabbages; all the threes are corned beef; and all the fours are onions.

The one who begins the game stands in the circle and calls out, "Potatoes and cabbages!" whereupon the "potatoes" and the "cabbages" must change seats. In the scramble, the one in the center tries to get a place for himself. If he succeeds, the player left without a seat is now leader. Ever so often, the center player calls, "Irish stew!" Then all the players change places.

CLAPPING THE IRISH—This is a quiet game, to allow the players to rest up. The guests are seated and divided into two groups. Each group chooses a captain and then decides on some Irish song, the rhythm of which they will clap out while the other side tries to guess what tune it is. The groups perform in turns.

Here is a list of Irish songs from which to choose. Some are far more "clappable" than others. Titles may be selected from the "Sweet Rosie O'Grady," "Tipperary," "Where the River Shannon Flows," "When Irish Eyes Are Smiling," "A Little Bit of Heaven," "My Wild Irish Rose," "The Wearing of the Green," "Kathleen Mavoureen," "Mother Machree," "Old Erin," "The Harp That Once Through Tara's Halls," "My Father and Mother Were Irish."

WHO HAS THE POTATO—This game is the old favorite, musical mystery. The players sit informally as for the previous game. One is sent out of the room while a small potato is hidden in some unlikely place, as, for instance, in the curly top of some pretty colleen's hair.

The seeker is called in to find the potato. He is guided by the group's singing of "Tipperary." When they sing softly, he is "cold." As he comes closer to the hiding place, the volume of their singing increases, reaching an all-time high as he almost touches it.

When he finally finds the potato, he becomes one of the "choir" while some other guest is chosen as seeker.

POTATO RELAY—Men and girls compete against one another in this relay. A equal number of players line up in column formation, the girls in one column, the men in the other. At the opposite end of the room, in line with its column, is a chair, around which that team's potato must travel. On the floor before each column of players is a potato. The two potatoes should be exactly the same size.

"On your mark! Get set! Go!" snaps the starter. At that signal, the first player in each column pushes the potato along with his left foot. He must not kick it, no matter how much he longs to do so! He must push it the length of the room, clear around the chair, then back to the starting line, when Player Two takes over, and so on until the last player of one team pushes his potato over the starting line, thus winning the relay.

LAZY POTATO CARRIERS—In this game, the same teams may be kept. Players sit in chairs placed in two long lines, facing each other, with enough space kept between lines for free action. Each player sits with his feet held close together, for this race requires really slick footwork. A potato—the more ball-shaped the better—is placed on the feet of the first player in both lines, and on the signal to start, he places it on the feet of the next player by clever manipulation of his own. If the potato falls to the floor, he must pick it up between his feet, never once touching it with his hands. If it rolls to some distance, he may rise and gently kick it back to a position near his chair. He then sits down and picks it up between his feet and deposits it on the feet of the next player. Feet encased in good, hefty men's shoes seem to have little trouble in holding a small potato on their polished surface. The trouble comes when they try to pass the rolypoly thing on to the feet of some dainty little lady who is wearing a size-four party shoe, with a pointed toe and a huge silver buckle.

The side that first gets its potato to the end of the line wins the contest.

OTHER POTATO GAMES—Any of the well-known "guff" golf games may be played with small round potatoes for the balls, the course being made as simple or difficult as the occasion requires. Walking sticks with curved handles may be used to hit the potato balls. Or brooms may be substituted, in which case the potatoes are swept over the course—or under the piano!

In the game of potato hoofing, the players carry the potato to the goal and back on the toe of the right shoe. Even then, the girl with the Cinderella foot sometimes brings home the spud before her large-footed admirer gets really started.

In the game of needling the potato, contestants carry the potato between two bone knitting needles, saying, "Knit one, purl one," all the time the potato stays put, and "Drop one!" when it falls. The knitting chant seems to upset the equilibrium of both player and potato.

COUNTING-OUT JINGLE—The following jingle provides a merry way to choose a captain, a partner, or "It." The leader stands before the players, and pointing to each in turn, repeats the counting-out rime:

> Riggidy, higgidy, wiggidy rig!
> Paddy dances an Irish jig
> While feeding potatoes to his pig.
> Riggidy, higgidy, wiggidy rig!
> O—U—T—out goes he!

(Or "she," as the case may be.)

PARTNER-FINDING GAMES—Tiny maps of the outline of Ireland can be cut from green construction paper, then cut in two, zigzag fashion, all different cuts. Guests match pieces of map to find partners.

Or two-part Pat and Mike jokes may be typed on paper, which is then cut in two. Each guest must find the other half of his joke.

Pat riddles may be used in the same way. The guest who picks from one Irish hat a slip reading. "What Irish city makes one think of a bottle?" searches for the guest who has drawn from another Irish hat a slip bearing the answer, "Cork."

POTATO REFRESHMENTS—For refreshments potatoes served in different ways or glorified Irish stew would be suitable; sandwiches cut in Irish shapes—pipes, pigs, shamrocks, harps, tall hats—with green fillings; green salads, candies, and dessert in the form of cakes with green frosting.

A menu for light refreshments could be simply Irish club sandwiches, ice cream and cookies, and mint punch.

DINNER MENU—A dinner menu is sometimes needed. Here is one that "wears the green."

Pear and Green Cherry Cocktail

Potato Soup with Parsley Garnish

Irish Stew   Green Peas   Pickles

Shamrock Salad with Wafers

Mint Ice   Fancy Cookies

Coffee

Green Gum Drops

MINT FRUIT PUNCH

Pour one cup of boiling water over one tablespoon of orange pekoe tea. Let the mixture stand ten minutes, then strain over one and a fourth cups of sugar. When it is cool, add the juice of five lemons and two cups of fruit juice, using one kind or several kinds. Chill, and when ready to serve, add an equal amount of ginger ale and garnish with mint leaves.

EXTRA IRISH ATTRACTIONS—Any attractions can be added, should the hostess want to use this party plan as a social, to be given in a church assembly auditorium or a club hall, both of which probably have a stage or platform.

There may be Irish people or an Irish organization in the community or town. They may be invited to put on an Irish folk dance. They are so generous that usually they willingly give much more than is asked. If they have Irish costumes, they may be urged to wear them.

Sometimes a dancing school will gladly arrange to have its pupils give Irish dances in costume. The instructors like to have this opportunity afforded them of presenting their most promising pupils before an audience. Not only is it good for the children, but it is good advertising for the school.

A fiddler and a pianist may be asked to play all the beloved old Irish airs.

An Irishman with a genuine brogue may be induced to tell the story of how Ireland got its name, telling the tale in his own way and words.

Of course, it is only an old Celtic legend, but in the green land of magic, long, long ago, couldn't it be true? This is how it has come down to us from the mists of antiquity:

Once the Emerald Isle was entirely covered by the sea, except for a short time, every seventh year. Whenever it reappeared, it seemed greener than ever. People couldn't believe that it would ever be totally submerged again, so they would build their homes upon it, intending to remain on the lovely island forever.

But always after a short time, it was swallowed by the sea again, not to appear for another seven years.

At that time, iron in any form was considered lucky. Today we consider a horseshoe lucky and wonder why. This superstition is a survival of the ancients' belief that iron subdued evil spirits.

Evil spirits were blamed for the sinking of the green island. Then, says the old legend, came an apparition—a good spirit— who told the inhabitants that the only way the island could be rescued from the sea was from someone to plant an iron shaft in its heart when it appeared from the under the sea.

A bold adventurer said he was willing to take the risk of thus doing battle with the evil spirits that were responsible for the sinking of the island.

When it next appeared, in all its glory of green, this brave man embarked on the sea. On reaching the island, he plunged his iron sword into the very heart of the island, and from then on, it never again disappeared.

Because of this legend, the island became known as "Ironland," later becoming Ireland.

LET'S GO A-MAYING!

Since time began, folks have been making bouquets of flowers that bloom in the spring—tra, la!—and weaving festive days into the floral chain that was already long before ever it twined the brow of Flora, Roman goddess of flowers.

A fragrant, unbroken chain, its beginnings lost in the mists of the world's dawn this tradition comes down to us in the form of May baskets, gift bouquets for friends about to embark on a voyage or matrimony, remembrance flowers for honored graves, and carnations for Mother's Day.

So here's to adding another link to the sweet old chain! Let's go a-Maying! Following is a group of May social affairs for mothers and others.

A MAY DAY BREAKFAST—The guests have to get up early in the morning to start a May Day right. It is a real thrill to meet in the dark, tramp to some picturesque spot, and there wait to see the sun rise. The hostess should walk the route beforehand, timing herself and allowing a little margin for the inevitable sleepyhead.

MAY BREAKFAST INVITATIONS—Invitations to this breakfast may be tied to the handle of a real, old-fashioned May basket and hung, in the time-honored way, on the door of each guest's home.

Or tiny May baskets may be cut from construction paper and filled with water-color flowers with a dainty envelope tied to each handle and containing this rimed invitation:

> A May Day surprise!
>   It's grand walking weather,
> Let's see the sun rise!
>   And see it together.
>
> Then scamper right back—
>   I hungrily ask it—
> To help me unpack
>   A May breakfast basket.

To these verses are added the name, the meeting place, the starting time, and a warning postscript, as "Be there on the dot. Like time and tide, we and the sun wait for no man." or, "No hitchhiking! No walk, no waffles!"

MAY DAY MENUS—These can be as simple or elaborate as the hostess wishes. Food can be served from a picnic hamper decorated to look like a dainty May basket, or from a modern chafing dish. If guests must rush off to class, job, or home duties, quick service should be planned.

The traditional menu is fried chicken with waffles and maple syrup. The first course could be in place—an orange or a grapefruit, cut basket shape, with a sprig of spring blossoms tied to the handle. Coffee and chocolate are served.

If the hostess wishes to make it a brunch rather than a breakfast, a May Day salad could be added, with sweet crackers and currant jelly.

MAY DAY DECORATIONS—Guests who, after seeing the sun rise, scamper right back to the home of the hostess, find that it, too, has gone a-Maying. It is gay with flowers. Vases of them are in the hall and living room. The dining room is a bower of blossoming branches.

MAY DAY CENTERPIECE—The table decorations are scaled to the overall plan. The centerpiece can be a simple little bunch of fragrant, woodsy flowers or a huge bowl of pastel-colored garden or hothouse blossoms, placed upon a mirror, with matching pastel doilies on the table.

Or the centerpiece can be an elaborate Maypole, partly wound with colored ribbons, each end anchored to an individual favor, such as a frilly May basket made over a nut-cup foundation, and filled with pastel-tinted candies or a tiny bottle of flower perfume.

There are several ways of making the Maypole stand steadily upright. One is to plant it in a glass dish or flower pot filled with sand.

SWEET SOUVENIRS—Edible bouquets may be made by simply twisting a few tiny gum drops of assorted colors into a square of cellophane. The twisted ends make a good enough stalk when reinforced with a toothpick or two, then wrapped around with tinfoil and thrust through a small paper-lace doily.

The girl who can make candied flowers or put up tiny glasses of apple and rose-geranium jelly has May Day favors at her clever finger tips.

Or—sweet, too!—the Maypole ribbons can be anchored to honest-to-goodness spring flowers, tiny nosegays for the girls, boutonnieres for the men, with a merry May wish, such as "May all your paths be flowery ones!" written on a dainty card, which is tied to each.

MAY DAY GAMES—The guests will be tired after their morning hike, so only quiet games are in order.

When flowery flattery is played all that is required is a sense of humor. The hostess hands each guest a card and a pencil, saying, "Please write your own initials on top of the card you hold." When all have done so, the cards are passed around so that nobody has his own.

"Now," says the hostess, "examine the initials on the card you have received. Don't tell whose they are! Next, write down the name of the flower, wild or tame, which you think the owner of the initials looks most like. But here's the laugh! The initials of that flower must be the same as the last initial on your card. The other initial must be used as the first letter of a descriptive adjective. Have fun with those adjectives, girls!"

Whe the guests have finished their literary creations, the cards are collected and given to the hostess, who takes them, one by one, and calls out the initials. As "W.P. Will the owner of those initials please rise and claim her card?" Where-upon Wilma Pancoast rises in all her two hundred pounds of well-corseted, well-coiffured, dignified efficiency.

"Wilma Pancoast," announces the hostess, "You look like a Wilted Pansy."

For the game of birth month flowers, every guest is asked to draw on the other side of his card a sketch of his birth month flower. In case he doesn't know his flower, the hostess has a list on hand, so that the amateur artists may know the worst. It reads: January, snowdrop; February, primrose; March, violet; April, daisy; May, hawthorn; June, rose; July, poppy; August, water lily; September, goldenrod; October, aster; November, chrysanthemum; December, poinsettia.

MAY DAY PRIZES—Any package bar of candy, about an inch thick, with a soft filling, makes a neat little chocolate candy tub in which a "daisy" can be planted. The daisy is a lollipop, which is given a yellow center and perky petals of crepe paper.

Tiny bottles of perfume make dainty prizes. If a hole is pricked in the cork, a wee artifical flower's stalk may be pushed through, making the favor look like a doll-size vase holding a single flower.

Mother's Day Showers

A SWEET BOUQUET FOR MOTHER'S DAY—Sometimes the guest of honor is one of those dear, aggravating mothers who see no reason why they should rate special honors for just being themselves. In which case, better get it over as soon as possible, with the least possible fuss!

A May breakfast shower is often the perfect solution, with the family gathered a bit earlier than usual around the table, and all the gifts, separately wrapped and tagged, but put in one receptable, carried in and presented by the youngest child or grandchild.

The container will depend on the nature of the gifts the children have planned to give. If frills—chiffon handkerchiefs, gloves, laces, costume jewelry, or perfume—they are put in a hatbox, trimmed to look like a fluffy May basket. If the gifts are the useful sort—the newest things in kitchen gadgets, for instance—they are arranged in a serviceable basket, with a huge artificial carnation to trim the top.

Mother, coming to the table, finds the family already assembled. Immediately she is greeted by the entire group singing to the tune of "When I Was a Lady:" ("Lieber Augustine").

> Here's to Mother Johnson, Mother Johnson, Mother Johnson,
> Here's to Mother Johnson, whose day is today!
> God bless her, we love her!
> God bless her, we love her!
> Here's to Mother Johnson, whose day is today!

The proper name for "Johnson," is substituted.

MOTHER'S CARNATION—Mother finds on her plate a card, reading:

> Mother darling, since it's Mother's Day,
> Won't you let us hand you a bouquet?
> Finest, grandest mother in creation,
> Take from us this family carnation—
> It's rather big, but someone had the notion
> It should be so, to match our own devotion.

Mother looks around for her prize carnation. One of the common variety is on every plate but hers. Then little sister marches in with the May basket, and mother gets her richly-deserved bouquet.

MAYBE PROMISES—These provide hours of secret fun in their writing, and sometimes a few twinges of conscience. Every member of the average family has some folly or foible that annoys mother—such as littering the family car; using the newest slang; smoking too many cigarettes; leaving roller skates and other dangerous toys on the stairs; slaming doors; using the guest towels; neglecting home study for television; coming in late from dates; monopolizing the telephone with sweet talk; forgetting to mail important letters; spilling talcum on the bathroom floor; never getting around to fixing that dripping faucet.

Each of the family misdemeanors is made the subject of a rimed resolution or a promise to do better, and written on individual cards to be read aloud by the culprit, at the table on Mother's Day.

They are meant to be funny, but spiced with a dash of truth. Members of the family may write their own; or each may enjoy writing a "maybe promise" for another.

For instance, mother has often scolded her teen-age son for constantly scrapping with his younger brother. So Big Bill writes on his card:

> Dear ma, in order to appease you,
> To my kid brother I'll be civil;
> I'll wear a halo, just to please you—
> (While he grows hoofs, the little divil!)

Other "maybe promises" could read:

> I promise, mother, nevermore
> Ever to bang another door.

> I promise, ma, sure as I'm born,
> This Saturday to mow the lawn.

The family car I will not litter;
I will not tease the baby-sitter.

I promise, mother, with the gang,
To moderate my use of slang.

For this day on, I'll try—good grief!—
To keep my phone calls fairly brief.

Dear mom, I'll heed all your "Bewares"
And clear my clutter from the stairs.

I promise, mother, that my buddy
And I will fool you yet—and study!

I promise to be careful, mum,
Of where I park my chewing gum.

I will not raise that awful din
When all the monthly bills come in.

Maybe I will not blow my top
When asked for women's things to shop.

I will not bring stray pups home, ma,
Unless you say I may—or pa.

Mother thanks the family, but says, with a chuckle, that she knows why these promises are called "maybes."

A LABOR-SAVING SHOWER FOR MOTHER—Many a mother has looked wistfully at the modern culinary treasures in the efficient kitchen of her newly-married daughter.

"Cooking should be fun, child," she says, "with labor-saving devises like this. Now, if you had married Dick when I married your dad——"

A labor-saving shower gives a happy chance to fix up that old-style kitchen by giving her every gadget she ever coveted, so that she can go fancy with carrots or cakes, and have the newest thing in can openers and cucumber slicers!

If mother isn't gadget-minded, but has her heart set on some daring extravagance, it is well to get dad in on it, too, and any other big-hearted man in the family. Then a large, spicy carnation is tied on the new electric refrigerator kitchen cabinet, and mother is called into the kitchen to get her bouquet.

To call her to a breakfast set with a beribboned outfit of chromium or aluminum is the thrill of a lifetime; and to invite her friends in to a surprise tea, with a complete new tea service, tagged "With love to mother, from the family," all set for her to pour, is another.

TABLE TALK—No formal program is required. Guests just sit and talk. The hostess may introduce such self-starting topics as, "How I first met my husband;" "What I weighed on my wedding day;" "The first meal I spoiled as a bride;" "The first quarrel;" "Why it was his fault;" "Our first home;" "The funniest thing my daughter ever said or did."

SEARCH FOR THE LONELIEST MOTHER—The loneliest mother may live in a beautiful home on the boulevard or in a humble shack near the railroad. Perhaps her only child is away in college for his first year or in the armed services. She may be a childless widow, a newcomer in the community, or for some other reason be entirely alone.

Sometimes the search for her is an annual affair, sponsored by some church group, such as the Women's Circle, the Young People's Society, the Adult Bible Class, or the teen-age group in the Sunday school.

It sometimes happens that there are several loneliest mothers, but two weeks before Mother's Day, one is elected by the look-out committee and formally invited by two young people, in person, to be the honored mother for that day.

If it is the Young People's Society project, two are appointed to see that the guest of honor is called for by car, conducted to the right department on Sunday morning, and placed comfortably at the front of the room. Everything is done to make her feel that she is a very special person and that the class is honored by her presence.

FLOWERS FOR ALL—Two girls stand outside the classroom door, one with a basket of carnations, the other with a tray of pins, and as the class members arrive, each is given a flower and asked to pin it on.

SPECIAL PROGRAM—The program is kept simple because it must be all over before church time. It starts with a mother song, given as a solo, followed by a brief prayer of thanksgiving for all mothers.

Then the teacher of the class introduces the guest of honor, and she is presented with an orchid corsage, to the purchase of which every member of the class has contributed. The teacher pins it on the loneliest mother, while the class sings, "Here's to Mother Johnson," as previously given in "A Sweet Bouquet for Mother's Day."

Next comes the singing of any favorite hymn—the guest of honor often has one—followed by the reading of Proverbs 31: 10-31. beginning "Who can find a virtuous woman? For her price is far above rubies." A boy and a girl, chosen for their clear diction, read alternate verses of this Scripture reading.

This is followed by another mother song and the reciting of one of Grace Noll Crowell's lovely Mother's Day poems, such as, "The Beautiful Gift," beginning, "What can a mother give her children?" Then comes a violin solo.

Now comes the time for the two short talks, carefully prepared and so well-rehearsed that they seem to be extemporaneous. These talks are given by a boy and a girl, on some appropriate topic, chosen by the teacher, such as, "How can we best help our mothers?" Or, "My favorite Bible mother, and why."

A SPECIAL DINNER—After the church service, the loneliest mother finds herself in a car on the way to the home of one of the class members, for a Mother's Day dinner. She is soon greeted by an informal, friendly family, and warmly accepted as one of them.

Later on, when she has had time to digest that big dinner, to rest and to nap, she is ushered into the family car for a local sight-seeing trip. Finally the Sunday school teen-ager and his parents drive the loneliest mother to her home. But she is no longer lonely. She has adopted him and his family as her own!

Bridal and Baby Showers

MAY BRIDAL SHOWER—Showers for a popular bride-to-be sometimes cannot all be fitted into April and overlap into May, when it is difficult to find a type of shower that she has not already had.

A rose-petal shower is a novel way to presenting her with

something of which she cannot have too many, especially if the honeymoon plans are for an extended trip or voyage.

The "petals" of the bouquet that is presented to her are pairs of stockings in all the new shades, the gifts of the guests. Each lovely sheer stocking is rolled loosely to resemble an open rose, then held in shape by being encased in pink tissue paper and given a little twist near the "blossom" stem, to keep the stocking looking like a rose. It can be tied snugly, if necessary, with narrow pink ribbon.

When all the "roses" are so wrapped, they are bunched around the head of an old-fashioned wooden darner, to resemble a Gay Nineties nosegay. The handle of the darner is then pushed through a paper lace doily, also the loose ends of the pink tissue paper that encases each "rose," and then this "stem" is wound around with florist's tulle and given a flashy bow.

Huge corsage pins are provided for this out-size bridal bouquet. They are large, old-style hatpins, pushed through spools of darning silk, so that the spools form the heads of the pins.

PRESENTING THE MAY BRIDAL BOUQUET—At lunch, when the bride-to-be least expects it, since no hint of the shower has been given in decorations or program, someone leaves the room, giving some plausible excuse, and comes back dressed in an outlandish bridal outfit, with lace curtain veil, and carrying the rose-petal bouquet, which she solemnly presents to the guest of honor, with the shortest presentation speech on record. She says:

> We just had a hunch
> To bunch 'em;
> Then came in a bunch
> For luncheon.

STORK SHOWER—A stork shower built around a baby's bonnet is suitable for May. The bonnet-shaped invitations are cut double from pink construction paper, and inside is pictured a spray of forget-me-nots, together with the verse:

> A baby's spring bonnet
> Ought to have a flower
> In the hood, or on it;
> How about a shower?

All necessary information is added.

It is easy to make it an old-time sit-down tea in the dining room, with the gifts arranged on a small table in the living room and opened later.

The color scheme is blue, pink, and white. The centerpiece is a dainty pink and blue cradle with a baby doll in it(guarded by a large toy stork, in its beak a baby's white bonnet, dangling by the strings, one pink, one blue. Any springtime greenery or trailing vine may be used to link the center one with a tiny toy cradle set at each place. Tied to the favor is a little white baby bonnet, with one blue and one pink string. These hoods are sweet in crochet.

The favors are filled with pink and white Jordan almonds, and into each is slipped a bunch of tiny gilt safety pins tied together with blue ribbon. Real flower petals are scattered over the cloth.

MAY BLOSSOM MENU—The menu should match the flower petals in delicacy. A fruit salad or orange sections, white grapes, and canned pears is easily colored pink, and with a bonnet of whipped cream salad dressing is delicious. With the salad go pink and white sandwiches, cut in bonnet shape. These could be cream cheese spread with currant jelly, or thin slices spread with strawberry jam.

Tea or coffee, and a cake decorated with pink and white icing completes the menu. Of course, the guest of honor cuts the magnificent cake. Then she is escorted to the living room to find a table piled high with gifts, all wrapped in tissue paper, or boxed and tied with blue and pink ribbon.

The hostess and the guests may "budget" the affair by agreeing beforehand that approximately the same amount be spent on each gift. Some clubs make it a rule not even to tag the surprise gifts with the donors' names. Others pool their pennies and buy a joint gift, such as a scale for weighing the little newcomer.

LET IT POUR

To go statistically and ecstatically springy—say it ten times without skidding!—there's a new bride every two minutes. Now if every bride-elect had twice as many showers in May as in April, what would be the rainfall—counting half a bride a minute—in June?

Well, like Cupid, who still insists that two can live as cheaply as one, we can't figure it either! But we can safely predict, with the weatherman, "frequent showers" — and plan accordingly.

Showers for the bride-to-be that suit and surprise should be the aim of the hostess. It is often wise to stipulate that approximately the same sum be spent on each gift; for not all guests can splurge, and some must skimp.

WHAT'S A SUITABLE SHOWER?—Does the lady dance better than she dusts? Then it's chiffon, not cheesecloth. What's her idea of a swell gift? Jade earrings or a sensible coffee-pot? What's her hobby? Does she wax eloquent on the subject of puppies, petunias, pickle recipes, or perfume?

The hostess will probably know, and can confide the bride-to-be's choice in species, style, and size to any of the invited guests who might not know. Especially size; for there is no rainbow in the shower that gives her stockings much too small or a size thirty-eight bra when she wears a thirty-two.

SURPRISE THE LADY!—It is the leakless shower that is never a washout. Hostess and guests can co-operate in a score of foxy ways to keep the honor guest from expecting the unexpected. One sure way is for the hostess to whisper in her ear the secret plan to give a surprise party for dear So-and-So—a mutual friend—and ask her if she could contrive to keep this friend out of the way or get her to the proper place at the right time. "I just hate to ask you. I know how busy you are. But I can always rely on you. You know how it is . . ."

This scheme works marvelously, and the stunned look of the harassed keeper after she has finally managed to herd her elusive charge to the party, where the truth suddenly dawns on her, adds hilarity to the surprise shower.

Standard showers—lingerie, fine linen, vanity, recipe, kitchen, bon voyage, cupboard, book, china, garden, stocking, handkerchief, and so on—can all be given that little twist, that difference which makes them remembered.

A Spring Shower Luncheon

This shower is a lingerie shower, all daintiness and fluff. The guests invited are the bride-to-be's most intimate girl friends.

SPRING SHOWER INVITATIONS—The invitations are written on pastel-colored cards. On the top left-hand corner is a carbon sketch of a chubby, bare Cupid standing on a black cloud. From his wings drip raindrops, as he empties from his upturned silver pail all sorts of feminine dainties. They drop, at intervals, down the card into an upturned umbrella, held to catch them by a pretty girl in a bridal gown and veil.

Somewhere between two of the falling pieces of lingerie is written or printed:

> In the spring a young man's fancy
>   Lightly turns to thoughts of love.
> In the spring a woman's fancy
>   Turns to bonnet, gown, and glove.
> In the spring Dame Nature's fancy
>   Turns to showers; that's for sure!
> In the spring my skittish fancy
>   Follows Nature's. Let it pour!

All necessary information is added, and, in parenthesis, "The fancier, the better!"

SPRING SHOWER CENTERPIECE—The centerpiece for the table is an upturned sunshade of any dainty color, hung above the table. From each rib drips a tinsel or silver paper raindrop. The sunshade shelters an exquisite Madam Pompadour doll with voluminous frilly skirts. They are full enough to cover many small, dainty gifts, such as blue ribbon garters, sterling lingerie clasps, evening hose, etc.

A small edition of the centerpiece doll, with full, frilly skirts of crepe paper, could stand at each place, as a favor. Should the shower be given in the evening, an electric bulb could be placed under Madam Pompadour's skirts, instead of the little gifts. A string of small Christmas tree bulbs placed under the skirts of the wee favor dolls gives a romantic, softly-glowing table illumination.

A Rainbow Shower

This shower is especially appropriate when the luncheon or tea is of a bon-voyage type, as, for example, when the bride-elect, after her marriage, is to reside in a distant town.

RAINBOW INVITATIONS—The invitations are written in violet ink on sky-blue correspondence cards, a water-color rainbow across one corner and silver raindrops across the other. Beneath this spring sky, is written or printed:

> It's a shower!
> Have you heard?
> Hush-sh-sh! A secret!
> Not a word!
>
> Chasing rainbows
> Should be fun;
> Come and help us
> Capture one.

The date, time, and place are added, also any other needed information regarding the individual gifts or joint gift.

FAVORS AND DECORATIONS—Guests' favors are rainbow-colored handkerchiefs, to weep into! A rainbow of ribbon or fringed crepe paper arches the table. At the end of the rainbow is a gilded flowerpot, full of gifts for the bride-to-be.

GIFTS—There are rare occasions when money is the ideal gift. It loses all taint of the mercenary and takes on the glamour of romance when it is put in tiny chamois-leather moneybags and stored in the pot at the end of the rainbow.

Frequently a joint remembrance is given to the going-away bride. It should be something substantial that will be a constant reminder of her friends back home, such as a chest of silver. In which case, the following may be substituted for the rainbow stanza:

> Let's go seeking,
> With the crowd,
> A silver lining
> In the cloud!

Sometimes a shower is given in connection with an evening of bridge or a club meeting which the bride-elect is in the habit of attending. In this case, there is less need for elaborate schemes to insure that the guest of honor will be there, and there is a better chance of a complete surprise, for she will see nothing unusual in the social gathering.

In such cases, the game or business goes on as usual, the surprise shower often coming just after refreshments.

If the shower is camouflaged as a bridge party, the tallies are rainbows, and the prizes something for rain and something for shine, such as an absorbing book of new fiction and a powder compact.

After the final bridge game, the guests are asked to look at the back of their rainbow tallies for distinguishing numbers. Somewhere in the room the hostess has hidden "clouds" with corresponding numbers. Each guest is to find her own cloud and look for its silver lining. If the one she finds bears a number that is not hers, she must hide it again with swift secrecy, so that its owner can find her own.

The clouds are gifts wrapped in black crepe paper, splashed with silver rain. They can be anything silvery, from chocolate mints wrapped in tinfoil, to silver boutonnieres or tiny silver frames containing snapshots of the bride and groom.

The bride-elect's cloud is put in so high a place that it becomes necessary for all to help her find it.

"Here it is!" cries someone. "My! What a heavy cloud! That ought to go in for silver linings in a big way!"

It surely does. For when the excited, but still unsuspecting, girl tears away the black cloud she finds its lining is a chest of lovely table silver, or a set of silver-backed brushes, a silver traveling clock, a pair of silver candlesticks, an umbrella with a handsome, initialed handle, or some such fine and lasting gift.

Basket Showers

SURPRISE KITCHEN SHOWER—This shower is always popular, for the handy container will carry gifts of almost any type. For the kitchen shower, it starts its travels as a new laundry basket. All the useful cooking utensils and tricky gadgets are put inside, each tagged with the giver's name and some nonsensical directions for its use.

A kitchen bouquet of copper scouring mops, with cake-turner and slice "foliage" and cooking spoon "blossoms," can accompany the flossy basket, and in all its glory it is placed on the doorstep of the bride-elect's home some sunny afternoon. When the lady hurries to answer the doorbell, she looks first at the semicircle of friends, smiling at her, and then at that amazing basket, and joyfully welcomes another surprise.

It is a good plan to provide lunch for everyone and pack it in that shiny new dishpan and bring iced punch or hot coffee in a thermos jug, but not the gift one. To be in keeping with the shower theme, all the guests may wear gingham kitchen dresses.

Cupboard Love Shower

Here is a basket shower that delights the bride who expects to start housekeeping at once. Each guest contributes homemade dainties from her own fruit cellar or pantry shelves—jams, jellies, marmalades, canned fruit, relishes, and pickles. This basket can be any kind of a large container that will be useful to a new homemaker. It could be a bushel peach basket, decorated with scalloped shelf oilcloth in a dainty spring design. Tied to the handle is an envelope containing the following rime, signed by all the guests:

> Of course we know that love can live
> On bread and cheese and kisses;
> But think of all the calories
> That sort of diet misses!
>
> Yes, think of all the tasty things
> We jell, preserve, and pickle;
> We hope that you can eat a few
> Without appearing fickle!
>
> Perhaps Dan Cupid thinks a gift
> Of home-canned eats is funny.
> Well, just you say it's cupboard love,
> We're feeling for you, honey!

May Flour Shower

This shower is a new dress for the recipe shower, and solves the problem when the hostess wants to invite guests whom she hesitates to ask to bring or send gifts that cost much money. Perhaps they may have been guests at several previous showers for the same girl, or have already contributed to a joint gift. Or perhaps they are not intimate friends.

In this case the hostess asks them to contribute something worth its weight in gold to a new bride—a pet recipe, proved and prized, guaranteed to please a husband whose mother is such a wonderful cook!

MAY FLOUR BOX—This box is the axis on which the party revolves. It is one of those small wooden cases, with indexed cards for the filing of recipes. The hostess picks—or paints —the box with an eye to the color scheme of the bride's kitchen. She encloses one of the blank recipe cards with each invitation.

INVITATIONS—The invitations show several little bags or packages of flour, cut from advertisements and pasted in place, and framed with a flower chain—daisies, forget-me-nots, roses, orange blossoms—in the form of two hearts entwined. Below the design is written the following:

> A floury shower
>   Of recipes, please,
> Calling for flour
>   In varied degrees.
>
> Please write a honey
>   On card I enclose,
> Worth more than money,
>   As any bride knows!

The invitation may add whatever else is needed, as "Recipe Shower for Mary." Or, if the hostess is elaborating on the simple form of the party, she can add a special request in the postscript, such as, "Bring an apron with you," or a kettle holder to make, or a dish towel to hem or initial, or a ten-cent kitchen tool.

DECORATIONS—The decorations consist mainly of flour bags, both paper and cotton. The latter can be dyed any color and strung as pennants, each sack bearing one letter of "Here comes the bride." For the table center, a doll's-house kitchen may be arranged, with a domestic little doll bride literally tied—by one hand, anyway—to the kitchen stove.

LUCKY-BAG FAVORS—The favors can be miniature sacks of flour—only they are filled with rice—and can do double duty as place cards if the name is written on a tiny label that is tied to the neck of each bag. If wished, an inexpensive little charm—ring, heart, coin, old shoe—can be put in each, for luck. Or tied to the neck of the bag, with ribbon matching the color scheme, could be one of the wee kitchen utensils that can be bought in sets at most dime store toy counters—a tiny rolling pin, cake tin, spoon, grater, etc.

Nuts and candies can be served in kitchen jelly molds. A suitable prize is a new cookbook, featuring cooking for two; or a souvenir scrapbook, well started with clipped favorite recipes from each guest pasted in, each one neatly— or amusingly — autographed. If the bride's kitchen color scheme is known, these books can sport matching or contrasting oilcloth or plastic covers, stenciled with her initials.

MAY FLOUR CAFETERIA—Perhaps it is an evening shower, to which the men are invited, and an informal way to serve the refreshments is in order. Then guests may line up and march into the kitchen, singing a "chow" song. Here each guest picks up a plate on which are sandwiches and a salad, and then marches back into the living room to find a comfortable eating corner. Kitchen maids, dressed in smart kitchen attire, bring them coffee and cream and sugar in plain kitchen china.

Later, the serve-self squad marches to the kitchen again, each carrying back his empty dishes, and trades them for ice cream and a little frosted cake. Each cake carries a flag bearing a different number. These are fateful numbers, the unsuspecting guests soon discover, when the hostess announces that those that have number 13 and 33 are to do the dishes.

MAY FLOUR GAMES—These games can be any old favorite with a kitchen flavor. The recipe-maker is a teaser for men. Each guest picks six "ingredients" written on slips from six different boxes and then tries to make a sensible recipe from his pickings, in a given time. Clowning is frowned on. Cooking is a serious business!

For other games, guests may try throwing ginger snaps into a round biscuit tin while toeing a distance line; threading raw macaroni "beads" against time; pegging dishcloths on a clothesline, in rival relay teams; dressing wooden picnic spoons as bride dolls; rolling or hitching a tin pie plate to and from a goal, using an old-fashioned hand can opener to hit or hitch with; or, in couples, attempt to peel an orange, the girl holding the fruit, the man doing the peeling.

MAY FLOUR RADIO HOUR—This is a stunt that results in some amazing recipes. Six girls do the broadcasting in one room. Each selects a masculine "cooking fan" to sit with the "public" in another room, pencil and paper in hand, to jot down the recipe she broadcasts. It all seems simple enough until the hostess announces that the cooking experts will broadcast simultaneously!

Pardon My Lid Shower

This fills the bill when the object is glee rather than gifts. It is a merry take-off on the arty millinery style show.

LID INVITATIONS—The invitations show a mannequin, with round circles of rouge on each cheekbone and no nose to speak of, wearing a shower cap, trimmed at the side with a hairbrush and comb. Beneath the mannequin is printed:

> Pardon my lid!
>   It's spring, you know,
> When hats go on
>   The way they go!

Inside the folder card is the formal announcement of the Hat and Chat Shoppe's private showing of original millinery models by Wera Fashion Plate, at the home of—(name and address of hostess).

GIFTS—All guests are asked to bring or wear an old-model hat—the freakier the better. All shower gifts are to be "something for the head," from aspirins to wave-setting fluid, from a pocket dictionary to nose drops. The final comic touch is that each gift is to be attached to the giver's ancient hat, masquerading there as part of the trimming.

Prizes are offered for the most ingenious, the most amusing, and the most "gosh-awful" lid.

PORCH-PREFERRED PARTIES

There are those who think nature is grand and who adore a picnic. But they prefer cream to caterpillars in their coffee and don't like sand in their shoes. They love a bacon bat, but loathe hiking a mile to fry their rasher. They enjoy watermelon, but don't see why they have to sit on nettles to eat it. In short, they like to rough it—but with all the comforts of home!

The porch party was made for them. The hostess plans it for any time her porch is coolest, but whether breakfast, luncheon, afternoon club affair, high tea, snack, or supper, she keeps it free and easy and happy-go-lucky, remembering that this is simply her picnic, without the ants and the poison ivy.

A Colorful Party

This party is the watermelon feed transferred from the wide, open spaces to the home back porch.

INVITATIONS—The invitations are melon-pink correspondence cards dotted with excited little pickaninny heads, bristling with braids, cut from black paper, and pasted in place. If the eyes and grin are first cut out, red and brown crayons can give more color to the faces.

Below the perky little heads the following is written or typed:

> Do you wilt with your collar?
>   Do you scorch with the town?
> Do you fade with the curtains?
>   Does the heat get you down?
>
> Then cool off at my party;
>   It's a colorful one!
> We'll devour watermelons
>   On the porch and have fun!

The day, date, and time are added, with the postscript, "Wear your coolest, most colorful togs."

COLORFUL DECORATIONS—A cool, roomy porch, with its wicker furniture, gay cushions, ferns and flowers, and fan-made breeze, is an ideal setting in itself for a hot weather party. But if the hostess wishes to go gala, she can do so by using the colored tot's favorite colors, red and yellow, against a background of cool green branches. Pickaninnies cut from black cardboard can be attached to candle holders and flower vases, to give a merry touch of color. The lights can be decked out in red and yellow tissue paper shades, to which have been pasted a couple of fat little pickaninnies, all rolling eyes and flashing teeth.

A COLORFUL PICNIC TABLE—An amusing centerpiece is a real watermelon patch, made of the natural vines bearing a few tiny, undeveloped melons. Gleefully robbing the patch are half a dozen little Negro dolls, dressed in cabin rags of red and yellow. Vines trail from the patch to the corners of the table. If pickaninny holders are used, one can be red, the other yellow. All this, of course, is merely to satis   vish to go gala. The melon slices could be brought in s   c. ff the ice to the guests as they laze on the steps or __ swing—and they would taste just as good as if served on the porch.

A COLORFUL MENU—Ice-cold red and yellow-meated watermelons are a feast in themselves. But sometimes the hostess would like a few extra items that carry out the same color scheme. In which case, the menu might include ham-and-egg sandwiches, or chicken sandwiches, candied sweet potatoes, tomato salad, and watermelon.

For a colorful service, there are paper plates and cups in matching colors. Or the ordinary white ones can have a gay paper frill pasted to the under side; and glasses or paper cups can be decorated with pickaninny cutouts. If there is a plump, jolly Negro servant handy, she may be dressed as a black southern mammy and allowed to supervise the melon carving.

COLORFUL MUSIC—This is the time for all the well-known southern melodies to fill the summer night—"Old Black Joe," "Dixie," "Massa's in de Cold, Cold Ground"—sung to banjo, accordian, or mandolin accompaniment. Sometimes a local glee club will gladly come and sing for their share of watermelon. There are lovely phonograph records of Negro songs and spirituals. The men at such a party frequently surprise even themselves at how well they can whistle

"Swanee River" together. Perhaps there is a real voice in the community that can do justice to "Old Man River."

COLORFUL GAMES—All games and contests should be of the cool and easy type, such as guessing weight and waist of some giant watermelon, brought in to be eyed and lifted before it is reduced to slices; guessing the number of watermelon seeds in a wine glass; or drawing the best pickaninny in the fewest strokes, or with the eyes closed.

There could be prizes for the widest pickaninny grin, the most colorful costume worn to the party, and for the coolest. Prizes are inexpensive trifles, such as, red and yellow bandannas, dice, lollypop banjos, and pickaninny licorice dolls.

Heap Big Injun Pow-wow

If there has been an epidemic of watermelon feeds, the hostess, by changing the invitation a bit, the setting, and the menu, can make it a corn, steak, bacon, or weiner roast, and still keep it on the porch.

INVITATIONS—For the corn roast, she substitutes an Indian in full war paint and feathers for the pickaninny heads on the invitations. The second stanza of the invitation is changed to read:

> Then keep cool at my pow-wow;
> It's a big Injun one,
> All ears, with the corn on!
> All chatter and fun.

DECORATIONS—Instead of the watermelon centerpiece, she has a tepee, with tiny dolls dressed as Chief Big Injun, his braves and squaws sitting around the campfire. Real smoke can curl from the top of the tepee if an incense burner is concealed inside.

For the occasion braves and squaws are given new Indian names drawn out of a tom-tom. They are written on scraps of yellow paper decorated with Indian symbols—thunderbirds, sunbursts, etc. The names are any absurd take-off on the beautiful Indian ones, like "Heap-much-fat," "Fallen-arches," "Screwy-in-the-skull," "Come-hither-eye," "Big-noise-no-do," and "Heap-much-talk."

Before refreshments are served, souvenir Indian head-dresses are distributed, with the request that guests don them for the snake dance to the table.

A competitive war dance between rival tribes may be featured, or any game of skill that depends on acccurate throw and hit, like archery, darts, quoits, etc. The evening may end with the singing of Indian songs, such as "Land of Sky-Blue Water," "Red Wing," or "In a Little Birch Canoe."

A Snow-Wonder Porch Party

This party has a delightful beat-the-heat theme. It is an old summer favorite.

INVITATIONS—The invitations may picture a snowy winter scene—old Christmas cards are a fine source—and offer guests a party at which everything is cool except the welcome.

DECORATIONS—The porch is a chilly sight, with white crepe paper everywhere, tufted with snowflakes of cotton batting, glistening with artificial snow. Very thin library paste will hold snow and frost in place.

A fringe of jagged paper icicles dripping from doorway and window ledges lowers the mental mercury. If flowers are used, all white should be chosen. For below-zero shrubbery, bare branches may be smeared with paste and thrust into a pan of white confetti. For snow underfoot, old dust sheets or tarpaulin may be spread on the floor.

ICE BREAKER—Guests, on arriving, are given a cardboard ice-pick, on the handle of which is written some ice-breaker suggestion, such as: "Shake hands with all you meet, shivering, 'My zero! What a winter!'" Or, "Slap every lady on the back, and say, 'Cheer up, sister! One of these days it's going to be summer again!'"

There should be a fresh piece of foolishness for each ice-pick, so that no two guests are breaking the ice in the same way.

PARTNER FINDERS—Guests find partners by matching cold weather similes which have been written in duplicate on paper snowballs. The men are directed to one end of the porch to draw from a pail, white with paper snow. The girls gather at the other end to draw from a similar one. Partners are told to find each other by admitting how cold they are.

Thus, Jack, drawing a snowball which read, "As cold as an earthworm," hurries to the girl of his dreams and asks hopefully, "Are you as cold as an earthworm?" His Jill, reading her simile, shivers, "No; I'm as cold as a snake!"

Other similes are: As cold as a dog's nose, frog, marble, cucumber, fish, summer fireplace, Greenland's icy mountains, pawnbroker's sign, iron, unsunned snow, an egg in a deserted bird's nest, or as cold as a New England audience!

COLD WEATHER MALADIES—When all have found partners, each couple is given a pencil and a "doctor's card"—a plain card headed, "Cold Weather Hospital. Silence, Please!" On the card is a baffling list of winter ailments, each one badly jumbled; for example, leemass (measles). Partners' attempts to help each other decipher the ailments must all be done in hushed whispers. There's illness in the house!

"Ummsp!" hisses Jack. "Where'd anybody catch a thing like that?" But Sallie, his bright little partner, knows! She holds her throat between her hands, puffing out her cheeks. Why, mumps of course! Gleefully he writes it down on their card.

Other patients might suffer from: 1. moonmc dolc; 2. zufinlane; 3. oninpemua; 4. repidhaith; 5. hownopig hugoc; 6. recalst erevf; 7. kecihncoxp; 8. siitngylar; 9. chrisibont; 10. nossllttiii.

The answers are: 1. common cold; 2. influenza; 3. pneumonia; 4. diphtheria; 5. whooping cough; 6. scarlet fever; 7. chicken pox; 8. laryngitis; 9. bronchitis; 10. tonsillitis.

The first prize might be a bottle of candy pills, or a glass jar of marble-size candy balls, the jar labeled, "Vitamins for That All-Gone Feeling."

COLD FEET—Players and leaders are seated in a circle of chairs. The leader has a white, fluffy wool ball. He explains that when he throws this "snowball' into some player's lap, that player must instantly begin telling a chilly story. What about? Br-r-r-rr! About that time in his life when he had the coldest feet, actually or figuratively speaking.

When he has told his bleak tale, he tosses the ball back to the leader, who immediately throws it upon the knees of some other shivering player. Appointing the right leader to throw the ball assures a good start, since he has been secretly asked by the hostess to come prepared to tell the first cold-feet story. Once the players get started, the stories will be spontaneous. There will be clamoring calls of "Say, now let me tell one!"

A suitable prize for the teller of the story that sent most sympathetic shivers down the most spines might be a pair of thick socks, marked, "Guaranteed all wool."

SNOW-WONDER REFRESHMENTS—The refreshments should look as cool as they taste. Any green salad or jelly looks cool on a hot day. A green cherry frozen in the center of each ice cube is a coolly decorative touch to the punch. Round cupcakes covered with rough white icing can be piled in a pyramid of snowballs.

For a North Pole sundae, a candy stick is inserted in a cone of ice cream. The cone can be roughened with minced shredded coconut and made wintry with drifts of marshmallow. It may be surrounded with jagged edges of wafers, behind which prowls an iced polar bear—an animal cooky.

A PIECE-FUL FOURTH

Want to take the smoke of battle out of Independence Day? Well, here's a picnic that is as piece-ful as a paper dress pattern or a patchwork quilt.

PIECE-FUL INVITATIONS—are written on a piece of paper quite obviously torn from a larger sheet. Pieces of red, white, and blue strings, their ends hanging loose, are threaded at intervals along the top, much as one makes a rag rug; and beneath this piece-minded fringe are the words:

> The world's just a bedlam;
>   Mad, I mean.
> So let's have a piece-ful
>   Picnic scene.
>
> A piece-minded party;
>   Come on, gang!
> We'll all go to pieces
>   With a bang!

P.S. Please come prepared to contribute your piece to the piece party. Will you play a piece?

The time and place of the picnic and any other necessary information are added.

PIECE-FUL PROGRAM—The program is easily planned by the clever hostess who knows the gift or hobby of each invited guest. If Dick goes gleefully to town on his mouth organ, she knows what "piece" to ask him for in that persuasive postscript. If Nellie can imitate a dog fight so that all the neighborhood cats scram for the housetops, the hostess can engage Nell's talent by the personal postscript, "Will you bark a piece?"

Promising piece-fulness for the campfire program can be found in almost any family picnic group. Mary, for instance, who melts one's heart with her mandolin music; Red, whose conjuring tricks don't always conjure; Grandpa, whose stories of pioneer days ought to be filmed; Joan and John, teenage twins with the latest steps in those terrible gymnastics they call dances; and Joe, who can whistle any tune after he's heard it once, and yodel, too, when the mood's on him.

PIECE-FUL DECORATIONS—The decorations can trim whatever spot the hostess picks for the picnic. Pennants—pointed pieces of red, white, and blue bunting or crepe paper, machine-stitched on lengths of tape—can be strung between tall posts bordering her lawn or draped between trees if the picnic site is a clearing in the woods.

If it is a brook or river picnic, the pennants can flutter from boat or bridge. If it is a picnic on lake or seashore, the pennants can be used to decorate the tent, beach umbrellas, chow booths, or car-parking lots.

PIECE EXHIBITS—A piece exposition, showing a rare display of pieceful exhibits, is possible if the hostess has chosen her cool, spacious porch to be picnic headquarters. The exhibits may include beautiful old pieced quilts, silk and cotton; patchwork and "crazy-piece" cushion tops; rag rugs on the floor. Perhaps in the whatnot some invited guest may have one of those fascinating spillholders grandma used to make by covering a cocoa tin with putty, and then pressing into it a fearful collection of mixed pieces—a watch spring, a baby tooth, a carpet tack, a collar button, fragments of broken treasured glass and china, or a safety pin.

Perhaps another collection of later date, may have a plate covered with cigar bands, nicely shellacked. Either could be the exhibit's piece de resistance.

More piece exhibits could occupy corners of the porch. Some of the invited guests may be ardent collectors of pieces; if not stamps, then shells, tiny china dogs, jugs, charms, souvenir spoons, picture post cards, snapshots, foreign coins, or dolls of all nations. All may be shown. If Mrs. Jones, who spent a winter shelling on Sanibel Island, knows the name of every shell in her collection, now is the time to introduce them formally.

A piece-ful atmosphere is fostered by host and hostess wearing arm bands and enormous badges, those of one reading "Piece Commissioner," and those of the other "Justice of the Piece."

PIECE-MEAL REFRESHMENTS—It is fun to start the meal with a shock by solemnly serving each couple one piece of cardboard—their tray—on which are two small pieces of pickle and two roasted peanuts.

Piece-ful refreshments may be any food in pieces: chicken salad, fruit salad, sandwiches cut wedge-shaped, sliced cake, peaches, or watermelon.

If there is not too large a group of guests, food can be served on odd pieces of unmatched china or glass. For a larger group, this occasion affords a fine chance to use all the oddments of paper plates and cups and left-over pieces from old picnic sets.

When the meal is over and night is falling, all the picnickers gather around the campfire for the big program of musical numbers, recitations, skits, and stunts contributed by the guests, winding up with group singing of patriotic and favorite old songs, with the best soloist giving "God Bless America" as the farewell piece.

GAMES—A piece-ful afternoon, with card tables set up in the welcome shade until the cool of the evening, when a snug campfire is just as welcome, is easily planned.

Any game played with pieces is appropriate—jig-saw picture puzzles, Chinese checkers, dominoes, cards, anagrams, lotto, tiddlywinks; or any of the old or new favorites in which pieces—dogs, horses, trains—progress or are penalized by the throw of a die.

Any piece-against-time game can be run as a progressive contest, with winning couple moving up a table. Thus, at one table, players could thread broken bits of macaroni on a piece of limp string; at the next, they could take prepared envelopes containing identically cut pieces of the first stanza of any patriotic song, and see which pair could first assemble the lines in the right order.

In fact, any game that features pieces is eligible: charades, in which pieces of words are acted; games in which each player adds a piece, as in consequences, or draws a piece, as in add-a-line art, or tells a piece, as in continued story, when each in turn takes up the tale where the previous author abandoned it.

Even the dear old picnic perennials can qualify if given a fitting name, such as iron-piece pitch for horseshoes.

Prizes for the games are called piece awards and consist

of anything that grinds, cuts, breaks or pulverizes, such as nutcracker, scissors, graters, or salad shredders.

Forfeits are demanded as piece offerings, and have to do with pieces. Thus one unfortunate guest is sentenced to brush confetti from here to there with a piece of feather. Another must eat potato chips by stabbing each chip with a hatpin and licking up the pieces to clean the platter.

Still another guest is handed a piece note torn to scraps, and asked to put it together again. When he does, the fellowing piece of sound advise is disclosed:

> Ef you want peace, the thing
> You've gut tu du
> Is jes' to show you're up
> To fightin', tu.

> —*James Russell Lowell*

MIXER—Piece-workers is a good mixer if the hostess wants everyone at her picnic to meet everyone else before they drift off in pairs or completely settle down as a cliquey foursome at some secluded table in the shade for the rest of the afternoon.

Each guest is handed an envelope with a different number written on the outside. Inside each envelope are six pieces of a picture, one of which miscellaneous scraps has a number on it to correspond with the number on the envelope. That is the "native"—the key piece. All the rest are "aliens."

Players are told to trade the pieces that obviously do not fit with their numbered one, until they have all six pieces of their own picture.

To get the equipment for this game, pictures are cut from the advertising pages of magazines such as a piece of jewelry, a piece of furniture, a piece of linoleum, a piece of farm equipment, or a timepiece. They are pasted on cardboard, then on each picture is traced the same number of irregular pieces, and each is cut as for a jig-saw puzzle.

The piece commissioner speeds up the piece-work by holding a timepiece on the workers and saying, "Piece in our time! Only two more minutes to go. Only half a minute. Two seconds."

STUNTS—A piece-at-any-price pie is a snack to serve whenever the party seems ready for it. It is a huge deep-dish pie, full of "plums" in the form of favors. The dish is an oval laundry basket. The crust is light brown wrapping paper ornamented with a pattern of decorative slits, from each of which dangles a piece of red, white or blue string. Each guest in turn takes a piece of string and pulls. The hostess can distribute the various stunts pretty much as she wishes, by fastening all the young folks' stunts to red strings, the women's to white, the men's to blue, and asking guests to pull the strings of their own color group.

Each plum pulled from the pie carries some price-tag stunt. For example, guests may be asked to perform any of the following stunts:

1. Demonstrate a person of the opposite sex going completely to pieces.
2. Give us a piece of your mind about the hats the ladies are wearing this year.
3. Repeat a piece of the Declaration of Independence. Go as far as you can.
4. Describe a set of dishes of a hundred pieces. How many of what?
5. Tell the various pieces that go into the making of a car. Or a television set, Irish stew, clock, radio, sewing machine, etc.
6. Did you ever have an amazing piece of good fortune? Tell us about it. Or have you a piece of good news? Let's hear it.

Numbers two and four are the type to choose for men; number six has exciting possibilities, such as announcement of engagements, trips, home-comings; also little family triumphs, such as John's new car, Jane's promotion, or Emily Brown's winning of another prize. Or the good news can be the simple statement, "Time to eat!"

How Piece-minded Are You? This is the old inventory-by-memory game, confined to pieces arranged, not too precisely, about the piece table: such as a piece of music, a piece of bread, a piece of wall paper; pieces of coal, sugar, kindling, chalk, rope, string, chain, ribbon, glass, fur, pencil, soap, rubber, cork, bone, comb, shoelace, rock, etc.

"Piece delegates" are asked to gather around the piece table for a three-minute survey. Then they are sent back to their respective seats, and each is handed a piece of paper and a piece of pencil and told to list two dozen or more pieces he has observed.

PRETTY PIECE POSTERS—People—young, to middlin', to old—love to demonstrate a hidden talent, which, they feel, might go places if given half a chance. Well, here's the chance to make that masterpiece so long clamoring to be created. Each artist literally throws his genius on canvas! Colored squares of kindergarten cardboard are on hand, also tubes of good library paste and bowls of gaily-colored confetti. The artist first lines in his picture, then smears it with paste and throws the confetti at it!

With the help of a sprinkling of bright green paper shavings, such as are left in boxes which contained fragile gifts, the artists can achieve some very exotic garden scenes.

When genius has burned itself sufficiently low, the posters, which should be signed, are collected and hung where all can view them with alarm.

A fitting title may be offered for the picture which receives most votes from an admiring public. When votes have been cast and counted, the blushing artist is asked to bring his picture up front so that the prize title can be pinned on it. The ceremony over, he is asked to read aloud the title. "Kindly Keep the Piece," he reads. The crowd cheers and jeers. He's welcome to it! They don't want it!

MORE MASTERPIECES—1. Piece souvenirs are fascinating to make. Guests are directed to a shady corner marked, "Piece-Work Done Here." There are long picnic tables, with benches drawn up alone the sides. On the table in shoe boxes, glass jars, and saucers are all sorts of pieces—beads, pipecleaners, feathers, crepe and tissue paper, rice, birdseed, toothpicks, light-weight cardboard, construction paper in various bright colors, sawdust, sand, old corks, fancy buttons, shells, etc.

In the toolbox are scissors, knives, glue, paste, Scotch tape, gummed tape, paper clips, paper stapler, crayons, box of water-color paints, and plasticine. Over the worktable hangs the sign, "Please piece together these trifles and make a piece souvenir. First prize—a surprise."

The surprise is the announcement that the winner may choose her prize from any of the surprising objects just completed as piece souvenirs.

2. Each artist is given a stick of chewing gum, a card, and an orange stick dipped in oil so that it will not stick. He chews the gum to the right consistency, then models it to resemble anything or anybody he chooses.

Plasticine can be used instead of gum. It is fun to hand to all contestants the same plasti-art kit, and see what vastly different results are achieved from exactly the same equipment. For instance, each package could contain plasticine in the same colors, four toothpicks, two fringe hairpins, an old fringe hair net, a pipe cleaner, two bobby pins, two black shoe buttons, four soda pop caps, and a rubber band wrapped around a used match.

Whatever the artist evolves from this mixture, the hostess should insist that it represents his suppressed desire, be it a model of a battleship or a baby.

3. Going to pieces is a game that may be preferred by some of the men. In which case, they may be given a box of empty thread spools and wooden clothespins and told to forage for what other material they need to show the world what a willing whittler can do when it comes to making something out of next to nothing. There should be a supply of whittling knives on hand in case the men do not carry their own.

COOTIE-DRAWING CONTEST—Guests draw the cootie's picture in pieces, a leg at a time, at the throw of the dice. As many card tables as needed are arranged, with four players at each table. The two sitting opposite each other are partners and race their opponents in a cootie-drawing contest. The common variety of cootie is shown in figure 4 on page 212.

There are rarer sorts, with feelers and a stinger, but the common cootie goes—and comes!—faster.

To start the game, the players take turns shaking a single die out of a glass. When the die turns up one spot, the player who threw it may begin his cootie by drawing a circle for its head. Until he shakes a one-spot, he cannot start to

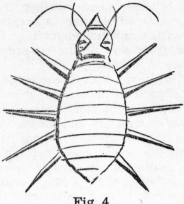

Fig. 4

draw. He sadly hands the glass to the next player. When he shakes a two-spot, he may add a body to his cootie's head, and so on until the insect is complete. Partners draw together on the same cootie. The drawing rules are:

> One spot for the head
> Two spots for the body
> Three spots for each arm
> Four spots for the facial features
> Five spots for the legs
> Six spots for the tail

Since the cootie has two legs and two arms, players must get three-spots and five-spots twice each.

Nor may a player draw a hit-and-miss cootie, such as first head, next a tail. Before he can continue to draw his cootie, the numbers must appear in the order given above. This is the rule that causes all the gnashing of teeth; for it certainly is preserving the wrong piece when a player throws six times in a row and gets the cootie's tail each time.

The couple first to complete their cootie might receive a bottle of insecticide as a prize, or a bottle of perfume or shaving lotion labeled insecticide.

A TEA-TOTALLY FREE AFFAIR

A three-penny tax on a pound of tea! That was the match that ignited the Revolutionary fire, and led the English Colonies of America to freedom. Fifty blanketed braves threw overboard the equivalent of fifty-thousand dollars worth of "the baneful herb" in less than three hours! What a tea party! Three hundred and forty-two chests of taxed tea steeped in the sea; and from that Boston brew there poured a new nation. So why not celebrate it with a liberty tea at a club Independence Day celebration?

INVITATION—The invitation may read as follows:

A free and independent nation,
  It seems to me,
Should have a birthday celebration
  Entirely free!
So let's declare our independence;
  Let's ring the bell!
Free air, free speech, and free attendance,
  Free tea, as well.

The verse can be written on correspondence cards, decorated with a carbon sketch of the Liberty Bell, the lines done with the red half of the typewriter ribbon. Or the cards can be of the folder sort, shaped like the Liberty Bell and tied at the top with a tiny red, white, and blue ribbon bow. On the cover is printed "A Tea-Totally Free Affair," and the time and place of the tea party, and on the inside is the rimed invitation.

DECORATIONS—For a tea, the decorations usually center in the table. They can go patriotic in a dozen pretty ways: white food on blue dishes; red crepe paper frills on paper containers; patriotic streamers running from a central basket of red, white and blue flowers to smaller baskets at the corners of the table. And there is a glory of patriotic flowers flying the flag of freedom around the Fourth—blue delphinium, bachelor buttons, white petunias, red carnations, white carnations, red roses and geraniums, and scarlet sage.

A perky little bow of red, white, and blue ribbon may tie a small cardboard bell to each teacup handle. The bell is cut double, the sides left open, if wished, to disclose a folded paper clapper, which is fastened to the top of the bell with a paper clip. The tongue is marked, "The Bell Told" and, upon opening it, the guest finds typed thereon a brief fact about some famous bell, headed with the request, "Please read or tell when called upon what your bell told." See Page 218 for facts about famous bells.

A Liberty Tea Bouquet—This is an amusingly different centerpiece. It is made of tea bags, each having a long wire flower stalk, and a frill of crepe paper petals. All the "tea-flowers" are bunched together and their stems wound with tin foil, then thrust through the center of a round lace paper doily, and tied with streamers of red, white, and blue ribbon, like an old-fashioned bouquet. Such a centerpiece could be awarded as a prize or given to the guest of honor or a special speaker or soloist, thus serving a double purpose.

Room Decorations—Liberty Bells should have the place of honor. If possible, the hostess may buy or borrow a good framed picture of this "best-loved relic in America," and set it on an easel where all must pass it or see it. The art teacher of the local high school and the students' poster club may be invited to provide dozens of drawings of the Liberty Bell. A prize offered for the best sketch or poster stimulates competition and arouses the youngsters' patriotic spirit.

Bells of all sizes and types are in order, from huge ones of crepe paper worked up on a wire foundation bought at the florist's—who has them in stock for wedding decorations —to tiny ones made in a jiffy from a paper cup. The "clapper" of the improvised bell can be anything from a tea ball, moth ball, or marble twisted in a square of paper, to a tennis ball, depending on the size of the bell.

Flower-pot bells have the sturdy quality of the weathered old Liberty Bell, and a party touch is given to the porch by a row of them, in graduated sizes, swinging from a horizontal rod made of a sawed-off broom handle gaily painted. Basket bells can be made of any wastebasket of jelly-glass shape. Peach baskets make a nice light frame around which to build a crepe paper bell. Patriotic bells of crepe paper to hang in doorways, from ceiling or chandelier, singly or in clusters of three, do not need any frame beyond a wire ring at the bottom, unless they are over eight inches in diameter.

LIBERTY BELL FAVORS—Favors that make useful souvenirs are little books listing the telephone numbers of club members. The cover is shaped like the Liberty Bell, and lettered, "Do give me a ring." The book may be tied with red, white, and blue cord.

LIBERTY BELL PRIZES—The prizes can be any sort of bell, from the lovely hand-painted Swiss cowbells to a set of tinkling Japanese wind bells. For the principal prize, a picture of Millet's painting, "The Angelus," is suitable or a framed colored portrait of the beautiful Bok tower.

REFRESHMENTS—Sandwiches can be cut in bell shape, and cookies also. The latter may be iced with chocolate, and the Liberty Bell crack may be white. A half pear, as it comes in cans, makes a delicious salad bell. Given a tongue of cream cheese or a preserved red cherry, it strikes the right note. It can rest on a bed of stiff red jelly, a slice of cake, or simply a blue plate.

Tea Party Games and Contests

DECLARATIONS OF INDEPENDENCE—Each guest is handed a little red program pencil and a blue-bordered square of white note paper, decorated with a gummed sticker of the Liberty Bell, under which is typed or written:

1. I declare myself free of ....
2. Because ....
3. And I resolve to ....
4. At ....
5. On ....

"This is a solemn occasion," announces the hostess. "I will give you a minute in which to think of something—or someone—you now declare yourself free of. When I signal that time is up, write it down in your best handwriting on the dotted line. Then fold it over, so that what you have written is completely concealed, and pass the paper to the next in line."

After all the papers have been passed five times, each time to a different signer, and all the dotted lines have been neatly filled in, each signer, in turn, reads aloud the declaration he holds.

For example: "I declare myself free of a head cold. Because I think a real lady should. And I resolve to lose ten pounds in ten days. At the liberty. On a money-back guarantee."

ARTY TO A TEA—Guests keep their pencils. The hostess passes around cards on which she has sketched the outline of a teacup, behind which stands the saucer or a plate. Carbon copies can be made from illustrations in newspaper advertisement or a mail order catalogue.

She announces that a prize will be awarded the "artist" who gives the plain chinaware of the sketch a pretty border design. There is one important rule. The pattern must be formed entirely of repetitions and variations of the capital letter T. Not an additional stroke or dot is allowed.

The prize could be a dainty tea towel, with a cup and saucer embroidered in one corner.

TEAPOT—This game is a variation of teakettle. One guest goes out of the room. The others decide on a verb which the absent one is to guess, such as shampoo, swim, sew, sing, study, skate.

The guesser is then called in and begins asking questions to find out what the verb is. He may ask as many questions as he wishes, of one person. He may dodge from one player to another.

Questions must be answered only by "Yes" or "No." When quizzing the players, the questioner uses the word, "teapot" for the verb which he doesn't know, but hopes he soon will. For example, "Can I teapot in this room?" Or, "Do you teapot at home?"

By following a plan of questioning designed to discover the time, the place, the action, etc., he soon finds out what the verb is.

TEA BALL PASS—To background music, guests pass a silver tea ball from hand to hand. When the music stops short, the guest holding the tea ball receives the pretty thing as a souvenir, on condition that it is paid for by whatever the hostess requests. This could be a song, a stunt, the telling of a story about some tea party attended, or by reading aloud to the assembled group the ancient tea advertisement, preserved under the tea cozy.

Under the tea cozy is a copy of an advertisement that appeared in England in the year 1660, announcing a new Chinese drink, called by the Chinese, "tcha;" by other nations "tay, alias tee." In part, the tea merchant's advertisement reads as follows:

"Tea removeth lassitude, vanquisheth heavy dreams, easeth the frame, and strengtheneth the memory. It overcometh superfluous sleep, and prevents sleepiness in general, so that without trouble whole nights may be passed in study. It is of great avail to men of corpulent bodies, and to such as eat much flesh. It clears a dull head, and maketh the frame active and lusty."

TEA-LEAF FORTUNES—It is fun to ask one guest who has a lively imagination and a quick wit, to come prepared to read the other guests' fortunes by the tea leaves left in their teacups.

RINGING THE BELL—A push-button bell, such as teachers use on desks, is placed on a table, and each guest in turn is blindfolded, given a fly swatter, and told to ring the bell by swatting the button. Three strikes are allowed.

Another way to ring the bell is as follows: A small handbell is hung just behind a suspended hoop. Guests are divided into competing teams of equal numbers. A "throwing" line is marked off about ten feet from the bell. It should be tried out for difficulty.

Each team in turn sends a player to toss a beanbag or a small rubber ball at the bell. Only one throw is allowed.

If a player succeeds in ringing the bell, it scores a point for that team.

THIRTEEN FOR LUCK—The hostess hands a pencil and paper to each guest. "Who knows the original thirteen states of the Union?" she asks guilelessly.

Practically every hand goes up, for that seems simple enough for anyone to know, and only half try.

"Write them down," she says, warning them to say nothing out loud which might help a groping neighbor and ruling that nobody is to help another, by, for instance, swapping states—a most unpatriotic trick!

It is surprising how few patriots have more than eight at the tip of the tongue—or pencil.

They are: New Hampshire, Massachusetts, Connecticut, Rhode Island, New York, New Jersey, Delware, Pennsylvania, Maryland, Virginia, North Carolina, South Carolina, and Georgia.

What The Bell Told

The following can be read by one person, or it may be divided up, as numbered, and typewritten on separate sheets of paper which are folded and inserted in the paper bells that are tied to the teacup handles.

1. By far the most famous bell in America is the Liberty Bell, which is on display at Independence Hall in Philadelphia. It was cast in London; brought to Philadelphia in August, 1752; cracked in less than a month by a stroke of its own clapper; was recast by local workmen and again cracked.

It was again recast, and finally the true liberty pitch was struck and the bell was placed in the belfry from which it was to "ring in and ring out the shifting scenes in the mighty drama of a nation's freedom."

It has made several journeys in its day. In 1777, when the British were approaching Philadelphia, it was taken down and carried to Allenton, via Bethlehem, for safe-keeping. Later it was brought triumphantly back and rang from Independence Hall for many years. In spite of the fact that the bell was cracked, it made triumphal journeys to expositions and world's fairs in 1885, 1893, and 1895; and in 1915 it was carried clear across the continent to San Francisco, the railway company building a special car for it, with buffers to prevent injury by jolts. This was the old bell's last trip, and on arrival in San Francisco, fifty thousand school children sang the national anthem in the streets as it passed, cannons saluted it, and the entire population turned out to do it honor. For fear of any accident to America's best-loved relic, a law was later enacted to the effect that it should never again leave Philadelphia.

"Old Liberty" weighs 2080 pounds. It is still suspended from the yoke on which it hung during the Revolution. Its inscription, which entirely encircles the crown reads: "Proclaim LIBERTY throughout all the LAND unto all the INHABITANTS thereof. Lev. XXV. V. X. By order of the Assembly of the Province of Pennsylvania for the State House in Philada."

2. The Independence Hall Bell was cast in 1876, the hundredth anniversary of the birth of the republic, for the tower of the Old

State House in Philadelphia. It weighs thirteen thousand pounds to represent the original states, and bears the same inscription as the Liberty Bell. It was cast by an American bell founder.

3. Two hundred thousand people of America contributed to the making of the Columbian Liberty Bell, cast in 1893 for the World's Fair at Chicago.

4. There is a garden of bells in California, where over five hundred bells of many dates and from many countries, hang, preserved in masonry built to house them. It is the largest and most interesting collection of bells in the world, and its collector was the late Frank A. Miller, of Glenwood Mission Inn, at Riverside, California. One beautiful specimen, dated 1247, is considered the oldest dated Christian bell, save one, in the world.

5. Paul Revere was a bell founder. A few years after the Revolutionary War, he built a furnace in Boston for the casting of bells, and his business was successfully carried on until he died in 1818, at the ripe old age of eighty-nine. One of Paul Revere's bells hangs in King's Chapel, Boston.

6. The first bell foundry in the United States was established by the Hanks family, ancestors of Abraham Lincoln on his mother's side. The family is still making bells. For a descendant of the old firm now carries on under the name of the Meneely Bell Company of Troy, N. Y.

7. The bells on the tower of St. Michael's Church, Charleston, S. C. have had an adventurous history since they were cast in London in 1764. The entire set has crossed the Atlantic five times, and two of the bells seven times. They were seized by the British in the Revolutionary War and shipped to London. But a Charleston merchant bought them and sent them back. In the Civil War, during the bombardment of Charleston, the bells were taken down and rushed to Columbia, S. C., where they were burned during the occupation of the town by Sherman's army. The charred fragments were tenderly gathered up and sent to London, where metal was added to recast them in the original moulds used a century before. In 1867 the eight bells came back good as new to be installed in their old steeple where, inhabitants said, they sang in their first home-coming peal, "Home again, home again from a foreign land!"

8. In ancient times, a silver bell was the prize awarded in races, and probably the expression, "bearing away the bell" originated in this custom. In after years, the prize became a cup, which is the bell inverted.

(Note: Most of these facts were taken from Coleman's "Bells," published by Rand, McNally & Co., Chicago, Illinois.)

LIBRARY HELPS

"To Think of Tea!" by Agnes Repplier, published by Houghton, Mifflin Co., 2 Park Street, Boston, Mass. (For fascinating facts about tea.)

"The Liberty Bell—Its History & Significance" by Victor Rosewater, published by D. Appleton & Co., 35 W. 32nd Street, New York City. (For authentic history, splendid readings, in prose and verse, and fine pictures of the Liberty Bell.

"Wedding Anniversary Celebrations" by Beatrice Plumb, Mabel N. Fuller and others, published by T. S. Denison & Company, Minneapolis, Minnesota. (For full, detailed and illustrated directions for making large, crepe paper bells.)

MERRY MEANDERS

The Independence Day party may provide outdoor summer fun for a class, a church or a club.

Over a century and a half ago, John Adams told Americans how to celebrate their independence: "With pomp and parade, with shows, games, sports, guns, bells, bonfires, and illuminations."

But, John, if they sprint, sizzle, or shoot from sunup to sundown, couldn't they relax under the stars in the cool of the evening? After going off with a bang all day, couldn't they meander by moonlight, so long as they wind up with a bonfire?

MERRY MEANDER INVITATIONS—The invitations for an Independence Day party are written on tinted cards, decorated to suit the occasion. The simple verse runs—or rather, saunters! —like this:

> Come, meander with us,
> Without frills, fret, or fuss;
>   The cooler the costume, the grander!
> We'll just saunter along
> With a bit of a song,
>   For a happy-go-lucky meander.

The day, date, time, and place and any other necessary information are added.

The card may be decorated with a sketch, sticker, or cutout, which is pasted in place, the choice being governed by whether the affair is a special Independence Day outing or simply a general July or August picnic; whether it will be by moonlight or starlight; the type of meander planned, and especially how guests are to get there—on foot, by bicycle, truck, or hayrack.

Will there be a moon? Then a big, magic moon may be pasted on and a merry face with a wicked wink inked in. If there is no moon, the card may be spangled with a few star stickers. If it is a July Fourth meander, the moon's head may be crowned with a patriotic bow or a few of the stars joined with a narrow red-white- and-blue ribbon.

For August, a watermelon, or cutout of a gypsy camp with a bonfire, will give the right spot of color. Adorable illustrations can be made for a straw ride. On paper which contrasts well with the tinted invitation card are sketched little hay wagons drawn by **plump horses. They are cut out** carefully and pasted on the card, with the top of the wagon left open to form a pocket. Into this pocket are stuck a few wisps of real hay, sweet grass, or fine straw, whichever is easiest to get; and then a driver, rural as a hayseed, and a joy-rider or two are added to complete the sketch.

Mixed Meanders—A meander is any sort of informal trip that spurns the route which is the shortest distance between two points. The objective is the picnic spot, which may be a clearing in the woods, a neighboring farm, the lake shore, or the lawn of some friend who lives some distance away. Only in this last case, perhaps the hostess may not be able to grant John Adams even his bonfire!

An Old-fashioned Straw Ride—The straw ride is the grandest meander of all! The hayrack is decorated with flags and bunting for the Fourth and with yellow streamers and goldenrod for August. The route that seems so haphazard is really carefully planned to every last detail, but nobody knows this but the hostess and her wisely-chosen helpers, one of whom is assigned to each conveyance. The loads are listed, so that each has its share of singers, natural "cutups," musicians, and "ballast." Any hostess who knows her crowd can quickly sort them out.

The party begins with the first "Gid-ap!" and each helper has his merry program, if not on paper, then in his head. If he can lead the songs, direct the simple games, and also act as lecturing guide en route, so much the better. If not, the girl with the ukulele or the boy with the mouth organ can lead the songs.

Meandering Travelogue—Someone is appointed to write and memorize fairly well a "spiel" about the landmarks, real or imaginary, passed along the way. If it is an authentic historical site, it should be given the honor due it. The party may be halted to sing patriotic songs. But if the locality boasts no such site, imagination may be allowed to make history. For instance:

"On your right, ladies and gentlemen, you see a little shack. Here was made the shot that was heard around the world. Five lead pencils were melted down to make that shot. They belonged to an ancestor of the farmer whose mortgaged fields we are now passing. Let's all sing to the tune of 'Merrily We Roll Along' our history-making song."

Whereupon the ukuleles and voices strike up:

> Merrily we jog along,
>   Jog along, jog along,
>   Merrily we jog along
>   Over historic ground!

Last lines may vary, to suit the occasion. For example:

> Past that first big shot.
> Over a Tory's tooth.
> Right over Bunker Hill.
> Sniffing some Boston tea.

LOVE YOUR LOCALITY—If it happens to be an August meander, the theme can be changed from patriotic to civic pride. Before every little four-corners is reached, the tour lecturer gives its absurdly exaggerated population; its industries— the making of mothballs or fly-paper, or the manufacture of patented scientific instruments for the discovery of buried golf balls; the raising and training of performing fleas, etc.

Or he tells of its celebrated residents, past and present. For instance: "On your left, ladies and gentlemen, is the home of the man who first said, 'How'm I doin'?' And that on the northeast corner of the southwest field is the palatial residence of a man who made his fortune on a shoe-string. He strangled his rich uncle with it, and he was the only heir."

The lecturer-guide should handle his job with an air of know-it-all importance. A megaphone, real or faked, gives a professional touch.

MERRY STOP-OFFS—Some meanderers plan to make a few stops on their round-about route to the picnic site. They arrange to serenade some lonely farm where lives an old-time neighbor or friend, often leaving a surprise picnic hamper of fancy foods. They stay long enough to play a simple ring game, such as Farmer in the Dell, or to sing a simple known stunt song, such as "Old McDonald Had a Farm."

Other stop-offs can be scheduled at places which the hostess knows are suitable, such as the playground of a country school, a wayside refreshment stand, a community park, etc.

AT THE END OF THE TRAIL—Here the merry meanderers find either fires burned down to a bed of glowing embers, just right for cooking, or "the makings," depending on the hour of arrival. The advance guard has not only built the fires, but has cut and pointed plenty of green sticks on which to toast the cheese sandwiches, the meat, and the marshmallows. They have piles of wood at hand, so that when the meal is over, a bonfire can be quickly built to give light, warmth, and a romantic glow for the evening's program.

There are a few logs for seats, a deck chair or two for honored guests, and plenty of cushions, rugs, and pure drinking water. Other needs are a utility lantern, a flashlight, a hatchet, matches, paper cups, and a first aid kit.

A hot drink always agrees better than cold with picnic food, and coffee is easily made. For between drinks, a refreshing fruitade is made by squeezing the juice from oranges, lemons, and grapefruit, sweetened to taste, and served with a sprig of mint.

MERRY MEANDER PROGRAM—For all joy rides the old rule still stands—merry songs going, mellow ones returning. Around the camp fire it is the same. The leading singers begin with popular favorites, peppy college and school songs, and camp parodies. But as the fire begins to die down to a soft glow, it is time for the old songs, even favorite hymns and spirituals; then "taps" as the parting benediction, before breaking up the crowd for the homeward trip.

A LANTERN MEANDER—This meander is a colorful hot-weather hike and picnic that young people enjoy. The group is invited to meet at a central place—club house, school steps, church, library, or home—about dusk. Here each couple is given a yard-long, forked stick on which is hung a lighted Chinese lantern. With these held high, the colorful procession trails off to the picnic spot, singing as they go. The singing seems spontaneous, but the song leader has planned the program beforehand, choosing leaders for each song.

When the supper spot has been reached, hikers push their sticks into the ground, so that the lanterns make an enchanting circle of color and light. Within this circle, a program of songs and stunts is staged. At the right time, a gaily-wrapped box is handed to each guest. Inside, each item wrapped in waxed paper, is a delicious meal. This could be a paper cup, with a scooped-out tomato fitted nicely into it, the red shell filled with chopped chicken, potato, and celery, mixed with boiled mayonnaise dressing. Another wrapped package contains two kinds of sandwiches—brown bread with cream and pimento cheese filling, and white bread with jelly filling. A roly-poly package turns out to be a stuffed egg. What! No cake? Surely. A dainty bundle discloses two delicious homemade cupcakes, a red and white peppermint stick stuck in each white-iced top, which is decorated with a few blue candy stars.

Thermos jugs containing red-colored punch or grape-juice are produced, with decorated paper cups.

MEANDER DE LUXE—Sometimes a group of appreciative women want to give a midsummer outing for a popular visitor or some hard-working member of the group who has earned a carefree party, such as a minister's wife or a stay-at-home teacher.

A delightful and easy way to do it is to plan a progressive porch supper, with each course served by a different hostess on her own porch.

The guests meet at the home of some member of the group whose place is centrally located. Here cars await at the curb, and the guest of honor and a few known to be especially congenial are ushered into car number one. The tour-director calls off the names of those who are to ride in the next car, and so on until the entire party is on wheels.

Arriving at Mrs. Blank's, the motorists find cool-looking tables set out on the porch and a warm welcome awaiting them, also the first course. Naturally, they expect the second to follow. But almost before they have finished, there comes the message, by messenger, telephone, or fake telegram, that Mrs. Brown expects them at her home at once.

Laughingly they pile into the waiting cars and set forth for Mrs. Brown's. Here, perhaps, is meat loaf, escalloped potatoes, hot fresh vegetable, jelly, and relish. Or, if the guest of honor is known to have a favorite meat dish, this is often substituted.

Again the call comes, and the guests are hurried off to Mrs. Smith's to eat one of her favorite salads. Then comes the last interruption. This time, they learn, it is Mrs. Sweet who is expecting them at once, before the ice cream melts.

When choosing a hostess to serve the dessert, one is usually picked who has the finest lawn, so that the ice cream and coffee can be served there, and the evening's program enjoyed in the open.

A TRAMP AFFAIR—This party is the young crowd's answer to the call of the open road. Invitations are printed on anything a hobo might use for stationery—scraps of wrapping paper, torn pieces of cardboard, and paper sacks. The read:

> This is the weather for loathing
> Civilized living and clothing,
>   And things that agree
>   With afternoon tea!
>
> This is the weather for tramping,
> Hoboing, roughing it, camping!
>   I've never hoboed;
>   Let's take to the road!

The invitation continues, "Bring stick and bandanna, and wear your tramping clothes," and supplies any other necessary information.

The meeting place is a garage or barn, which makes a good hobos' hangout. Here the girls take scraps of paper from one rubbish can, the boys from another, and match for partners. Thus the boy who draws the scrap reading, "Weary Willie," looks for "Weary Wendy." Dusty Dick looks for Dusty Dot. Moth-eaten Mose looks for Moth-eaten Moll, and so on until all are paired off. Each then ties his red handkerchief, tramp-fashion, to the end of his stick, and the couples hike off to look for a hand-out.

The head hobo is the leader, and is already informed as to location of friends' houses along the way where food has been previously deposited. Each house bears on gate or pavement the tramp's easy-mark sign, E.Z. The head hobo assigns a different "chief whiner" at every stop to do the actual knocking at the door and begging for food.

At the first door, sandwiches are handed out, each bundle wrapped separately in waxed paper. These the tramps put into their respective bandannas, swing their bundles back over the shoulder, and amble off to the next stop. In this way they "beg" pickles, cookies, candy, etc., according to the menu planned, from as many different back doors. It is fun to arrange for a few "slams" so that the staggered hobo finds the door slammed in his face before he has had a chance to tell of his starving wife with ten children and a boil on the back of her neck!

When all the food making a good square meal, has been collected, a fire is built, and the hoboes sit around it to enjoy their pickings. This fire can be built in a chosen picnic spot, a vacant lot, or the Weary Willies and their hungry mates can tramp back home to the back yard, garage, or barn from which they started. They may boil coffee in the shabbiest-looking receptacle that can be found, and serve it in tin cups.

A SUNSET TEA FOR THE FOURTH

There are unpatriotic feet that ache just as much when they are stood on for hours watching the big parade as they do at the end of a black-letter day of plain, everyday house cleaning.

There are community programs for a sane and strenuous Fourth that have the men in the family marching in the blistering sun all morning and the children running races all afternoon.

A sunset tea is a celebration that calls for a chair for everyone on a breezy lawn, a long, cool drink in the shade, and not too much of anything else.

INVITATIONS—If the party is to be a small, intimate one, the invitations can be hand-written. If it is to be a larger affair, they can be "redily" typed on plain white note paper, with the typist using the red half of the ribbon.

They can be illustrated with a carbon sketch of a few cups and saucers across the top. In the corner a tiny bow of red, white, and blue ribbon can be tied, and if the hostess is still feeling artistic, she can scatter small flag-blue stickers around the border. The simpler, the better!

The invitation reads:

> Come share a quiet Fourth with me,
> A simple six o'clock high tea;
> We'll dance the old steps on the green—
> The two-step and the waltz, I mean—
> And show without the fizz and fuss
> Just what Old Glory means to us.

A postscript may be added, with the program in mind, such as, "Bring your favorite victrola record with you. If you can't decide, bring two!" Or if the program calls for amateur night music, the performers may be reminded to bring their musical instruments.

COSTUMES—The hostess might wear a decorative colonial costume. The two ladies, chosen for their charm and poise, to pour tea and coffee at the elegant service table, can be dressed in period dresses or in dainty, full, ankle-length frocks, with fichu and ruffles.

The pretty girls who assist guests to help themselves at the table—two, if the crowd is small, more, if large—wear similar gowns. The girl who serves iced tea, lemonade, and punch at the garden booth is in period dress or in dainty attire of the garden party type.

If the program includes a group of old-fashioned songs, the girl singers add to their charm if they dress in the sweet old costumes of a bygone day.

PORCH AND GARDEN DECORATIONS—The hostess may unearth all the old Japanese lanterns, leftovers from previous parties, stored in attic, garage, or family "glory hole." They are hung in trees and shrubbery, as shades over electric bulbs or to glow softly over their own candles so that they dot the dusk of a starlit evening.

For the festive Fourth, two long bamboo fishing poles are arched over the garden gate, and two fancy lanterns hung thereon. Other arches of bamboo, trimmed with flowers and vines are lovely and may be placed along the main path from gate to lawn, from porch to garden, to dancing green, or to mark any point of interest. To light a table, two pliable bamboo poles may be lashed to opposite table legs and looped overhead to form an arch, from which a colorful lantern is hung.

THE PARTY SETTING—At the very first sight of the party locale, guests should feel relaxed and rested. The cool green of the lawn soothes glare-and-dust-wearied eyes. Small tables are set out in the shade, grouped informally about "the green"—an open space reserved for entertainers and evening dancing. Each table is covered with a white cloth, and in the center of each is set a blue bowl of red salvias or any other red flower the garden grows. Table favors could be homemade paper fans, or boutonnieres or red, white, and blue garden flowers.

At the center of the group of tables is a flag pole from which floats Old Glory, and at sunset time, the flag is lowered by scouts, to the strains of "The Star-Spangled Banner," played by an old-time fiddler.

Wicker and deck chairs, settees and garden seats are scattered in cozy groups under the trees and through the shrubbery. A few rugs and cushions are thrown on the grass for the youngsters who find any sort of chair too formal for the Fourth. A securely-tied hammock adds to the take-it-easy atmosphere.

Every table is supplied with incense or joss-sticks so that patriotic mosquitoes can be persuaded to celebrate somewhere else.

The decorating committee has raided the garden of hostess and neighbors, and great bowls of cool blue and white blossoms are everywhere—bachelor's buttons, blue delphinium, and white petunias. Here and there may be a touch of red—roses, geraniums, scarlet sage, carnations—but not too much of it.

Red, white, and blue balloons bob on strings to help focus the eye on the speaker's stand or any other point of interest, where they will not tangle with the lanterns. Any place can be zoned off, or in, by red, white, and blue paper streamers looped from tree to tree or from pole to pole. The balloons can be given to the children as party souvenirs when they are no longer needed as markers.

Sometimes a natural incline in the garden provides a pastoral stage for the evening's program, the only drawback being that there is no shrubbery near it, behind which the performers can hide until their number is announced. In which case, woodsy screens can be made to wing out from the stage by nailing chicken wire to posts placed the right distance apart, and then threading the mesh with trailing vines, wild flowers, and bushy green branches. But decorators should beware of mistakenly gathering poison ivy!

THE SERVICE TABLE—The service table is placed on the porch or in the loveliest garden spot, and is set with the prettiest tablecloth. Flanked by silver candlesticks or candelabra, there should be a distinctive centerpiece, either of choice flowers, or of a patriotic scene in miniature, as a doll dressed as Betsy Ross, busily stitching the first flag.

The tea service, silver and old, if possible, is placed at one end of the table, with the needed china, silver, and dainty table napkins.

The coffee service—also heirloom silver, if possible—is

placed at the opposite end of the table, together with cups and saucers, plates, silver, etc.

Cake and sandwiches are put on the table, displayed on old-fashioned china, and candy and the like in early glassware.

SERVING—Two friends of the hostess, asked well in advance of the day, pour the tea and coffee. They greet each guest as she comes to them to be served. The hostess, footloose and hand-free, is at liberty to welcome new arrivals and see to the cool comfort of all.

Guests, when led by the guest of honor—such as the oldest present, the speaker, a silver-haired war veteran, or the minister's wife—help themselves to sandwiches and cakes or other dainties from the dishes on the table, then carry these refreshments to the little tables, or stand or sit in groups for a neighborly chat as they enjoy them.

Two pretty girls in costume replenish the plates of sandwiches and cakes, remove and replace soiled dishes, bring in fresh tea and coffee if needed, and, later on, clear the little tables.

THE PROGRAM—No hefty sprinting! No heavy thinking! The program should be as effortless as possible and as informal, with long, lazy intervals between numbers, for just doing nothing at all. In any group there are people who just love to sing, some with good leading voices. A week or so before the Fourth, one or two have been asked to get their singing crowd together and prepare a program of patriotic songs for the night of the tea. Guests are invited to join in the choruses, but are not high-pressured. If they don't know the words, they are assured that it doesn't matter. They can hum, "la, la," or whistle the tune. Such selections could include "Dixie," "Battle Hymn of the Republic," "America the Beautiful," "God of Our Fathers," and "America."

A record player hidden behind the shrubs, but well within good hearing range of most of the guests, could fill all intervals with favorite records brought by the guests and pooled for the enjoyment of all.

A male quartet is naturally keyed to such an occasion. The members can be asked to come prepared to sing some

Negro spirituals: "Swing Low, Sweet Chariot;" "Heab'n;" "Deep River;" "Go Down, Moses," or any other in their repertoire.

Pretty girls from a local choir or glee club, in picturesque period costumes, can sing a collection of old-time songs, such as "The Lass With the Delicate Air," "Flow Gently, Sweet Afton," "Ben Bolt," or any other beloved old-timer.

Harmonizers supply comic relief. They are the amateurs who, accepting the kind invitation of the hostess, brought along their banjo, fiddle, accordion, "sax," or pocket comb, and now stand ready to "harmonize away from home." They play "Turkey in the Straw," "She'll be Coming Round the Mountain," or "Pop Goes the Weasel," with—well, abandon!

OUTDOOR PLAYS—The young folks could give a skit or a short outdoor play. The scenery is all there, and a forest screen as a background for the performers is easily made in the same way as the wings, previously described.

Stage lighting and spotlights are smoothly managed by the high school lads, and frequently a patriotic playlet, given as part of a school program, can be reproduced with little effort.

DANCING ON THE GREEN—A program of old-time dances may be planned. Copies of the program are typed and pasted to the back of gay souvenir paper fans.

The stately minuet and the lancers may be featured even if it means bringing in outside talent, also the Virginia reel. Fill in with the lovely old waltzes and a few two-steps, with an occasional schottische and polka.

The old-time fiddler may have to give place to a three-piece orchestra, but he should be kept in the foreground as atmosphere.

EXTRA GAMES—The following are a few games to tuck away in a mental pocket, in case they are needed for a non-dancing group.

"Who can name the forty-eight states?" the hostess asks guilelessly. Practically every hand goes up, for that seems simple enough for anyone to do, and only half try.

Each guest is given paper and pencil. All are warned

against thinking aloud, and by so doing, helping a groping neighbor; nor are they to boost their own score—or a dear friend's!—by swapping states.

If even one of the patriots produces a perfect forty-eight, he—it will probably be a traveling salesman—truly deserves a good prize, such as a desk-size American flag in a fancy holder. A second prize could be a jigsaw puzzle of a map of the U. S. A.

The hostess then asks those who failed to name all the forty-eight states to name the thirteen original states. "That should be easy," she says. It is surprising how few have more than eight of them at the tip of the tongue or the pencil.

The thirteen American colonies which became the original thirteen states of the Union were: New Hampshire, Massachusetts, Connecticut, Rhode Island, New York, New Jersey, Delaware, Pennsylvania, Maryland, Virginia, North Carolina, South Carolina, and Georgia.

MISSING WORD CONTEST—The will to concentrate on guessing games is almost nil, with the thermometer around ninety degrees, but here is another easy one.

The hostess hands out slips of paper on which have been typed the last two stanzas of "America," with a number of blank spaces where the words are omitted.

"Simply fill in the blank spaces with the right words," coos the hostess, then gleefully watches the guests' faces as they cope with those blanks!

GROUP SINGING CONTEST—This is one of those ever-popular sing-downs. Guests are divided into two choirs, with some effort to make a fair division of voices and talent. After the good leading voices and the ones who can't carry a tune in a basket and the men's and women's voices are fairly well distributed, the two rival choirs are told that they are now to compete in a "sing-to-the-finish," to see which team can outlast the other.

Every song rendered must feature a different state, such as "Illinois," "Beautiful Ohio," "The Eyes of Texas Are upon You," "Marching Through Georgia," "My Maryland," "My Old Kentucky Home," "In the Blue Ridge Mountains of Virginia," "Michigan, my Michigan," etc.

As soon as one team has finished its song, the rival team must instantly start singing its selection. No song may be repeated.

The side which successfully sings down the other receives the prize—a box of throat lozenges.

WHAT STATE ARE YOU FROM?—Charades were popular in colonial days, so guests should do a bit of dramatizing.

The company is divided into two little theater groups— the Columbias and the Uncle Sams. Each group selects a director. Then each director draws from a box a slip of paper on which is written a different state abbreviation. He and his group then prepare to dramatize it. When the groups have been allowed sufficient time for rehearsal, a bell is rung—and the show is on.

The director of the Columbias announces, "We are from *this* state." Whereupon all his players begin washing one another's necks, behind ears, hands, etc. The word is obviously "Wash." But the audience may be full of bad guessers. Finally one actor uses his package of cigarettes as if it were a tablet of soap, and "Wash," yells the audience in one enlightened body.

Abbreviated state names easily dramatized are: Ark., Conn., Ill., Kan., Mass., Me., Miss., Md., Mo., Ore., Pa., Tenn.

IMPROMPTU SPEECHES—Is there a glib, amusing speaker in the group? Is he never at a loss for words? The hostess calls him to the speaker's stand—a soap box will do—gives him a secretary, and hands her a box containing a number of folded slips of paper. These slips, the hostess explains, are notes from his constituents. They contain hints on what he'd better talk about, if he wants their votes!

He may choose his own topic and begin his speech on his own. But after a few well-rounded sentences, his secretary will hand him one of his constituents' notes. He must glance at it, and then, without losing his oratorial stride, introduce its words into the content of his speech.

After he is on an even keel again, his secretary will hand him another note, and so on until all have been embodied in his speech without ruining its continuity. Each folded slip of paper contains either one word, such as "Scat!" or a disconnected phrase, such as "Grandma told me—," a proverb, such as "Silence is golden," or quotation, such as "Give me liberty or give me death!"

The only break the speaker is allowed is an occasional life-saving sip from a glass of ice water. If members of the audience have been allowed to write the notes, their glee in watching his struggles to digest their particular tough tidbit is fiendish!

WISHING YOU A LOVELY EVENING!—The wise hostess will make alternative arrangements, so that if it should rain, the sunset tea need not be postponed.

Guests depart to the strains of "America" played by the old-time fiddler, or "Taps" played by the scout bugler from the distant dusk of the garden.

A KID 'EM ALONG SOCIAL

Here we have a jolly break-up lark for the summer crowd at lake or camp, also a rollicking rally for sun-tanned vacationists, back home for school or business.

KID 'EM ALONG POSTERS—The posters show a bold sketch of the little red schoolhouse, with its bell clanging vigorously, while children dawdle on their way schoolward. Beneath the sketch is printed:

> We kid ourselves and kid our friends,
>   Till every other land considers
> That ours is just a nation of
>   Incurable and chronic kidders!
> We like to kid ourselves—that's sure!
> So let's be kids at school once more!

All necessary information is added, also any special postscript, as "Prizes offered for the most kiddish togs and talk," or, "Bring your favorite wheeled toy with you."

Sometimes the committee in charge wish this to be an old-style box social. In which case, the postscript could read, "Bring your own school lunch in a box, tagged with your name or nickname."

KID 'EM ALONG SIGNS—Signs all over the premises meet the "pupils" more than halfway. "School—Go Slowly! Dangerous Children!" reads the first. A lighted sign over the garage reads, "Parking Space for Roller Skates, Scooters, Tricycles, and Kiddy Cars. No Dogs Allowed." Another might read, "School Property. No Fighting, Scuffling, or Loud Talk Allowed on the Premises. By Order of Ima Strictun, Teacher."

KID 'EM ALONG SCHOOL RULES—Lists of rules may be prominently placed where they will catch the eye; as, for instance, on the front door, in full glare of the porch light, in the lobby or entrance of hall, or in the dressing rooms. Several copies of the rules may be posted, each in a different place.

The list could include:

> Do not catcall, whistle, roughhouse, giggle or
>   whisper in hall.
> Hang coats and hats on the proper pegs.

Coats and hats found on the floor will be con-
fiscated.
Throwing of spitballs is prohibited.
Tiptoe to your seat in class.
Quiet, Please!

SPECIAL RULES—A director or hostess who knows the crowd
intimately can prepare a second list of special rules, each
a sly dig at some guest's well-known little pecularity—
funny things that make the "roasted" one laugh more loudly
than anybody else.

For instance, Mrs. Brown has a new grandson, the first
in the family, and so, of course, the most miraculous baby
on earth. So Rule One reads: "Ida Brown is forbidden to
mention 'Iccle-bitty Bobby.' "

Other rules on the list might read:

Lottie Letts is forbidden to talk about her reduced weight,
diet, or calory-intake.

Bob Smith is forbidden to argue about the new garbage
tax, nitwit women drivers, or what passes for music these
days.

Sam White is forbidden to recall, with illustrative anec-
dotes, what a cutup he was at school.

Sarah Gray is forbidden to compare her pet parakeet
with other dumb birds she knows.

SUGGESTION BOX—If wished, a suggestion box can add its bit
to the general joshing. It can be placed on a card table just
below the list of special rules, with a card near it, reading,
"Pupils are invited to write here their suggestions for special
rules for other children enrolled in this chool. Suggestions
need not be signed, but write plainly, please."

The box can be a shoe box, with an ample slit cut in the
lid, before it is fastened shut with gummed tape. A trap of
paper slips and pencils are on the table.

At refreshment time, these unsigned special rules are
read aloud, to the hilarious hoots of all, including the victims.

KID 'EM ALONG SCHOOL—In the hall or near the classroom
entrance is a big wire basket, marked, "Please dump here
your dignity, your chewing gum, and anything you may be

eating. Any child seen throwing apple cores or orange peel at other pupils will be severly punished."

The social room or hall is made to resemble the interior of the country school of less standardized days than these. If no real blackboards are available, large sheets of black paper may be tacked up, to which are pasted crooked letters and figures cut from white paper. Shabby wall maps and a battered globe may be added.

On the walls are hung exhibits of the children's art—crude drawings, some badly crayoned, of persons, animals, and objects. Each effort is signed by the pupil's name, written by the teacher. All names, of course, are those of the guests.

Viewing this exhibit is one of the hilarious features of the evening, highlighted by such shouts as, "Do come and look at this pig the pastor drew!"

The part of the room or hall set aside to be the classroom is cleared of easy furniture, and stiff, straight-backed chairs are substituted. They are arranged in rows in two groups, with an aisle between. The name of a guest is pasted on the back of each chair.

By using this method, the guests can be neatly divided, with girls and boys alternating, into equal teams, and with the natural leaders and cutups, the shy and the brash, fairly equally divided.

TEACHER'S DESK—Teacher's desk stands facing the class and is elevated, if possible, on an improvised platform, if there is no stage. It is supplied with a schedule of lessons (the program of events) pointer, ruler, chalk, a few fool's caps, and—most important of all—a pushbutton bell. A shining red apple adds an amusing touch.

ACHIEVEMENT CHART—The scores of rival classroom teams are marked on this chart. It should be a blackboard or a large white poster on which the scores can be marked in black crayon.

MISS IMA STRICTUN—It is a lot easier to act the typical old maid schoolma'am if dressed for the part. Miss Ima could wear horn-rimmed glasses, no make-up, a severely prim hair-do, and a grim expression. As for her dress, any wasp-waisted, high-necked, long-sleeved bodice would do, with a long, wide, old-fashioned skirt and flat-heeled shoes.

SNEAKY TATTLETALE—Sneaky is the apple-polishing chief monitor who gleefully reports all rule-breakers, writing their names and crimes in his little black book. His hair is neat, slick and shiny. His suit and shoes are immaculate, in striking contrast to those of his classmates. He speaks in an assumed prissy tone. If the crowd is large, he has other monitors to help everything run smoothly. They wear arm bands, lettered "Monitor."

Occcasionally, a black-listed pupil gets even with Sneaky by pinning on his back a card reading, "Kick Me!"

QUIET, PLEASE!—Miss Ima Strictun meets her pupils at the door with such greetings as, "Bob Jones, pick up your feet!" Or, "Mary Jones, show me your hands, I knew it! Stay after school and clean the ink wells.! Jane, use your handkerchief! Who coughed? Well, whoever did, don't do it again! I won't have you coughing germs all over the place. Tom, tie your shoelaces! Mary Jane Bates, are you chewing gum?"

PEP MARCH—This is really a dress parade to show off the juvenile costumes of guests. If prizes have been offered for the most kiddish costume or the best wheeled toy, the three judges are in the reviewing stand, making notes. Otherwise, it is just a peppy, singing march, to get things started off on the right foot.

Miss Ima explains that after a long vacation, school children need conditioning. Therefore, monitors will line them up for marching, and, at the sound of the bell, all are to march around the hall, singing to the tune of "For He's a Jolly Good Fellow" the words:

> All the best things come from study,
> All the best things come from study,
> All the best things come from study,
>   And we're for study, too!
>
> CHORUS
> And we're for study, too!
> And we're for study, too!
> All the best things come from study,
> All the best things come from study,
> All the best things come from study,
>   And we're for study, too!

When she raises her hand, all marching is to stop, while she gives them a new line to sing. Then they are to resume marching, singing the new line.

New lines announcer, "All the best things come from reading," or writing, arithmetic, geography, history, etc.

If the attendance is large enough, guests may be led through the simpler figures of the grand march, a monitor leading each line.

The last verse brings the guests, singing, to the "classroom." Monitors, who have familiarized themselves with the seating arrangement, help guests find their right chairs. All sing, as they march to their seats:

> Now it's time to go to our classroom,
> Now it's time to go to our classroom,
> Now it's time to go to our classroom,
> And show what we can do!
>
> CHORUS
> And show what we can do!
> And show what we can do!
> Now it's time to go to our classroom,
> Now it's time to go to our classroom,
> Now it's time to go to our classroom,
> And show what we can do!

When all are seated, Teacher rings her push-button bell for silence. School has started. She announces that this year she has a new plan for the class, hoping that a little more competition will keep them on their toes mentally. The pupils sitting on the right side of the aisle are to be known as the kidders; those on the left, as the stringers, and the two groups are to compete. After each event, the result will be marked up on the achievement board.

READING TONGUE TWISTERS—Teacher turns the blackboard, and the pupils see written thereon a list of tough tongue-twisters. She picks her victims at random, first from one side, then from the other, asking each to stand up and read, without hesitation, the sentence she indicates with her pointer. After each pupil's recitation, she marks down on a card on her desk, a plus sign or a zero, according to how he acquits himself. When all have read, she totals the score of each group and announces the winners.

While Teacher is chalking up the winning point on the achievement chart, monitors hand around to all members of the class, winners and losers, half-lengths of liquorice strings, twisted into knots.

Most groups have lists of favorite tongue-twisters. Here are some that never fail to tie the tongue in knots:

The seat ceaseth, and it sufficeth us.

She stood at the gate, welcoming him in.

She sells sea shells.

Mixed biscuits, mixed biscuits, mixed biscuits.

Round the rugged rocks the ragged rascal ran.

What size shoes would the sunshine shine, if the sunshine could shine shoes?

What eat ye, gray geese? Green grass, gray geese

Five frightened fans fanning Fanny furiously.

READING CONTEST—Teacher explains that whereas the last lesson was a test in enunciation, this is one in expression, the winning mark going to the group which throws the most real feeling into the passages read.

A monitor has previously found an exciting story of the wild west thriller type and neatly chopped it into sections, placing the amputated pieces into a box and shuffling well.

He passes the box around, and each pupil helps himself to a piece of the narrative. When all are supplied, Teacher gives the signal for the occupant of the first chair to rise and read his piece with as much dramatic fervor of tone and action as he can achieve. When he has finished, he sits down and the pupil next to him rises to "elocute." The rest of the class follow in order of seating.

Since the first reader probably drew a paragraph from the middle of the story, and the second, the happy ending, the continuity of the western is decidedly scrambled, and it is this, together with the exaggerated "oral expression" of the readers, that makes it all so funny.

Teacher may find the contest a tie. In which case, she chooses the best reader from each side to re-read his portion and this time, backwards, please!

WRITING GAME—Papers and pencils are passed around by the monitors. Teacher announces that pupils are to write with their left hands a sentence which she will put on the board. If there are any left-handed pupils, they are to use their right hands. The sentence she writes is, "I would rather be right than President."

When finished, they are to correct the following sentence: "dll Jork band mo lay nakes wack pa aull oy." (All work and no play makes Jack a dull boy.) Or any other proverb in which the initial letters of words have been transposed may be used.

SETTING-UP EXERCISES—Teacher complains of the dullness of the class and suggests a relay race to wake it up. She announces that at the sound of the desk bell, the first one in the first row on each side of the aisle is to run clear around his own row and touch off the one in the next seat to his and then sit down. This second player runs around the row of chairs, then touches off the third, and so on, until the last player is back in place. Whichever group first gets its last runner back in place scores a point. Then the second rows on each side of the aisle compete in the same way, and so on until all have run. The side with most points to its credit is marked up as the winner.

DRILL DEMONSTRATION—If the relay cannot be run off because of lack of space between rows of chairs, the following trick can be substituted. Teacher chooses a representative from each side. She asks each in turn to do the exercise alone. The pupil may sit in a chair to do it, raising the "clock" foot off the ground, to perform; or stand, steadying himself by placing his left hand on Teacher's desk.

"Move your right foot around in a circle clockwise," says Teacher, "as if it were the hands of a clock, Slowly! Good!"

She allows him time to practice the foot motion. Nothing to it, he thinks.

"Now," she directs him, "'keep your foot going in that direction and at the same time make the figure 6 in the air, with the forefinger of your right hand. Like this. Now, together. No! No! Your foot is going in the wrong direction! Try again."

Of course, it can't be done—but they will need a lot of convincing! When both have failed—also volunteers who rushed up to show them how—Teacher marks zero for both sides on the achievement board.

ARITHMETIC—Teacher asks the pupils to arrange the figures 1 to 9 so that they will amount to 100 when added together. They are to work out this example on the paper handed to them by monitors. The first one to do this correctly is to receive a giant lollipop. This lesson will hold them for a while. So if the director or hostess has to see about the chocolate for refreshments, she can put the monitors in charge and slip away.

The following is one way of doing the sum:

$$
\begin{array}{r}
15 \\
36 \\
47 \\
\hline
98 \\
2 \\
\hline
100
\end{array}
$$

Another is:

$$
\begin{array}{r}
32 \\
57 \\
\hline
89 \\
6 \\
4 \\
1 \\
\hline
100
\end{array}
$$

RECESS—Recess comes when the social is about two-thirds over, preferably in the playground. The playground can be a part of the social hall, set aside for this purpose, a church basement, a roomy porch, or an adjacent room which has been cleared to make playing space.

Teacher announces that this is a free play period, and that each child may play as he pleases, but that Sneaky will be on duty to record any breaking of the rules. She offers a prize for the best team yell, rehearsed during recess time. Monitors are at hand with suggestions, if any are needed, which is very doubtful. The following is an example, to be sung to the tune of "Turkey in the Straw."

Oh, the Kidders' team
Is the smartest and the best;
We keep things going,
And we never take a rest.
And we have one yell,
And we yell it all together,
And it goes like this:
"The Kidders forever!"

The stringers and kidders may recruit members of their respective teams to practice the yells they will be called upon to give either at refreshment time, or during the closing exercises which follow.

REFRESHMENTS—These are individual school lunches, prepared in advance, leaving nothing but the chocolate to be made. Each lunch can be put up in a quart ice-cream carton, with an all-day sucker tied to the handle. Monitors serve the hot drink—chocolate or coffee. Or, if a soft drink or milk seem more juvenile, each child can be handed a bottle of pop, or a child-size bottle of milk, such as are served in school cafeterias, with a straw through which to drink it.

A deluxe lunch box contains mixed sandwiches, meat and sweet, also a stuffed egg, a piece of fried chicken, stuffed celery, pickle, and a cupcake.

A simple school lunch consists of sandwiches, gingerbread man, animal crackers, all wrapped in waxed paper, and a candy stick, wrapped around with anything that makes amusing reading, such as a bright child saying, or a schoolboy howler.

PARTNER FINDERS—Teacher may prefer to have pupils eat as partners, rather than in a big group. Here are suitable ways to provide each girl with a "chow chum." Dunce caps can be made in duplicate color or pattern and matched for partners, or tiny toy slates can be given as souvenirs and partners chosen by writing a simple addition sum on one slate, its answer on another. Crepe paper bow ties and hair bows may be made in duplicate colors, a different shade or mixed shades for each couple. They are taken from two boxes, and then the guests match for partners.

Spin-the-platter is a more uproarious method of finding partners. On separate slips of paper are written a different nickname for each boy, such as Fatso, Slim, Freckles, Goggles, Red, etc., which are put in a box. The same list of nick-names is written on a poster where the girls can study it. Each boy takes a slip from the box, being warned not to tell what name he draws.

A girl now spins the platter, which could be a tin pie-plate, at the same time calling out the nickname she fancies. The boy who has drawn that name rushes forward and tries to catch the spinning plate before it falls to the ground. If he suceeds, he takes the spinner as his partner for refreshments. If not, he pays a forfeit, but is still allowed to keep the girl.

EXCUSES—While the children are eating their lunches, Teacher pounces on first one, then another, demanding, "Why didn't you do your homework last night?" Instantly the startled culprit must have a pat excuse, starting with, "Please, Teacher, because—" and giving a reason in words beginning with his own initials. For example, Richard Arthur Brown stammers, "Please, Teacher, because I was—er—er—robbing a bank."

CLOSING EXERCISES—Closing exercises tie the program's loose ends. The special rules found in the suggestion box are read. The result of the class contests is announced. The yells are called for and given. The cup—a tin one—is awarded.

Sneaky is called upon to read from his little black book the names of rule-breakers, and their misdemeanors. Guests hear themselves blacklisted for such preposterous things as talking too much; not talking enough; for sneezing; for dressing too young for their years; for having freckles, or dimples, or red hair. "Outrageous!" they protest.

But, as Teacher points out, discipline must be maintained —or what will this country come to? She announces that she will mete out a mass punishment. They shall pay the penalty collectively.

SINGING FOR THEIR SINS—All the culprits are lined up, and Sneaky divides them into two choirs, an equal number in each, and tells each group to choose its own director. One group is to be known as the kidders, the other as the stringers.

Then Teacher tells them they are to compete to see which group can outdo the other in singing original words to a dear old tune that everybody knows.

The soft background piano music of "Auld Lang Syne" is played, Teacher explains that the choirs will perform in turn, each singing four simple words to the tune of "Auld Lang Syne."

She writes on the board the four words for the stringers. They are, "I can string beans," Then she writes the words for the kidders, "I can kid gloves."

These words, she explains in her best academic manner, are easily substituted for the words of the old song, beginning, "Should auld aquaintance be forgot?" and fitted to the tune.

To prove this, she sings a sample in falsetto or bass:

> "I can string beans, I can string beans,
>   I can string beans, I can;
> I can string beans, I can string beans,
>   I can string beans, I can.

Teacher announces that in order to pay fully their debt to society, the song must be rendered with great expression, both vocal and facial.

After the first choir has performed, the second one does its best with "I can kid gloves," sung to the same tune.

Teacher is not satisfied with the result. She complains that the singing dragged. Therefore she must ask both groups to sing together the same two lines, but this time to the tune of "Turkey in the Straw."

"It is not so simple as the first," she admits, "but it can be done. Ready? Sing!"

GOOD-BYE, TEACHER—Miss Ima Strictun dismisses the class in orderly fashion. She insists that all the children stand and sing to the tune of "Good Night, Ladies:"

> Good-bye, teacher,
> Good-bye, teacher,
> Good-bye, teacher,
>   We' re going to leave you now.
>   CHORUS (faster)
> Bitterly we weep aloud,
>   Weep aloud, weep aloud,
> Bitterly we weep aloud,
>   Boohoo to leave you now!

A CHRISTOPHER ROBIN'S OUTDOOR FETE

This is an outdoor party for children, at which they meet Christopher Robin of storybook fame and play in the Enchanted Woods with Winnie-the-Pooh and all the adorable animals they met in the house at Pooh Corner.

It can be cut down to party size, with the hostess using only one or two of the attractions, or exanded into a church, club, or community fete for a large group of children.

GUEST OF HONOR—Of course, the party is in honor of Pooh, that beguiling "Bear of Very Little Brain," because there couldn't be any party without him. For isn't it written that the magic forest can only be found by those who are "Friendly with Bears?"

Any super-sized top Teddy Bear can impersonate Pooh. For a necktie, he can wear around his neck a tag labeled "Winnie-the-Pooh."

POOH-ISH INVITATIONS—For the big community affair, the invitations could resemble one of the famous notices "brained out" by Rabbit. Printed in childish, irregular letters and entirely without punctuation and with misspelled words, it could read as follows:

"Notice a Party of cristoher robins Friends at the House at PoOH CorNER for Winnie-the Pooh, a Bear of Very Little braiN who makes Hums. There will be Honey and Haycorns and Thistles and StrengThening Medicine For Roo and crumS for Very Small AnimalS under the tabel By ordeR KEep to the LeFt. Prospessers will Be Tressecuted Sined Rabbit."

For the small party, instead of the Pooh-ish notice the invitation could show the sketch of a chubby Teddy Bear, and below the sketch, the following:

> I could have a happy party
>   Greeting you.
> Could you have a happy party
>   Meeting Pooh?
> Rabbit, Piglet, Wol, and Tigger
> Creatures Small-for-Short and Bigger?
> (Eeyore's big, and Kanga's bigger
>   Much than Roo.)

> P.S.   If you could, then join my party,
>   Toodle-de-doo!

Both the notice and the invitation should carry at the foot all necessary information as to day, date, time, and place of the Pooh affair.

THE MAGIC FOREST—The magic forest can be any woodsy place, where there are trees and trails and an open space for games. Boards are nailed up bearing the names of all the places so well known to Christopher Robin's friends. At the entrance to the woods is a notice printed in Rabbit's wobbly letters, reading, "To the Magic Forest." At another suitable location, are posted directions, "To the Hundred-Acre Wood." This is where Owl lives, and the children will enjoy searching for his little wooden house stuck up in the fork of a tree and marked, "The Wolery." If it can be given a letter box marked "Letters Only" and a bell placarded, "Nock Ring Also," gleeful shouts will acclaim such cleverness. A crepe paper owl, plumply stuffed and with shoe-button eyes, would be an irresistible touch.

THE HOUSE AT POOH CORNER—This is the home of Eeyore, the donkey. It is made of a few pieces of round sticks, arranged hut fashion. Everyone will remember how Owl accidentally took Eeyore's tail to use for a bellpull, and how very despondent Eeyore was until it was found and nailed back in place. So the picture of a tailless donkey is tacked up and each child in turn in blindfolded while pinning a paper tail where the donkey's tail should go. If a real donkey — or even a Shetland pony — can be borrowed or rented, it can be stabled here with a dependable "groom," and the children given rides.

CHRISTOPHER ROBIN'S HOUSE—The house is in the base of a huge tree trunk. It has a green front door, with its owner's name printed on it. It would be a delightful idea to make a real little room of compo board and green branches. Here the small son of the hostess could "live," impersonating Christopher Robin; and if it is located near an open space, games could be played and refreshments served in Christopher Robin's garden.

POOH'S HOUSE—Pooh's house is a little playhouse near by. It could be a small garden tent, furnished with a few comfortable chairs and some shelves on which stand rows of jars, each labeled "Honey." One chair could be plainly marked "Piglet's Chair." Bread and honey sandwiches could be served here.

KANGA'S HOUSE—This is also the home of little Roo and Tigger—the tiger who, "Whatever his weight in pounds, shillings, and ounces, always seemed bigger because of his bounces." Pictures of kangaroos and tigers adorn the interior. A small toy kangaroo sits in a high chair before a table on which stands a huge bottle labeled. "Strengthening Medicine for Little Roo."

A Kanga and a Tigger game are played here. For the former, the children see who can hop farthest on one foot.

Tigger doesn't growl, purr, or bark, but makes a strange noise in his thoat, like "Worraworraworraworra." The children are asked to "worraworra" in turn to see who can sound most like a tiger. Then each child is given a balloon as a bouncy present from Bouncy Tigger.

RABBIT'S HOUSE—Rabbit's House is any convenient clump of bushes that a busy and brainy rabbit might choose in which to "think important thoughts." It should be hung with rabbit notices, the largest one announcing that a "Serche is being Organdized to look for Small Beetle, called Small for Short."

Suspended by a thread from the lower branch of a tree in a roped-off area is a shining black beetle. The children are turned loose in this restricted zone to search for Small. The child who first discovers him must say or do nothing to disclose his hiding place to the rest. Instead, he must just whisper it to Christopher Robin and then sit down. One by one, as the others spy Small, they also seat themselves until finally all the seekers become sitters.

THOUGHTFUL SPOT—Thoughtful Spot is halfway between Pooh's house and Piglet's house. The children find it by following the trail as marked out by guide cards. Here rugs are stretched on the ground around a small chair occupied by the largest Teddy bear that can be procured. Almost lost in a large chair sits little Piglet, with a paper sack marked "haycorns" between his paws.

If an understanding grown-up could be stretched out on one rug, lazily eating honey drops from a large glass jar and ready to read aloud first one and then another of the Pooh books, the children could easily be persuaded to rest awhile and listen. Then, as they each munch a honey drop, she could read from her book some of Pooh's best "hums"— those captivating verses that came to the little fat bear as he rambled in the woods.

REFRESHMENTS—"Time-for-a-little-something" is a Pooh-ish term for refreshments. With him, it was a synonym for honey. For the children, it should be ice cream and cake, but if there is any way of giving each a tiny pot of honey as a memento of the party, it would be a lovely Pooh-ish thing to do.

POOH'S TRAP FOR HEFFALUMPS—If there is time for one more game before they go home, the children may hunt for Pooh's trap for Heffalumps. Should there be a dried-up pool or a natural depression in the woods, it can serve as the trap. If not, a small hole can be dug in some unexpected corner. A square piece of board on which is printed, "Trap for Heffalumps, Made by Pooh" is laid face down at the bottom of the trap. When this is turned up, it discloses a box containing little packages, in each of which are sticks of plasticine, colored beads, and a few toothpicks. Each child is given a package to take back to Thoughtful Spot. Here the children sit around a table to make a Heffalump out of the plasticine, beads, and toothpicks. Since no one knows exactly what a Heffalump is, the results are surprising.

SEARCH FOR POOH'S NORTH POLE—If there is still time, the children may search for the North Pole. Nobody could tell it from any other wooden pole stick in the ground if it were not for the inscription on it: "North Pole Discovered by Pooh. Pooh Found It."

THE SIREN CHARM SCHOOL PARTY

Charm is what it takes! Ladies may be complexion, clothes, and calory-conscious, but to be irresistibly bewitching, they should attend the Siren Charm School and learn how to be charming in ten easy lessons. Here is something new in Halloween fun.

CHARM SCHOOL ANNOUNCEMENTS—The invitations are sent out on orange-colored cards or note paper, decorated with a sketch of two black witches, brewing charms and spells in their black cauldrons.

Beneath the beguiling couple is typed or written:

> The two siren sisters,
>   In spell-binding sessions,
> Tell how to be charming
>   In ten thrilling lessons.
>
> Their very bewitching
>   Black-artistry thrills you;
> You'll learn to be charming,
>   I'm sure—if it kills you!

The day, date, time, and place or the class are added, and the time is stressed, the lessons start promptly.

THE SIREN SISTERS—Ima Witch and Bea Witch are the proprietors. Ima is married to one of those sultry foreigners— a devilish fine fellow, with horns and hoofs, known as His Satanic Highness in sulphuric society, but just plain Old Nick to his friends. Bea, the younger witch, a notorious charmer, is amusing herself with her cats and bats between "affairs." Sphinx, the school cat, completes the staff.

THE SIREN CHARM SCHOOL—The school is the basement, attic, laundry, barn, garage, or whatever informal spot is best suited for the party. It is given charming illuminations, such as blue lights under cauldrons on tripods, set in corners of the room. In the windows, with a hidden flashlight focused on them, are pictures of movie and television "sirens," all dressed up for the occasion in black witch's hats. By experimenting with red, blue, or green tissue paper, fastened over a flashlight, the best color for atmosphere can be readily ascertained.

CHARMING SETTING—The classroom decorations are designed to stress the Siren Sisters' sinister *black*ground—the ancestral cave in the wet, wild woods. Branches, little and big, tacked every witch-way, are made to look weird when draped with dangling festoons of finely-fringed black crepe paper.

An eerie ceiling can be made by handing tennis nets overhead to form the foundation, then lacing light branches and twigs through the mesh and hanging irregular lengths of finely-fringed gray and black paper, to resemble Spanish moss, on the branches. Bats, cut from black cardboard, and suspended by black thread to the overhead net, add to the mystic atmosphere.

The Siren Sisters' coat-of-arms consisting of crossed brooms, is displayed in some prominent place, such as over the doorway, mantel shelf, piano, or refreshment table.

On any level ledge, there is a row of cardboard streamlined cats, with here and there a sitting, stretching, or yawning puss, each marked with an appropriate charm pointer, for example, "Learn to sit gracefully!" or "Reach for beauty!" or "Learn to relax." A row of walking cats carries the advice, "Streamline your hips by walking five miles a day "

Each of several of the cats should wear a tag on which is plainly printed a name, such as Smut, Inky III, Snowball, or Tabby.

Since cultivating a memory for faces, and where one has seen them, is a charming asset, students will be required, as part of their class work, to list from memory the cats and where they were met; so some of the creatures should be ratfully placed in unexpected places.

For instance, if a pumpkin face is used in decorations, instead of cutting out the features, a small black cat's-head sticker can be stuck on the pumpkin for each eye, a kitten's head sticker for the nose, and a black bat sticker with full-stretched wings, for the wide mouth. It is amazing how few notice those cats!

THE SIREN SISTERS ATTIRE—The sisters wear the usual witch outfits: tall, pointed hats, full skirts of red or orange, each with a wide, black, circular cape. Long, streaming, unkempt locks can be made of unraveled rope or lengths of worsted.

A tooth can be blacked out, or a complete new set of orange-peel teeth inserted. The right accessories for the best-dressed witch, or course, are brooms and cats; but spider earrings and snail-shell necklaces are in excellent taste, and a dead mouse as a boutonniere is a charming fancy.

SPHINX, THE CAT—Sphinx is the Siren Sisters' chief assistant and can be impersonated by a husband, brother, sweetheart or chum. He wears a cat's head mask and anything else of a catty nature which he can be bribed or bullied into wearing. He acts as doorman, mascot, butler, janitor, and sound effects man. He wears a bellhop's coat, lettered across the shoulders. "The Siren Charm School." He hates Old Nick and has not absorbed enough charm to hide the fact. He spits cattily at Old Nick on sight.

THE CHARM CURRICULUM—The games of the evening should be planned to suit the individual group of guests. But here is a sample. The hostess can use or adapt all the "studies," or choose only those she prefers or for which she has time.

CHARMING FACES—*A make-up contest.*—Ima Witch tells her her students that careful make-up is important to the charm-seeker. Therefore, each is to try for an alluring, or arresting, new make-up, using the beauty helps provided for that purpose. "Powder rooms" are assigned for the make-up contest, or dressing corners—sheeted-off alcoves, with mirrors, and a well-lighted table containing the cosmetics. The wider the choice of cosmetics, the better. Theatrical make-up boxes, minstrel kits, as well as the usual rouges, powders, lipsticks, beauty aids for the eyes, and so on may be used.

But for those who prefer an arresting make-up, there are bottles of white shoe polish, bowls of flour, patches of red tissue paper for circles of color, lampwick black for eye shadow, etc.

When Sphinx blows his siren which is a noisemaker students enter the main classroom, bringing their new faces with them. After the first shock, Ima Witch brings each in turn to the front and asks for the criticism or approval of the class. This, she explains, must be specific. Charm students must learn to increase their powers of expression! It is not enough to say the exhibited face is ghastly, out of this world, or lousy. Ima Witch demonstrates what she means.

Exhibit One is Bob Brown, who has made himself up as one of radio's most popular blackface stars. Ima Witch surveys him critically, her head on one side. Then she says in a heavily judicial tone of voice, "I think the mouth is a little over-emphasized. A small, soft Cupid's bow would be better. And I think the whites of the eyes should be rouged to make his nose less snub and his ears less like an elephant's. Of course, the real make-up problem here is in the face itself. Consult a plastic surgeon."

Ima Witch encourages her students to be free and "objectionable" in their criticism of each model's make-up as it is brought before them. With glee, they carry out her instructions.

At the sound of the siren, the class is dismissed for a brief recess, so that those who wish to, may remove their war paint.

CHARMING CLOTHES— *A Style Show*—Bea Witch now takes charge. The would-be charmer, she announces, must be clothes-conscious. "Start a new personality by looking like the person you secretly yearn to be," she urges them.

In one closet are costumes for the men; in another, costumes for the girls. "Twenty minutes," she says, "are allowed in which to array yourselves as radiant new personalities! What a charming challenge!"

If there are no closets—as when the party is being given in a garage or a cellar—then dressing rooms may be screened off with sheets. If the party is being given in a home, guests may be directed to different rooms to don their new personalities.

In each dressing room and on clothes horses and in laundry baskets is the wildest collection of discarded hats and clothes—with hilarious accessories!—that ever a merry-hearted hostess gleaned from her own and her neighbors' cast-offs.

It is fun to assemble full outfits of widely different characters, as for a play, then scramble them. The hostess starts by taking her guests, one by one, and mentally giving each that new personality. Tom can be a hobo; Bill, the villian; Percy, the dude; Sam, the soulful poet.

Then she mentally casts the girls and dresses them right down to the last detail, be it a gypsy tambourine or a Mardi Gras mask. Not that anyone will dress as planned! She may expect to see the hula-hula dancer's grass skirt worn with the halo hat intended for Princess Margaret, and Tom the hobo in Percy's monocle.

Sphinx gives the warning siren. "Five minutes more," he shouts, "to work on that new, vital personality! Make it snappy!"

At the second siren, the style show is on. Bea Witch calls on the students, in turn, asking why they think their particular costume expresses their hidden personality. After each has recited, the class is asked for frank, free criticisms. Again "slanguage" is ruled out as having no descriptive value. Anyone using such words as "sloppy," "swell," or "corny" is put on the black list, and later on, must pay a stiff forfeit.

Then students go back to their respective dressing rooms, discard and—it is to be hope!—hang up their costumes.

CHARMING VOICES—Does your voice smile or file? Ima Witch sets about finding out. First, those telltale vowels! "On the count of one, two, three, and four, hold the breath," she tells the class. "On five, explode into a loud sound of A. Broad A, please! After that, more breathing for four counts. Then the sounds of E, I, O, U, in turn. Now, repeat, holding the nose. Now shout all the vowel sounds, in their order, together, please. Terrible! Begin again! On the count of —"

Finally, Ima Witch tells the class to say, "Coo—ooo," and, keeping the mouth in that rounded shape, to coo, "Do I look like a goldfish?"

"Well, rather," she answers, "but not so intelligent."

THE CHARMING WALK—"The charming person," announces Bea Witch, "has a graceful walk." She hands out oranges, while Ima puts a good march record on the phonograph. Each student balances an orange on the top of his head, and, standing in line, awaits the signal to begin marching. At the sound of the siren, all march. When it sounds the second time, they turn smartly in place and march in the opposite direction. As soon as the orange falls off the head, the marcher drops out.

As soon as the students fall out, Bea Witch starts them off in couples, oranges on heads, to march again.

THE AISLE OF CHARM AND POISE—If the guests are young and venturesome—or just venturesome!—this is for them. If not, it may be omitted.

"The orange drill to improve your carriage," announces Bea Witch, "was just a practice session for the next important demonstration, which will give you an opportunity to show the perfect poise of a charming couple under all circumstances. His Satanic Highness will conduct you down the aisle. Form in couples, please."

The aisle is the old obstacle walk, so long a favorite of Halloween pranksters. It has previously been prepared in a passageway or long hall. It is dimly lighted and full of pitfalls, all designed to upset the equilibrium of those who walk gingerly along it. An old bedspring hidden under a rug; toy wooden blocks; a coil of garden hose; a stretch of anything that breaks when stepped on, such as soda crackers or eggshells; the bulb of an old auto horn placed where a foot is sure to find it—all these are poise-shakers.

Old Nick prods on the slow ones, marking all for their show of poise and grace while walking down the aisle. All get a zero.

THE CHARMING PERSON IS A GOOD LISTENER—This game gives the hostess a chance to introduce all the well-known horrible sounds one expects at a Halloween party.

Sphinx is in charge of the sound effects, aided by Old Nick. They can work out a hair-raising series of sound effects. The students sit in the dark and in a deathlike silence, listening. Suddenly they hear chains rattle, or a window raised; then a dull thud, and a heavy body falling down the stairs, to wild screams. Black silence follows, broken at last by loud, agonized groans. Then more black silence, except for a shuffling sound that comes ever nearer, to the accompaniment of puppylike whimpers.

Then, in the hall, a hollow voice cries, "Help! Help!" This is Old Nick, somewhere outside, shouting through a length of garden hose, the other end of which he has slipped through a small opening in a window.

Then a drowning man chokes his last in the darkness. This is especially horrible, unless one happens to know it is the Sphinx gargling his cider.

A wash boiler, crashing down on the laundry floor, can bring the demonstration to a close.

The lights are turned on. Cards and pencils are handed out, and class members are told to prove they are good listeners by listing all the sounds they heard and recognizing them for what they really were; thus, "The infernal machine —a wound-up toy, running down under a muffling pillow or rug."

CHARMING CONVERSATION—The charming person is a good conversationist. The students all sit in the dark, while Ima Witch starts telling a love story about a heroine whose devastating charm was all a matter of never being at a loss for a word. Bea Witch, from time to time, flicks a flashlight full in the face of one of the students, who must immediately go on with the story until the flash picks out another.

Students who fail to pick up and continue the story with suave smoothness are later given exercises to make their tongues more agile.

For them, a blackboard is produced on which is written, "Which witch wishes a whirl on Will Wile's wheel, while Will whittles witches' whips?" Each student is required to read this sentence rapidly five times.

THAT CHARMING VERSATILITY—The charming person is versatile. The students take from a box slips of paper on each of which has been written a simile, as, for instance, "As flickering as a flame." When his name is called, each must rise and, without a word, pantomine his simile. If anyone thinks it is easy to "flicker," he should try it!

When all have performed, Ima Witch reads off the complete list of similes, giving all a chance to guess who pantomimed which. Some of the similes would have stumped a

Barrymore; for example: Artful as the devil; purry as a cat; clean as a new broom; brilliant as the moon; pale as the stars; light as air; still as the graveyard; spooky as a ghost; wise as an owl; blind as a bat; ugly as a witch; round as a pumpkin; sour as a lemon; hard as a nut; slippery as an eel; sly as a fox; lively as an elf; and screwy as a corkscrew.

THE CHARMING QUIZ—The charming person cultivates a memory for faces and where one has seen them; and for names.

Students are given five minutes in which to become familiar with all the cardboard cats used in the decorations, and to count them.

They are then called back to class, handed paper and pencil, and asked to answer the following questions in their best handwriting:

1. How many cats in the room, not including humans?
2. What charm-pointers did the cats give?
3. Give the names of cats you met on the cat walk.
4. State exactly where you met each one.

Students are asked to sign their charm quiz before handing it in.

MORE MEMORY TESTS—Old bed sheets are hung up. Bea Witch calls the girls and stations them behind the sheets, with sufficient space between them. The short girls may be stood on stools or boxes, further to mystify the guessers.

A slit is made in the sheet, through which each girl, at a signal, thrusts her nose.

This is Forget-me-not Lane; and each man, in turn, strolls down it, pausing before some nose to say, "Oh, now do you do, Miss............?" naming the girl he hopes belongs to the nose.

If he is wrong, Ima Witch marks the error against his name on the roll, and each mistake brings his mark down a grade.

He is given three chances at three different noses. Three bad guesses give him D on his report card, and fellow-students may inflict any forfeit they choose on him for thus disgracing the class.

However, should he guess right the first time, his reward is the lady-with-the-nose as his partner for refreshments.

After each man has shown his lack of observation, the girls, in turn, stroll down the lane, trying to remember the names of men by their noses; or their feet, which show at the foot of the sheet; or their hands which are thrust through cuts in it. In the latter case, men should remove their rings or wrist watches, since these objects might provide clues.

CHARMING TABLE DECORATIONS—The table decorations feature a witch-and-cauldron table center piece, with a tall, black witch's hat standing at each plate. If given a cat's-head sticker at the peak and a curved tail of slashed black paper, the hat becomes a cat. A favor can be placed under each hat, such as a tiny bottle of perfume labeled, "Siren's Spell," or a rolled and beribboned charm school diploma, which is really an individual fortune, written by the hostess who knows the dream of each guest's heart and takes this way of foretelling that it is on the way.

REFRESHMENTS—The menu can contain the usual Halloween stand-bys, each labeled to suit the occasion. The doughnuts are marked "Wedding Rings;" the pretzels, "True Lovers' Knots;" the apples, "Eve's Seduction;" the cider, "Love's Potion."

A BEAT-THE-JINX DINNER

This dinner originally was planned to celebrate the ninetieth birthday of a distinguished judge who was born on a Friday the thirteenth, and who had a "triple jinx" on him, since this was the thirteenth time in his long life that his birthday had fallen on a Friday!

The theme can be used, however, for a Halloween dinner, or adapted under some such title as "An All-Jitters Dinner."

BEAT-THE-JINX INVITATIONS—The invitations show a sketch of a bulletin on which is pinned a calendar page of the birthday month, with the day and date ringed in heavy black.

The pin that secures the page to the board is tagged "Lucky Pin." Sketched in one lower corner of the board is a dangling rabbit's left hind foot, and in the other corner is the picture of a horseshoe.

Below the bulletin board is sketched an open stepladder, on top of which stands a black cat with upstretched tail. To the right of the ladder is printed in bold, black letters, "Come and help us beat the jinx!" The day, date, time, and place are added, each printed on a different leaf of a big four- leaf clover, growing from a patch of grass sketched in the righthand corner of invitation.

BEAT-THE-JINX DECORATIONS AND FAVORS—The decorations feature all the popular superstitions, but each bad luck omen is "de-jinxed" by having a good luck charm attached to it. Thus the much-cracked mirror has sprays of four-leaf clovers festooned across it; the toy black cat on wheels that is drawn across the path of arriving guests drags a rabbit's foot in its wake; the stepladder in the doorway, under which all guests must pass, is decorated with real and cardboard horseshoes.

The decorations are in clover-green, black, and silver. The centerpiece is a silver basket of thirteen jinx flowers, made by attaching to each green wire stem, a blossom consisting of the number thirteen, cut from black paper. Even the green foliage is "jinxed," for each leaf is formed of two pipe cleaners, dyed green, one of which is used straight, the other bent to shape a long, narrow figure three.

Scattered over the tablecloth are symbols of good and bad luck-silver horseshoes, green four-leaf clovers, and the number thirteen in various sizes, cut from thin black cardboard.

The favors are little silver baskets, made over a nut cup foundation, with the fatal number thirteen, in big black figures, wired to each. The baskets are filled with rock candy. A small green label, shaped like a four-leaf clover, tied to each handle, reads, "Broken mirrors!"

BEAT-THE-JINX PROGRAMS—Since the programs may be kept as precious mementos, time and thought go into their making. The green cover carries a reproduction of the sketch on the invitations, done in bold black.

On the occasion of the celebration of the judge who had survived ninety birthdays of the thirteenth day of the month, the first inside page was headed, "Papa's Lucky Day," and then gave the date of the present birthday being so joyfully celebrated, and below it a list of all the past years when his birthday had fallen on the double-jinx of Friday the thirteenth. After each such lucky date was printed which of his birthdays it was, as fifth, fortieth, sixty-eighth, etc., and where he was at that time. At the foot of the page was printed, "This one beats the jinx!"

For the hostess giving a general beat-the-jinx dinner, this first inside page could be used to give a few of the most interesting lucky thirteen historical facts, thus making room on an inside page for the printing of the menu. Such "luckies" could be:

The thirteen colonies, which revolted from England in 1776, became our great nation.

The cornerstone of the White House was laid Oct. 13, 1792.

The Stars and Stripes became the national flag on January 13, 1794.

"The Star-Spangled Banner" was written September 13, 1814.

The two inside pages of the souvenir program are neatly typed and paragraphed. They read:

Did You Know?

That the ancient Hindus started the superstition that thirteen people sitting at one table was unlucky?

That, at one time, there were people in Paris called "Quatorzes" (Fourteens) whose sole occupation was to hire out as the fourteenth guest at dinner parties?

That Napoleon shunned the number thirteen in every form and caused himself untold worry on this account?

That European hotels frequently number Room 13 as 12½ or 12A? And that many large American hotels skip the thirteenth floor?

That many clubs exist today called "Lucky Thirteen" to defy the old idea of bad luck?

That the license tag for Leon County, Florida is numbered 13, but that Tallahassee persons may select 68, if they prefer?

That you would rate very smart if you could name the thirteen original colonies?

The fourth page of the souvenir program gives more facts about the number thirteen. It reads:

Other Famous Thirteens

Thomas Jefferson was born April 13, 1743.

The District of Columbia was made the national capital on December 13, 1791.

Richard Wagner was born in 1813, composed thirteen operas, finished "Tannhauser" on September 13, 1860 and saw its debut on March 13, 1861.

The source of the Mississippi was discovered on July 13, 1832.

The last battle of the Civil War was fought May 13, 1865.

Cyrus Field laid the first Atlantic cable on July 13, 1866.

Thirteen ships sailed for France in the first transport of World War I on July 13, 1917.

If wished, just thirteen of these historical thirteens can be printed on the program, the rest being recorded on posters, one fact on each, and placed about the room to serve as conversation pieces.

BEAT-THE-JINX MENU—This was not printed in the original souvenir program. Since many of the invited guests were elderly, a simple, light dinner was served. A Halloween dinner for younger digestions might be: small individual chicken pies, with the number thirteen pricked out on the crust; potato croquettes; stuffed apple salad, with the number thirteen either pasted or cut on the red apple skin, each apple topped with a black paper witch's cap, on which has been pasted a terrifying evil eye; mulled cider and hot gingerbread, topped with whipped cream.

If a more simple menu is preferred, it could be:

Frankfurter in Finger Rolls

Waldorf Salad in Red Apples

Brown-Bread-and-Butter Sandwiches

Ice Cream Sandwiches

Candied Orange Peel

Cider

To make the ice cream sandwiches, a slice of orange ice cream is placed between two slices of devil's food cake, iced with orange frosting.

BEAT-THE-JINX DINNER FUN—Guests are given pencils and cards, on the top of which is printed a large 13. They are given their choice. They can list all the superstitions they know, trying for a total of 13; or they can list the names of the thirteen original states.

Guests may be asked to come prepared to tell a true incident when a bad—or a good—omen warned of something that came to pass.

To beat any jinx that may befall them for attending the dinner, guests are invited to hunt for the lucky pins hidden around the room in various places. As they search, they are to chant:

> See a pin, and pick it up,
> All the day you'll have good luck.

When a pin is found, the finder is to change the chant to:

> See a pin, and pick it up,
> All your life you'll have good luck.

The pins can be safety pins, some of them tiny gilt ones, other out-size. Having found one, guests are asked to pin their luck on shoulder or lapel.

If the dinner is a small family affair, these lucky pins can be real ones, such as can be found on costume jewelry counters—tie pins or brooches of horseshoes, wishbones, four-leaf clovers, rabbit's foot, etc.

Thirteen Popular Superstitions

It is bad luck:

1. To spill salt, without throwing a pinch of it over the left shoulder.
2. To brag without immediately touching wood.
3. To walk under a ladder without whistling.
4. To pass on the opposite side of a tree, without saying, "Salt and pepper" to avoid a quarrel.
5. For two persons to pass on the stairs, without pausing to shake hands, to avoid bad luck for both.
6. For two people to look into a mirror at the same time without smiling.
7. To change a garment put on wrong side out.
8. To open a umbrella in the house.
9. To break a mirror. (Seven years of bad luck!)
10. To take the last piece of food on a plate.
11. To have a black cat cross one's path.
12. To rock an empty rocking-chair.
13. To hear a dog howl continually at night.

DO TELL

Do tell! Why, of course. But how, when, where, and whom? Some prefer the conventional style in the following assorted announcement parties. First comes the formal press announcement. For this, the engaged girl's parents inform the society editor of the home newspaper, whereupon the notice appears, with a photograph of the engaged girl.

Then there is the formal tea, the betrothed couple receiving with the girl's mother. Or the girl's father may make the announcement at a party given for the girl and her fiance.

The least formal of conventional ways of telling is by word of mouth to friends at home and by notes to those who are out of town.

INFORMAL ANNOUNCEMENT PARTIES—But for those who like to be gaily different, there are no end of tricky ways of telling. The informal announcement party is just as likely to be given by a thrilled maiden aunt or a married sister as by the bride-elect and her mother. Frequently the party is given by the engaged girl's best friend, just to show she's a sporting loser. This is especially fitting if she is to be the maid of honor.

When? Since the idea is to "spring it," the problem that confronts the hostess is how to keep it a surprise. There is usually a little Miss Nosey in every group, with an annoying habit of guessing right. The wily hostess plays safe by making some usual or regular meeting—club, lunch, bridge, tea—the occasion at which the announcement is made, thus circumventing Miss Nosey's nose for news.

Where? The most appropriate setting for the announcement party is the home. But if it is not a June wedding and midsummer heat is driving people to woodland trails and breezy beaches, announcements can be made just as effectively as the big moment of a mystery meander in the woods; of an Only Pebble Splash on the beach; of a lazy-daisy picnic in the meadows—where the daisies *do* tell!— or of a just sew get-together on the shady porch where friends are invited to bring their sewing and idly rock while sipping tea or a cooling fruit drink.

Who? Who should be told? The informal announcement

is usually made at a party attended by the bride-elect's dearest and most intimate friends, and so is mostly an all-girl affair—lunch, bridge, or tea. But should her special circle of friends prefer it, it can be an evening affair with the men invited.

How? There are countless ways of telling the good news: By some game or contest. Or the centerpiece, the favors, or the dessert may give it away; or some casual little stunt when the party is almost over may literally "spill the beans" or "let the cat out of the bag."

THE CARDS TELL—Perhaps the newly-engaged girl's friends are card fiends, and if they don't play bridge it isn't a party. Then she can let them play as usual, and when the right moment comes to spring the secret, she can simply say, "Girls, I'm going to put all my cards on the table! But don't look at them until I give the word."

She then deals rapidly from a prepared pack, seeing that all the cards fall face down, until the pack is dealt. Each card is from a heart suit, with a tiny snap of the happy pair pasted either in a heart, or in the center of each card, and under the picture the announcement, simply worded; for example, "Mary and Joe engaged."

CARD COTTAGE—If it is a bridge luncheon, a clever center-piece that does not immediately give the secret away, is a card cottage. Its foundation is a cardboard box, with playing cards pasted on outside walls and roof. A picket fence cut from scorecards or made of bridge pencils surrounds the little house. Inside the yard stand two little Cupid dolls, one wearing, sandwich board style, two queen of hearts playing cards; the other, two king of heart cards.

Playing cards, laid like a flagstone path, meander from the card house, and as far across the table as they need go, in order to spell out the telling message, all the cards lying face down.

When the hostess is ready to reveal the secret, she says, as before. "My cards are on the table." She points to the path of cards. "If you want to read them," she adds, "just turn them up, one at a time, starting with the end one, nearest you, Nell.

Nell turns up the card and is surprised to see, instead of the usual clubs or spades, a large capital Ietter printed on a square of stout paper which has been pasted over the spots on the card. Still that initial letter "E" holds no special significance to the guests, who probably conclude they are about to play some new alphabet game. The girl next to Nell turns up the second card, the next guest the third, and so on, until the word "engaged" is spelled out on the table.

Excitedly now each guest, in turn, turns over a card until the girl's name is spelled—backward, if wished, to add to the suspense. Finally the cards reveal the name of the lucky man, and good wishes are in order.

PICNIC HAMPER SURPRISE—Invitations show a big picnic hamper with a question mark above it, and below:

> What's inside it?
> Don't ask me!
> I'm not telling;
> Come and see.

The date of the picnic is added, and any other necessary information, such as the meeting place, the time of departure, or the location of the picnic site.

The picnic menu is kept secret, so guests are led to suppose that this is the big secret surprise indicated by the question mark above the basket shown in the invitation. This picture, however, is just a smoke screen to hide the real purpose of the picnic, which is the announcement of the engagement.

When the right moment comes, the hostess produces a picnic hamper of the usual fitted type. "It seems time," she remarks, "to let the cat out of the bag!" She raises the lid and takes out a small burlap bag, from the neck of which protrudes the head of a toy cat. She loosens the string that ties the mouth of the sack and releases the cat. Tied to its collar is a label which had been concealed inside the bag. On it is written the good news, such as, "Bessie and Bill are engaged."

THE TRYSTING TREE—The trysting tree is a way of announcing the new engagement should get the gold medal for studied simplicity. The picnic guests are led to a tree trunk in which have been freshly cut the initials of the betrothed pair, within the time-honored double-heart frame, and topped with a bunch of wood violets.

TATTLE-TALE TABLE—At this engagement party, tea or buffet supper, the favors do the telling.

The invitations for this party are printed in a first-grader's tipsy letters or childish scrawl on children's stationery, and read: "Dere frend, i got sumthing on teecher's pet, and i am gonna tell it nex munday nite. Will you cum and here me do it or are you to scared?" The notes are signed by the hostess, using the same childish print or handwriting.

In the center of the table is a replica of the little red schoolhouse, with a doll dressed as a typical old-time school-ma'am on the steps. Flanking the school are tiny toy slates, one for each guest. These are the "tattlers," for on each is written, in schoolboy letters, "Dick to Marjory"—or whatever are the names of the engaged couple—and on the other side of the slate the word, "Ingaged", with rows of crosses for kisses below.

ROSES-FOR-LOVE TEA—For the month of June, the announcement could be made to a group of girl friends at a rose tea. The room and the table are beautiful with vases of tea roses, so the guests see nothing unusual when each is presented with a dainty corsage of sweetheart roses, tied with narrow pink and white ribbon.

But soon some discerning guest notices that one end of that ribbon is caught within the heart of her corsage. She draws it out, and discovers that it is tied to a ring! Of course, the diamond is genuine glass; but what a surprise! All the guests immediately begin searching in their own corsages and find their rings. Then the hostess pulls the ribbon from the heart of her rose corsage, and out comes her solitaire.

"Girls," she insists, "mine wasn't bought at the dime store. Mine is the real thing!" Upon examination, this proves to be so.

AN AUTO ANNOUNCEMENT PARTY—This party is suitable for an evening, when the men are included in the invitations.

The invitations are written on correspondence cards, decorated with cutouts of automobiles. Beneath the pictures is written:

> We auto have a party,
> We really auto, so
> I think you auto come because
> Of things you auto know.

All necessary information is added.

Any auto game is suitable for this party, such as a contest to see which couple can write the best account of the accidental meeting of an imaginary hero and heroine, of their falling in love, his proposal of marriage, the wedding and honeymoon. Also in the writing of the story they should see who can use the names of the most makes of cars.

Or guests may compete individually to see which one can jot down in the shortest time the best original slogan for any midget continental car.

Prizes are rolls of candy life-savers, marked, "Spare tires," or packages of chewing gum, labeled, "Emergency tire-mender."

The centerpiece may be a toy garage, roomy enough to hold a miniature candy-filled car for each guest, and a tiny toy truck for the engaged couple. These toys can be bought at most dime stores. The garage can be homemade by covering a card box, and cutting out little doors in both sides and ends. Across the front and back of the garage is a sign, reading:

U Auto Know Garage
All Kinds of Pairing and Repairing Done
Dan Cupid, Proprietor

Dan is there in person, his Kewpie doll chubbiness garbed in the cap and overalls of the mechanic. He stands at the door, a toy rubber tire wired to his hands.

To each toy auto is tied a length of real, honest-to-goodness string, not ribbon, the other end being tied to a "Drive carefully" card at each guest's place at table.

When the hostess gives the word, her guests tug at their strings and so pull their cars out of the garage. Each little candy-filled auto comes out easily enough except the telltale truck which has been fixed to balk.

For the all-girl party, the truck can be put in the garage crosswise with the door. If it is a mixed party of girls and their escorts, the balkiness of the engaged pair's car is easily achieved by fastening it to the string of her fiance's car, so that both will be pulling in different directions, and a tangle inevitable.

The couple's car trouble will get it the spotlight, also much bantering advice, such as. "Step on the gas, Bill!" or, "Back her through the rear door, Jane!" Finally, in a burst of speed, out jerks the contrary little toy truck. On its side is a crazily-lettered card reading, "Just Engaged! Bill and Jane" or whatever happens to be the names of the newly-betrothed pair.

A NEWSY ANNOUNCEMENT PARTY—This party is a jolly means of announcing the engagement at an evening affair to which both men and girls are invited.

The invitations are written on white correspondence cards, bordered with a strip cut from an old newspaper and pasted around to form a frame. Inside the frame is printed, " 'Some tell, some hear, some judge of news, some make,' says Dryden. Come to our Newsy Party, and do all four."

All necessary information is added regarding the place, day, date, and time of the party.

The evening's entertainment begins when men and girls draw from boxes of duplicate slips and then match for partners. On these slips are written various departments of a newspaper, such as editorial, front page news, sports, advertising, fashion, club news, comics, and so on.

It is arranged that the hostess and her partner get the slip reading, "Front Page News." Also in the men's box is one slip reading, "Mr. Ed I. Tor, Editor-in-chief," and in the girls' box, a slip, reading, "Mrs. Dick Shunary, Assistant Editor."

It is announced that a new newspaper is to be launched, called "The Party Line News," and that in half an hour's time the editor will call for material from the various departments and expect to get good copy, and not lame excuses. If any member of the staff feels that he can do better work in another department, five minutes will be allowed for an exchange of jobs.

All items of news must be of strictly local interest, preferably about those attending the party. Also writers need not stick to facts. Indeed, a vivid imagination is the chief requisite, and those writers excelling in it will win the coveted awards.

After the paper is out, it is read aloud. Then comes the front page news—the announcement of the engagement, made by the editor-in-chief. "The only bit of true, genuine news in the whole paper," he announces, "is the headline news that Mary and Joe are engaged, and that's what the party's about! Congratulations are in order."

TELLING BY TELEPHONE—Sometimes the men tell! Agreed that they have their nerve, but it has been done. The telling telephone call is one method which has the full connivance of the bride-elect. The monthly bridge party has gone smoothly along, with nothing to mark it from any other social get-together of the same group of girls. It has reached the dawdling-over-the coffee stage, but not quite the moment for the first covert glance at a wrist watch. Then the telephone rings.

"You take it, Lil," says the hostess. "You're the nearest."

Lil does. Her face expresses cordiality, surprise, then puzzlement. She holds the telephone mouthpiece against her chest and speaks to her hostess. "Alice, listen. It's Dick Vincent. He wants me to tell you he's on the line if you want us to congratulate him. What's he talking about?"

"Oh," says Alice, with a fine show of casualness, 'I hadn't got around to that yet. He means his news—we're engaged! Better congratulate him, Lil!"

A telling telephone call, especially if it's a party line!

RAPID FIRE METHODS OF TELLING—Sometimes the girl wants to "spring it" with as little fuss as possible. She can do it the jigsaw way. She merely writes the news on as many silver cardboard hearts as there are guests, then cuts each heart into irregular pieces before slipping it into an envelope. She hands around these envelopes between cups of tea and offers a prize for the one who first puts two and two together and makes a match of it.

SPILLING THE BEANS—There are a number of quick clever stunts for announcing the engagement. The hostess can spell out "Jack and Jill engaged"—of course, using the right names—by printing one letter on a lima bean until she has the entire message inscribed on the total number of beans. Then she puts the lettered beans into a box.

After the guests have arrived and chatted awhile, she tells them that she has a new game they might like to try. It is played with lucky beans.

She brings in the box of beans and, as if by accident, upsets them all over the table or floor.

"Oh, there!" she cries, with well-feigned annoyance. "I've spilled the beans!"

Instantly her guests hurry to help her pick them up, while the distressed hostess tells them how many there ought to be. Not one must be lost!

Some observant guest will notice the letter on the bean he picks up and comment on it, whereupon the hostess confides that this was the game she intended them to play. The idea was to make a sentence of the lettered beans—an important sentence of four words, the key word of which was to be, "engaged."

Again, a little sister may rush in and release two toy balloons, which, when caught, are found to have the names of the betrothed pair on them.

Or, simplest of all, the hostess can exclaim at any time during a routine gathering of the clan, "Oh, girls, I want you to see my new hat!" She rushes upstairs, brings down a new hat box and opens it. "There" she exults, "Thank goodness, the lid's off!" Inside is a bridal veil!

A NOTE-ABLE EVENING

This is an evening of entertainment for members of a choir or any other musical group who are looking for a frolicsome time and not intending to take their talent seriously.

NOTABLE INVITATIONS—The invitations show a quartet of "notable" singers lustily performing. They are amusing little silhouettes with hourglass bodies, lines for feet and arms, and a musical note for the head and neck. Tiny music notes issue from each "noted" head, from where the mouth might be, wafted on little lines to show their source. See Fig. 3.

Fig. 3

A border of notes may be drawn below the sketch, or may be made to signify footlights if the little black "notables" are singing from a stage.

Below the sketch, is printed the following invitation:

A NOTE-ABLE AFFAIR

To be held on ...., at .... Whether you are a semibreve or a demisemiquaver, we hope you will join the other "notables," and tune up.

Make a note of the time, 8:00 p.m. sharp!

That's the pitch. Bring your own key with you.

NOTE-ABLE DECORATIONS—Music, a yard wide and fifty feet long, is tacked on the walls. It is simply a roll of plain white paper. The notes, rests, etc., are cut from black gummed paper and stuck in place.

The music and words of any well-known, appropriate song may be marked on this blank music "page," such as "The More We Get Together," to the tune of "Lieber Augustine."

Musical notes of all sizes, cut from black construction paper, are the main decorations, with here and there the picture of a popular radio or television star, vocal or instrumental.

TABLE DECORATIONS—Refreshments can be served at a booth, boldly lettered "Bar," its white background decorated with black musical symbols.

If refreshments are to be served at a table, the centerpiece can be a musical box; and the favors, either dimestore toy musical instruments or noisy trifles, such as bazookas. Song sheets and cutouts of black music notes can be scattered on the table.

MUSIC MUSEUM—This guessing game is for the early-comers. As they arrive, the Maestro, who is the official greeter, hands each a pencil and a card which is numbered, as for a dance program, from 1 to 10. On top of the card is a clue, reading, "In the Music Museum you will find ten different objects, each of which has some musical significance, as, for instance, a piece of heavy string (chord). This explanation is followed by the column of numbers.

The exhibits in the Music Museum are arranged on a table to which newcomers are directed. Each exhibit has marked on it a distinguishing number.

The exhibits could be: 1. Tape measure; 2. Watch; 3. Razor; 4. Anyone's full name written on a piece of paper;; 5. Door key; 6. Chin rest from a violin; 7. Chocolate bar; 8. Piece of ruled paper; 9. Rubber band; 10. Card bearing the number 20.

The correct answers are easy to guess. They are: 1. Measure; 2. Time; 3. Sharp; 4. Signature; 5. Key; 6. Rest; 7. Bar; 8. Lines 9. Band; 10. Score.

More difficult exhibits to guess would be High C, Pitch, B flat, Brace, Choir, Solo, Dotted quarter.

MUSICAL ADVICE—This is a good game to start things off on a temperamental note. Two inexpensive song books are taken apart and duplicate pages put in two boxes. Men take a page from one box, girls from another, then match for partners for the first round of discussion.

The couples group themselves informally about the room. The Maestro explains that he will announce various topics for conversation, all of them of great interest to true music lovers. When a chord is struck on the piano, each couple must immediately begin to converse about the announced topic.

In a few minutes' time, a discord will be struck on the piano, whereupon music lovers must instantly change their talking-partners, ready for the next topic to be announced.

The Maestro warns them that there will be "teachers" circulating throughout the group, taking down the names of any who are not discussing the topic with the right amount of gusto.

Amusingly controversial topics can be listed by any choirmaster from his own experience. Here are a few favorite samples: 1. How to get to choir rehearsal on time; 2. How to sing, or play, by ear; 3. How to sing above a cold; 4. How to sing falsetto. Demonstrate; 5. How to improve the choir robes; 6. How many inches to open the mouth when singing "Ah." Demonstrate.

THE MUSIC GOES ROUND AND ROUND—If a singing start is preferred, guests stand in a circle, all facing in. On the back of each is pinned the name of a different well-known song. The songs can be old favorites or the newest hit on radio or television, just as long as they are familiar to all.

While the guests are in this formation, the Maestro stands in the center and sternly announces the rules. He explains that when the signal is given, singers must all start singing together; and when the second signal is given, to stop singing, all singers must instantly stop—and all together. There must be no solo notes, or hangovers to give away clues to alert ears. "Teachers," he announces, "will be on hand to penalize any offenders, who will later pay stiff forfeits for any breaking of this rule."

Guests are then asked to turn in the circle so that each can read the title of the song pinned on the back of the person who is just ahead of him.

At a signal from the Maestro, all must start to march around in circle formation, while singing at the top of their voices the song that is written on the slip in front of them. At the same time, each must try to catch what song the singer back of him is singing, and thereby learn what song is pinned on his own back.

After three or four minutes of this decidedly mixed chorus, the Maestro signals for the singing to stop and questions each in turn, "What is the title of the song you were backing?"

Those who fail to answer or who answer incorrectly pay a forfeit at refreshment time or after.

MUSICAL REST—Throat lozenges are passed around. Singers may be invited to visit the bar for a rest—and a glass of fruit punch.

SINGING PICTURES—The Maestro calls all musicians back to a test in creative ability. Sheets of drawing paper, pencils with erasers, and small, sealed envelopes are handed to guests. Inside each envelope is a folded slip of paper on which is written the name of a different song. Guests are warned to keep the titles they have been assigned a secret from the others. Each guest is to illustrate the song title that is written on his slip, signing his sketch on the back with his initials.

After ten minutes or so, the papers are collected numbered, and then thumb-tacked up in the "picture gallery."

Each artist is then given a card on which to write, after its distinguishing number, his guess as to what song the sketch illustrates.

A prize ribbon is pinned on the illustration recognized by the most guests. Another is pinned on the artist who guessed the most titles correctly. These blue ribbons are the cutouts of a musical note, which are pinned on by the stem. They can be cut from blue felt or from construction paper, and make a good souvenir.

LIFE PORTRAIT OF THE CHOIR DIRECTOR—If the guests are trained musicians and know the score, they might enjoy making a directed drawing of the choir director. There are several methods, some quite involved, and if a guest has a favorite one, he could give the directions to the company, using as many musical terms as possible. If not, here is a simple method which the Maestro can announce, step by step. He could say:

"First, of course, his head. (You may use your erasers freely!) Shall we make it of two braces? The top is a slur. His hair? Oh, that is made of trill lines. His ears are inverted bass clefs. Now for his handsome features! His eyes are holds; his nose, an inverted accent mark; his mouth, two ties, with staccato marks for the teeth."

He pauses here to ask, "Any questions? Any requests that I repeat any of the directions? Remember that the best portrait receives a prize."

After a brief pause, he resumes, "Then we will proceed. The choir director's neck and tie are a tenor clef sign. Now for his manly frame! His body is formed by two upright ties; his legs and arms are diminuendo marks and his hands and feet are flats. Now he's complete except for the buttons on his coat. These are repeat signs."

A reasonable amount of time is given for the floundering artists to complete the portrait, but all requests for another piece of drawing paper, so that they can start all over, should be refused.

The prizes could be sheet music or a phonograph record; or some small symbolic prize, such as a key ring or a box of rubber bands.

GIRLY SONG CONTEST—The guests are divided into two equal teams. After they are in separate groups, the Maestro explains that this is a sing-down of songs which have as their titles the names of women.

Each group is to choose a leader to direct the singing, and then at a signal, one group will sing its "girly" song; and when it has finished, the other group will sing its selection.

When one choir fails to recognize another song with a

girl's name in its title, it is officially "out," and the other choir is proclaimed winner.

Suggested songs are: "Annie Laurie;" "Oh, My Darling Clementine;" "Juanita;" "Nellie Was a Lady;" "Li'l Liza Jane;" "Oh, Susannah;" "When You and I Were Young, Maggie;" "Little Annie Rooney;" "Mary Had a Little Lamb;" "Darling Nelly Gray;" "Mistress Shady;" "Sweet Genevieve;" "Reuben and Rachel."

Do-It-Yourself Musicians—This stunt is a fill-in, just to give voices a chance to rest. Each guest is given a stick of colored plasticine and asked to fashion any musical instrument from it. In a box from which any amateur sculptor may take what he wants, is a collection of helps: spools of coarse thread for fiddle strings, bottle tops, toothpicks, orange sticks for tools, paper cups, scissors, brass paper fasteners, etc.

The Week-day Round—This old favorite stunt song is a wonderful trap for the unwary, resulting in many victims for the forfeit feature. It is sung to the tune of "K-K-K-Katy." The guests are divided into seven separate singing groups and seated. Then each group is given the name of a different day in the week. The words of the song are:

> Oh, Mistress Shady, she is a lady,
>   She has a daughter whom I adore;
>   Each day I court her—
>   I mean the daughter!
> Every Sunday, Monday, Tuesday, Wednesday,
> Thursday, Friday, Saturday afternoon,
>   At half past four.

All the groups sing together the whole song until reaching the names of the days of the week. Then each group bobs up, in turn, to sing its own special day—Monday, Tuesday, etc.—and having sung it, immediately sits down.

Then the entire company join in singing, "Afternoon, at half past four."

This stunt song is repeated, and each time it is sung faster, so that the bobbing up and down of the busy weekdays becomes both confusing and convulsing. Mistakes of individuals or groups are recorded for future punishment in the form of forfeit-paying.

FORFEITS—Any stunt that even remotely has to do with music will do as a suitable forfeit. For example, he may:

1. Sing "Gaily the Troubadour," accompanying himself on the tennis racquet.

2. Sing in coloratura style the following:

> A tooter who tooted the flute
> Tried to tutor two tooters to toot.
> Said the two to the tutor,
> "It is harder to toot, sir,
> Than to tutor two tooters to toot."

3. Demonstrate his musical pitch by repeating "Music hath charms to soothe the savage breast," saying every other word in a falsetto voice, and the alternate words in the deepest tone he can muster.

4. Propose to any guest present, singing his proposal ad lib, to any tune the lady suggests.

5. Speak on the subject, "The most difficult instrument to learn to play is second fiddle," and do so with a caramel in his mouth.

6. Sing a lullaby to any musical instrument, which is bonneted with a sheet of music and cradled in his arms.

REFRESHMENTS—Little oblong cakes can have a music staff traced on their white icing. Lines can be traced with a toothpick that has been dipped in melted chocolate. Currants can form the notes.

Ice cream can be served in little homemade containers, shaped like drums. Olives become edible notes when given a toothpick stem. For a supper, any dish that can be eaten with chopsticks is suitable.

PROGRAM TRIMMINGS

Sometimes the monthly meeting can become altogether too regular. Some little extra is needed to add sparkle and zest, nothing elaborate—just some timely trifle that sort of trims the regular order.

Such little extras can take the form of responses to roll call; the singing of some well-known song that seems written especially for that particular month; or the introduction of a simple game or stunt related in some way to the red-letter days or general activities of that month.

Here are a few suggestions to spark the imagination and ingenuity of leaders of such groups of women.

Response to Roll Call

JANUARY—Each club member gives a New Year's resolution for organization's work, or tells of some piece of work she started some time ago and intends to complete this year, so help her!

FEBRUARY—Each member tells of an incident in her life when she was left in the dark, either literally or figuratively speaking.

MARCH—Each member tells an Irish joke or gives a good housecleaning short cut which she can personally recommend.

APRIL—Each member tells what she likes and dislikes most about the spring of the year.

MAY—Each member tells about her first doll, its name and fate.

JUNE—Each member tells a funny incident that occurred at her wedding, or at another's.

JULY—Each member tells what she would like America, her town, her family, or herself to be free of.

AUGUST—Each member names her favorite camp-fire dish, and if unusual, how to make and cook it.

SEPTEMBER—Each member tells the nicest thing that happened to her the past summer or relates the peak experience of her vacation.

OCTOBER—Each member states some special bit of good fortune she wishes for the organization.

NOVEMBER—Each member tells the chief thing for which she is thankful at this stage of her life.

DECEMBER—Each member brings to the meeting an inexpensive, homemade Christmas novelty, home decoration, or Christmas tree ornament, displays it, and gives a two-minute talk on how she made it. Or each member brings her favorite Christmas card greeting and reads it aloud to the group.

Songs to Sing at Meetings

JANUARY—"Auld Lang Syne;" "Time on My Hands."

FEBRUARY—"Yankee Doodle;" love songs.

MARCH—"My Wild Irish Rose."

APRIL—"I'm Always Chasing Rainbows;" "I've a Rainbow Round My Shoulder."

MAY—"Mother Machree." "Oh, That We Two Were Maying!"

JUNE—"I Love You Truly;" "Moonlight and Roses."

JULY—"America."

AUGUST—"Bringing in the Sheaves;" "Moonlight Bay."

SEPTEMBER—"School Days;" "I've Been Working on the Railroad."

OCTOBER—"Keep The Home Fires Burning;" "Shine On Harvest Moon."

NOVEMBER—"Come, Ye Thankful People, Come;" "Doxology; "Turkey in the Straw."

DECEMBER—"Jingle Bells;" "There's a Song in the Air;" Christmas Carols.

Quick Games and Stunts

JANUARY—Each member is given a paper pie plate and a black crayon, and told to mark the face of a clock on the plate, setting the hands at whatever time is written on the back of the plate.

FEBRUARY—Each member is asked to draw a groundhog seeing its shadow.

MARCH—Each member is given a stick of green plasticine, and told to mould from it a St. Patrick's Day model—a pig, pipe, potato, shamrock, harp, hat.

APRIL—Each member must try to fool three persons before the meeting ends.

MAY—Each member is blindfolded and attempts to draw a daisy on a large sheet of paper thumbtacked to the wall. The number of petals to be drawn is clearly stated.

JUNE—Each member is given some white tissue paper, pins, Scotch tape, and a paper spoon, lollipop, or a headed clothespin to dress as a June bride.

JULY—Each member is given pencil and writing paper and told to draw a sketch of Statue of Liberty as she remembers it, putting the right object in each hand. The right hand holds her torch; the left, a law book.

AUGUST—The members form two groups of equal sizes. Then, in turn, each group tries to see which, in unison, can give the loudest and most realistic hay-fever sneeze.

SEPTEMBER—The leader has a set of alphabet cards, and lifts

one at a time with a quick, upward sweep from the pile, so that all seated can see it at the same time. The first player who shouts the name of a work implement or utensil, stating whether for farm, garden, kitchen or general housework, receives the card. When all the letters are gone, the member who has the most cards receives the whole set as a prize.

OCTOBER—Each member is given a paper sack and told to make a Halloween mask for herself from it. At hand are scissors, library paste, crayons, whisk broom straws for whiskers, a saucer of mixed buttons, bottle caps, and a ball of string.

NOVEMBER—Each member is given an oatmeal box for a drum and a pencil for a drumstick, and told to beat out the tune of "Turkey in the Straw." A few paper horns may be distributed to help the orchestra along.

DECEMBER—Each member is asked to bring a white elephant gift to be put in Santa's grab bag from which each one in turn, draws a gift.

PROCEDURE POINTERS

There was a time when a banquet was, as the dictionary defines, "a feast; a ceremonious public dinner or supper." In other words, it was an elaborate meal, with probably a dull speech or two following it—a plain "they-met-and-et" affair.

But no longer! Now the banquet must have a novel theme, just as does the social, prom, or party.

The theme is first announced in invitation or by poster. Then it is carried out in the decorations, both of reception room and banquet hall, in the design of menu cover and program, and in the table decorations and favors.

The toasts are chosen to tie in with the general theme, also the speeches, care being taken to notify the speakers of the theme and of the time allotted them. Sometimes the toastmaster and waitresses are costumed in keeping with the theme, as gypsies, for instance, for a gypsy banquet.

The soft background music and special vocal and instrumental numbers are all selected with the theme in mind. One song that is especially appropriate may be chosen as the theme song for the evening, as "School Days" for a back-to-school banquet, guests marching in to the table singing it, hearing it several times during the course of the evening, and, finally, as they say, "Good night."

Even the after-banquet program—dance, concert, movie, stage play or informal evening of games—is planned to tie, however loosely, to the theme.

There are several other ways to accentuate the banquet theme; for example:

THEME ENTRANCE—The introduction of the theme makes the important first impression. A huge symbol of the theme is built on the threshold, or within the reception room, or as the "door" to the banquet hall, so that guests must step through it to enter. For the spring flower banquet, a swinging white gate, and a picket fence, dripping with real or artificial blossoms; for the Mother Goose banquet, an enormous shoe, with the Old Woman who lives in it caught in the act of hanging on it a "house for sale" sign; for a heart's-ease banquet, a huge pansy-decorated valentine; for a best-seller banquet, an immense open book; for a boxers' banquet, an arched doorway made of gaily-wrapped boxes of all shapes and sizes, each labeled, "Do not open until Christmas!"

THEME STAGE SCENE—Some banquet halls have a stage, even scenery and footlights. With imagination, clever lighting, and living characters in costume, a vivid dramatization of the theme can be presented in such settings as a pirate's den; a gypsy camp; a circus, with concessions, clowns and all; a covered wagon; a mountain shack of a general store, with a hillbilly band on the steps.

THEME TABLE ARRANGEMENT—Tables need not always be straight up and down. They can be placed four-square around a central, spot-lighted table; or they can be placed to form a triangle, a plus sign, or a letter, as H or V. They can be arranged to form a fan for a Japanese banquet, or as the spokes of a wheel. Round tables can be used to make designs. They can be assembled to form shamrocks for a St. Patrick's Banquet; or for an aviation banquet long tables may be arranged to form the wings and body of a plane, with a round, drop-leaf table forming the nose.

THE THEME SPOTLIGHT—The decorating committee puts out its best efforts to make the speaker's table outstanding. Not always is the centerpiece an artistic creation of rare flowers. Sometimes it is tied tightly to the theme of the banquet, and so could be a collector's model of an old sailing vessel; or a miniature replica, done to scale, of a proposed new dream building—church addition, library, hospital, or gymnasium. The spotlight is turned on this centerpiece, drawing all eyes. Often the theme is underscored by a set of murals on the wall back of the speaker's table or by bold chalk or poster paint drawings.

The spotlight is effective when turned on the central scene, framed, like the picture it is, by the square of tables set around it. This beauty spot might feature an improvised fountain or a tranquil pool of water lilies, or a ring of gauze-winged fairies dancing around a Maypole. Or into the softly-lighted spot of light, which changes color to suit each musical number of the program, strolling singers may come to play string instruments between the courses or while they are being served.

THE THEME FAREWELL—This is a much appreciated extra. There is someone at the door to shake hands with the departing guests. As he does so, he says something that ties in with the theme of the evening. As, "Good night. Happy landing!" after the aviation banquet. Sometimes with the handshake goes a small, inexpensive memento of the occasion, often a complimentary gift from a neighborhood merchant, such as a package of seeds after a spring-planting banquet, or a map of the city after a know-your-town banquet.

For a small and cozy banquet, a joke or thought from an inspiring poem that is related to the theme may be typed on tinted note paper and handed out as a farewell favor.

A sample joke for a Thanksgiving banquet:

Waiter. Chilly tonight, isn't it?
Diner. No, thanks; none of those Spanish dishes for me!

A sample thought from an inspiring poem, for any banquet with a flower or garden theme.

I never see a garden anywhere,
That I do not see God walking there.
—Grace Noll Crowell

Committees and Their Duties

How many committees are necessary? That depends. An elaborate dinner and dance may need as many as fourteen or more sub-committees, including secretarial, cloak room, floor, prize, etc. Whereas a simple affair may require only the big four—food, fun, frills, and fanfare, more formally known as menu, program, decoration, and publicity. If tickets are sold, another is required—finance; and if favors are to be made or bought, and the frills committee spurns to handle such trifles, then a favors committee is added.

THE SOCIAL COMMITTEE—The steering organization appoints the necessary sub-committees, according to whether the affair is simple or elaborate, and after considering the type and theme of the entertainment; whether admission is free or by ticket; whether the meal will be home-cooked and served by members of the sponsoring organization in its own hall, or prepared by outside caterers, or served at a hotel at so much a plate. These various conditions have a bearing on how many committees will be needed and frequently on the amount of work and responsibility they must carry.

The aim is to appoint enough committees to make light work of the most pretentious program, and to make sure that no little group of willing workers is worn out, while others, equally willing, have nothing to do.

DUTIES OF EACH COMMITTEE—The duties of the various committees vary under different circumstances. For instance, sometimes the food committee has charge of not only its usual duties, but also of the placing of the tables, which is often the coveted privilege of a decorating committee, desirous of arranging them in some novel way that ties in with their decorative scheme.

THE THREE W's—No wheels can turn until the three important W's are established—what? when? where?

The first step is to decide what type of a social affair to give and a novel theme for it. Next, it is essential, in many cases, to "clear the date" as early as possible, for if the banquet or party is to feature some red-letter day, such as Valentine, St. Patrick's, Thanksgiving, other organizations probably will be planning social affairs for the same date and also trying to get the same place for them.

Often just a telephone call is all that is required to secure the right date and place for the party. Sometimes a special sub-committee is appointed for this purpose. The members go in person and make all necessary arrangements. This go-see vanguard seems to have no official name. Why not call it the where-and-when committee?

As soon as the social committee knows positively that the place and date can be announced, then the necessary machinery can be set in motion.

Following is a list of the various committees and their main duties. The social committee chairman chooses only those necessary for the smooth success of the entertainment planned.

PROGRAM COMMITTEE—This committee goes into action immediately. Speakers and performers usually have a tight schedule of engagements and need several weeks' advance notice. If the affair is a banquet, the committee arranges for speakers and toasts. If it is a party, then for the games, either appointed one of its members to plan and direct them, or selecting someone else who is qualified. If it is a dance, then for the orchestra.

Should there be much music on the program, this committee is named the program and music committee, and the members most qualified assume all responsibility for the music, both at the meal and for the formal program that follows.

MENU COMMITTEE—For light refreshments, this committee frequently not only plans the menu, but bakes the food. And a chairman who can skimp and not seem to is a treasure.

For a large banquet or dinner, this committee works hard. It plans the menu, arranges for the serving of the meal, and if there is no special clean-up committee appointed for this very necessary service, sees that everything is left shipshape in the kitchen.

For a small dinner, the menu committee also sets the tables; but for a large banquet, another group of women, called the table committee, is in charge of this task and works in close co-operation with the decoration committee, or whichever group is assigned to the decorating of the tables.

In starting its work, the menu committee usually first meets to discuss various suggested menus and estimate the cost of each. Perhaps some member thinks she can get a special price on the meat or some other item on a proposed menu. She is authorized to go ahead and do her best.

At a second committee meeting, if this is a pay affair, there may be reports on how many tickets have already been sold, and what is the estimated attendance at the banquet. Reports on any cut in costs are made.

Usually at this second meeting a definite menu is decided upon; also who is to serve the meal. Waitresses are sometimes in costume, to harmonize with the theme of the banquet.

Then comes the matter, always of vital importance to this committee, yet periodically the same old struggle: how to get in the reports of the ticket-sellers a few days before the night of the banquet, so that the volunteer caterers will know, at least approximately, how many meals to shop for, prepare, and cook.

PROGRAM PRINTING COMMITTEE—This committee plans and makes the souvenir programs. Members submit their original ideas for a cover design, some offering made-up samples. These tie in with the theme of the banquet, are illustrated with some artistic or amusing sketch, and carry the name and date of the banquet.

When one of the designs has been selected, the committee makes the necessary number of covers, usually of colored construction paper.

Later, when the menu and program committees have completed their plans, and it is certain there will be no further change in them, the program printing committee proceeds to print, type, or mimeograph the menu, table events, and songs on the inside pages, and then assembles them in their attractive covers, tying them with silk cord or ribbon.

Sometimes this artistic committee generously undertakes to make the table favors also.

DECORATION COMMITTEE—Occasionally this committee is divided into two groups. One has charge of the room and stage decorations, the other of the table decorations, concentrating on the speakers' table. They work closely together in developing the theme of the banquet or dinner. They are especially careful to guard against fire hazards, using only fireproofed paper and seeing to it that no exits are blocked by decorative designs.

This is a most important committee, which, by its ingenuity, can transform the ugliest hall into a fairyland that insures, by its very atmosphere, a gay and happy time.

PUBLICITY COMMITTEE—This committee is the one that never stops working until the guests are crowding in at the door. It makes original, arresting posters to announce the event, placing them wherever they will be seen by the most "prospects," on bulletin boards in church and school, and in local store windows and shopping centers.

It runs notices about unusual features of the banquet in local papers, church bulletins, school papers, and the like. It sometimes sends out theme-decorated letters of invitation to a selected mailing list, or has printed and distributed interest-arousing handbills that advertise the banquet.

It may be able to induce a local radio station to give a brief announcement of the affair or persuade the friendly manager of the neighborhood movie theater to flash the publicity item on the screen. Friends who have jobs dealing with the public can be very useful to this committee.

Several nights previous to, and on the night of, the banquet, the committee attracts the attention of the passing public by placing large signs, illuminated by electric lights, outside the place where the banquet is to be given.

TICKET COMMITTEE—This committee sells the tickets or distributes them to group leaders to be sold. It tries to prevent the menu committee from going slowly mad by getting recent reports on the number of tickets sold. It is often asked to collect the tickets at the door on the banquet night.

PRIZES COMMITTEE—This committee is a boon when several good prizes are to be awarded. It shops carefully with good taste and good sense, to select the perfect gift.

FINANCE COMMITTEE—The more elaborate the affair, the more necessary is this committee, and the more important. It holds the purse strings, reviews and passes on the proposed expenditures of the various sub-committees, draws up a budget, finds ways to balance it, hold down expenses even under pressure, and keeps careful accounts right up to the last minute. It is often a committee chairman's worst headache, but it keeps the banquet out of the red.

RECEPTION COMMITTEE—This committee gives the gracious touch that often is remembered longest. It greets the guests and sees that strangers, if any, are introduced to warm, outgoing people and made to feel at home.

At the close of the evening, members of this friendly committee are again at the doors, to speed the parting guest and give the evening some such happy ending as a smiling, "Good night. And thank you for coming. Hope you enjoyed us as much as we enjoyed you!"

SUGGESTIONS FOR CHURCH SUPPERS

In church circles, the solution of all financial worries seems to be, "Let's have a church supper." The problem is how to make it different, how to make it sparkle, so that it is not just another old church supper.

Following are brief suggestions gathered from church supper chairmen, suitable for each successive month in the year.

JANUARY—The meal may be called a Seasonable Supper, featuring the four seasons. One table, as spring, has decorations of growing bulbs. The waitress representing March wears a St. Patrick's Day costume; the one representing April, a jester's costume; and the one representing May, a May Queen costume. The favors are tiny calendars.

The second table may be arranged as summer and decorated with crepe paper flowers and butterflies. The three waitresses are: June in a rose costume, July in an Uncle Sam costume, and August in a summer girl costume. The favors are Japanese fans.

The third table is arranged as autumn, with decorations of autumn leaves. The three waitresses are: September, dressed as a school girl in a high school blazer; October, wearing a Halloween costume; and November in a Puritan costume. The favors are pretty school pencils.

The fourth table represents winter, with decorations of cotton snow. The three waitresses are December, dressed as Santa Claus; January as Father Time; and February in a valentine costume. The favors are tarlatan bags of candy.

FEBRUARY—The supper may be called a Presidents' Supper, featuring Lincoln and Washington. The table decorations are bunting, a log cabin, and a cherry tree. The waitresses wear colonial costumes. The favors are little cardboard hatchets.

MARCH—This supper may be called an Irish Supper, featuring Pat and his pig. The table decorations may be green, with pigs made of Irish potatoes and matches. The waitresses are dressed as colleens. The favors are candy pigs. Appropriate music consists of "Mother Machree," "A Little Bit of Heaven," and "Tipperary."

APRIL—For April, there may be a Jest-So Supper, which may feature jokes. The table decorations are dolls dressed as circus clowns. The waitresses wear a jester's cap and bells. The favors are "rubber" pencils or any other trick novelty.

MAY—For May, there may be a Bird Supper, which features birds. The table decorations are birds cut from colored cardboard and twigs supporting hay nests full of candy eggs. The waitresses wear bluebird crepe paper costumes. A few canaries in cages may be borrowed for the stage. The favors are bird whistles. The music consists of bird records.

JUNE—For June, there may be a Graduation Supper. The table decorations are piles of ribbon-tied diplomas and midget books, with a cardboard model of the little red schoolhouse as a centerpiece. The waitresses are dressed as sweet girl graduates. The favors are little mortar boards cut from shining black cardboard and filled with candy. The music is "School Days."

JULY—A Jungle Supper is suitable for July. The decorations are ferns, rubber plants, cannibal heads (coconuts with hideous faces painted on them), and native cymbals (small, new pot covers trimmed with gay tassels of fringe crepe paper). The table centerpiece is a native straw hut. The favors are tiny cardboard canoes. The prizes are little war chiefs with date heads and feet, raisin arms and legs, clove features, and fringed paper costumes. The waitresses wear elaborate native headdresses, gold cardboard nose rings, ropes of beads, and grass (crepe paper) skirts. Tom-toms provide the music. If a poster is needed, it could show a picture of a jungle camp, with a white explorer being cooked alive in a native pot. The caption could be "Is It Hot Enough for You?"

AUGUST—The supper for this month may be called a Cooldown Supper. The costumes are informal, with the men in shirt sleeves and the women in play suits. The table centerpiece is a snow-and-ice winter scene. An all-cold meal may be served. The favors are tiny paper parasols. The music consists of moon songs.

SEPTEMBER—The September supper may be called a Get-busy Supper. The table decorations are schoolbooks, tools, or anything that suggests resumed household tasks, such as brooms, electric irons, toy laundry equipment, and packages of soap powder. The waiters and waitresses are high school students in work clothes, the boys being in overalls and the girls with their heads tied up in dusting handkerchiefs. The favors are working utensils for a doll's house. The music may be "I've Been Working on the Railroad."

OCTOBER—The October spread may be called a Halloween Supper, being wholly lighted with candles and eaten by candlelight. The table decorations and centerpiece are fancy candles. The waitresses wear caps and aprons decorated with cutouts of colored candles. The favors are tiny orange candles in black cardboard holders. A few candle games may be played. Halloween should be featured on the menu. The music includes "In the Gloaming."

NOVEMBER—The November supper may be called a Thanks-a-Million Supper. The table decorations show a few musical notes and the printed words, "Come, Ye Thankful People, Come." The waitresses are dressed as Puritan girls. The favors are little bags of candy corn. The music may be "America the Beautiful."

DECEMBER—The supper for December may be called a Greeting Card Supper. The hall and the table are decorated with used Christmas cards. The waitresses wear aprons with pockets made of sewed-on Christmas cards. The favors are tiny, handmade memorandum books, with covers cut from greeting cards. The music consists of Christmas carols.

STUNTS FOR THE FELLERS

Sometimes it is a club or fraternity banquet, to which only men are invited. Here are some stunts that have been successful at such affairs.

STARTING THINGS OFF WITH A BANG—The boys are warned that the proceedings will start promptly at a certain time and that anyone not there on the dot stays outside until after the first course—"and we mean it!"

It is oysters on the half shell, and no sooner has the last dish been served than all the lights suddenly go off. Then there is a terrific clap of thunder, made by the hidden orchestra, followed by three cracking pistol shots. There is an instant lull in the conversation.

"Gosh! What a storm" blink the boys, thinking uneasily of all those slippery oysters to be eaten, maybe, sight unseen, in the pitch darkness.

Then a spotlight is thrown on two lovelies in the balcony. They are draped in red, white, and blue. The orchestra, also hidden in the balcony, strikes up the national anthem, which the boys, led by the pretty girls, join in singing.

Or instead of "The Star-Spangled Banner" the girls, suitably costumed, may sing the college song or a club or convention favorite.

SINGING WAITERS—Some of the boys in the organization dress up as waiters and serve the dinner, having been fortified with a good square meal beforehand.

Let us assume that there are six men down on the program to give brief after-dinner talks. Before each one speaks, the singing waiters line up in front of the stage and sing some funny, fitting verse about him, the words set to a well-known old or new popular tune.

NO SMOKING—The meal over, the boys good-naturedly full, they light their big cigars, and lean back for a good after-banquet smoke.

Suddenly three or four men dressed like firemen barge in and order everybody to stop smoking. They have such an air or high-handed authority that the astonished boys hardly know what to think.

"How come?" demands one, up in arms at this new violation of a man's personal liberty.

"A new fire ruling, just passed," snaps the most bumptious of the pseudo-firemen. "No smoking! It a fire hazard. Put out that cigar, you fire-bug!"

The firemen pass through the hall, browbeating the weak-hearted, then proceed to the platform and put on their speciality—a "hot" singing or dancing number.

CUT-GLASS CUTUP—This stunt is guaranteed to give the boys a real shock if there is a presentation of something breakable to be made.

Besides the genuine article, a cheap fake gift of something easily breakable is purchased. Then, during a serious speech of presentation, "Clumsy Charles" is seen to enter with an important air, carrying the fake gift, poised on the fingers of his hand, held high, apparently so that all can see it. Then—horrors!—he stubs his toe, and as the audience gasps and shudders, the cut-glass bowl or decanter, or whatever it is, crashes to the floor, breaking into fragments.

The boys, still choking on their cigars, hear the chairman bawling out "Clumsy Charles" on the side, and mutter, "Bang goes five bucks!" or whatever sum they contributed to the disaster.

Then someone else brings on the real gift and presents it.

RISE PLEASE—After the show, the Master of Ceremonies announces that someone—the chef, the waiters, the actors, the orchestra, the dishwashers—would appreciate a contribution. Rather than pass the hat for small change, the management would very much appreciate a few larger contributions.

"Everyone who will give ten dollars, please rise." As nobody stirs, the emcee says to the orchestra leader, "Let's have 'The Star-Spangled Banner.'"

MY HAT—This stunt is a mirthfully murderous way of adding to the fund a club is raising for its charity work. It needs: a temperamental auctioneer who means what he says; box of old clothes, presumably donated for the cause; a couple of cheap new hats; a strong table on which is placed a chopping block, and a meat cleaver.

Also, unknown to the club members, while the meal is being served, all their hats have been sneakily gathered and now repose in a second big covered box beside the auction block.

"Gentlemen," announces the chairman of the meeting, "the old clothes have been gathered, and we are going to auction them off here this evening."

The auction is turned over to a burly member, who is in the know. He steps to the table, puts the chopping block on it, and the big sharp meat cleaver on top of that. He reaches in a box and lifts a hat for a bid.

"What am I bid?" he barks. Everyone hesitates. The auctioneer doesn't wait a second for them to warm up. He slams the hat down on the block and lets drive with the cleaver, and with one stroke cuts the hat completely in two. Of course, this is one of the cheap new hats bought for the purpose.

The next hat is taken from the box. It is that of Andrew Peters, president of the club. Andy recognizes his hat, and with a wary eye on that meat cleaver, quickly bids a dime for it.

"What a piker!" jeers someone. "Well, after all, it is my own hat!" points out Andy.

Other members gleefully bid against him, unaware that their own hats will soon be on the block. The secretary finally buys it for sixty-five cents.

Another hat is lifted. Nobody seems to recognize it, But, since it is a new hat, the bids quickly reach twenty-five cents, but the auctioneer yells, "Heck, fellows! We can't sell such a good hat for two bits" As he says it, he lets drive again with the meat cleaver and cuts the hat slap-bang in two! This is the second of the two hats bought for the purpose.

After that, it is amazing how quickly the men bid for those hats as each recognizes his own. Some, in their zeal, buy as many as three. The owner is forced to pay at least the bid-in price before his hat is turned over to him. The average price of the hats is a little over a dollar.

Thus a nice little sum is realized, and at the same time the men enjoy a stunt that they can kid one another about for a long time to come.

HERE'S YOUR HAT, BUT WHAT'S YOUR HURRY?—If the crowd is small, good-natured, and in no rush to get home, this stunt gives an exciting end to a jolly evening. But a plain-clothes man should be placed in the cloakroom to see that nobody walks off with the Mayor's foreign-made hat!

The mischief is started in the checking arrangements for hats and coats at the door. Some practical joker slips out during the evening and shifts the hats around, so that when the boys present their checks, each will get the wrong hat. A small thing to excite a man so much!

ASSORTED CHRISTMAS BOX SOCIALS

Clubs or churches wishing to use the Christmas box plan, under which gifts are collected for distribution, may give a social or a party, drawing upon "A Boxy Banquet" for suggestions for such decorations, games, refreshments, etc. as meet their requirements. See page 120.

There are scores of such Christmas box social affairs. Following are a few of the most successful:

A PRINT-BOX SOCIAL—Books and magazines make lasting gifts. The books can be new, or may be good used books in first-class condition. They can be paid as admission to the social or given in the usual way.

Guests can club together to pay for gift subscriptions to some magazines they know the favored one will like. Or each can give a subscription to a different magazine previously decided upon, to save duplication.

A print-box social or party is sometimes given to get books for a new library for church or club or to add new books to a library already established.

THE GOODY-BOX PARTY—This party is a lovely Christmas surprise to spring on someone who has little time for fancy cookery—the business woman, the away-from-home girl who lives in a couple of rooms or a kitchenette apartment.

The goodies are all dainties, beautifully done up in gay tin boxes. Each guest prepares her own specialty, or takes it from her shelves of home-preserved fruit, jam or jellies. When the boxes, all tinseled and ribboned, are opened by the thrilled recipient, they disclose homemade cakes, cookies, candies; assorted jellies in jovial little jars; relishes in Christmas colors; jars of mincemeat; boxes of roasted nuts and stuffed dates; gorgeous small cakes, cellophane-wrapped; plum puddings in novelty bowls, all ready to reheat; squat glasses of cranberry conserve. All made-in-the-kitchen gifts, by cooks who know how!

Sometimes it means nothing to the giver but taking the goody from her pantry shelf. She never misses it. But it means much to a girl or boy whose homesickness has settled into a longing for homemade strawberry jam, or salad dressing like what mother used to make.

THE STOCKING BOX PARTY—There is usually a champion knitter in any ladies' aid, guild, or young people's society. She is asked to knit a doll's-size sock in holiday colors, for each member or guest. These are distributed or sent with the invitation, so that each person can wad a dollar bill into the tiny toe.

At the party, guests tie each little sock with a tag reading:

> I thought you might
> Be out of socks,
> So I send you some
> As a Christmas box.

There is a box on the table marked, "Christmas Socks Box," and into this go all the little full socks. The box is then wrapped, addressed to its destination, insured, and mailed that night, if possible. The party then goes on, happier than ever, playing any of the boxy games planned for the boxy banquet.

The inmates of old People's homes love to get these little socks, not only because of the novelty, but also because the extra pocket money may be used, if permitted, to buy that ice cream cone, chewing gum, or the stamps that they have been wanting for a long, long time.

A TOY-BOX PARTY—This party is for the benefit of children Santa might forget. The admission ticket is one toy, and before the party breaks up, the hostess must, figuratively speaking, "deliver the goods." That is, she must have assigned competent, reliable people to pack the toys and see that they are delivered on time to their destination. To come back in the New Year and stumble upon the toys still in the church basement closet is a sad experience.

CHATTER-BOX PARTY—Is there a shut-in on your street? It's quiet enough in her room. This party goes in a body to her home, and gives her as much chatter as she can stand. If she has a phonograph, her unexpected guests take her a new talking record or an old favorite. If she hasn't a radio, they buy her one, on time. A talking bird or a singing canary makes an excellent gift.

TOOL-BOX PARTY—For a youngster who is a hammering carpenter, this is the sort of Christmas party to give him, with his sisters and his brothers, his uncles and his aunts contributing the tools for which he yearns.

STAMP-BOX PARTY—If his hobby is stamps, he will like this sort of a party, and he will bless his friends and relatives for adding, in this novel, happy way, to his prized collection.

CHRISTMAS TREE BOX PARTY—Sometimes the real evergreen Christmas tree is in one place and the party in another. In this case, a tree may be made of the boxes of candy which are to be given to the guests. They are of uniform size and shape. Each is wrapped in dark green paper and trimmed with gay Christmas seals. The boxes are arranged in a pyramid to form a geometrical tree. Tree ornaments are hung from outside corners, or Christmas tree light may be draped to outline the shape. A large ribbon spool may be put on top in place of the usual star, with lengths of silver ribbon or tinsel cord dangling from it.

If there are additional favors—popcorn balls, doll-lollipops, tarlatan stocking, filled with toys and trinkets, and the like—they can still trim the tree by being thumb-tacked into the edge of a box.

When the time comes to distribute the gifts, Santa himself can take down his tree, one box at a time. Or boxes can be wrapped in red crepe paper, chalked white around the edges to resemble bricks, and built into a most effective fireplace, through which Santa and his bag can carefully emerge.

PUZZLE-BOX PARTY—If there is a lad who must sit for hours in a wheel chair, this is the party for him. Guests carry his every sort of ingenious puzzles to help him while away the long hours.

A WORK-BOX PARTY—At this party the gifts are all up-to-date kitchen gadgets for mother, who likes to decorate cakes, cookies, and carrots.

AN AUTO-ACCESSORY BOX PARTY—This is a special party for the man who pays the bills. Dad has been hankering for new gadgets for his car, but never buys them. Now is the time to buy them for him and make a party of it. He'll love it.

Then there is the paint-box party for the little girl who loves to color, and a beauty-box party for the big girl who colors her cheeks.

A FAMILY CHRISTMAS BAZAAR

Oh, that bugbear of the Christmas rush—the shopping list! With Cousin Violet who has everything, and Cousin Mattie who has nothing; and a bachelor uncle who doesn't smoke, and loathes slippers; and a spinster aunt who—the very idea!—doesn't care for canaries, goldfish, imported teas, or fancywork!

Oh, the mad, blind dashing about in crowded stores and the dragging home with aching feet, a cold in the head, and the wrong gifts, with nobody in this joy-crazed world to care a whoop!

Nobody? This bazaar was planned to help the harassed gift buyer do her Christmas shopping early and easily.

BAZAAR POSTERS—The posters are made of green or red Bristol board and decorated with a whole family of shoppers —grandma, mother, dad, and the twins—all cut from white paper and pasted in place. Above them are two lines of fluttering pennants, each carrying a single letter, in red or green, of "A Family Christmas Bazaar."

Below is printed the following:

> This family bazaar is planned
>   To save you money, time, and woe;
> To help you shop, you understand,
>   For families that somehow grow
> To be the most unusual ones
> When time for Christmas shopping comes,
>
> We aim to please—like Santa Claus!
>   Each one upon your Christmas list;
> The country cousins, aunts, in-laws;
>   You'd die if one of them were missed!
> We know how difficult they are,
> And hence our family bazaar.

The date, place, and time of opening are added and the poster is displayed and in prominent places well in advance of the opening date.

BAZAAR DECORATIONS—Since the Christmas rush seems to start earlier every year, a decorative scheme should be chosen that will not burden the committee members, all of whom possibly will be suffering from that rushed-to-death feeling that comes with the first "Do Your Christmas Shopping Early" warning of the season.

The crepe paper pennant trim has been called the busy decorator's friend. Hundreds of wedge-shaped pieces can be cut out in a few minutes. As one worker cuts, another pins the pennants on lengths of tape, while still another attaches them permanently by machining along the tape.

When these long lines of gay, fluttering streamers of pennants are looped across the room from booth to booth in open doorways or as valances over windows, they make a most effective decoration.

Clever posters can be made for the various booths, each poster featuring the picture of that particular member of the family—dad, mother, daughter, son, grandchild, friend, etc.—in whose Christmas gifts the booth is specializing. Suitable pictures can often be cut from covers of popular magazines, especially those that feature character pictures for which the subject not only sits, but tells a story in the process.

INFORMATION BOOTH—This booth, placed prominently and labeled so that all can see, is presided over by Santa Claus himself. He should know his stock so well that customers can bring to him the most hard-to-please person on their lists and instantly get excellent advice and reliable information as to where a suitable gift can be obtained.

CHRISTMAS MAIL BOOTH—This booth sells Red Cross stamps, stamps for any other good cause, and packages of foreign stamps for the collector; also stamp albums, fancy stamp dispensers, mail baskets, postal scales, ballpoint pencils, boxes of quality stationery, note paper, Christmas cards, etc.

Here also are displayed all sorts of Christmas seals, tags, and stickers; also a fine line of fancy wrapping papers, ribbon, cord, tinsel, colored cellophane paper. Christmas boxes for the mailing of gifts are sold here, too, also such practical needs as balls of string, rolls of sturdy brown wrapping paper, parcel labels and tags, and white tissue paper.

Behind a table on which are all the requisites, stand assistants, prepared and ready to gift-wrap any article purchased at the bazaar. They have on display samples of the various styles of gift-wrappings, with the price for such service.

GRANDMA'S BOOTH—If possible, there should be a silver-haired, gentle old grandmamma on show in Grandma's booth, even if sales, change, and light conversation are made by a younger woman who assists her. Here are sold things which are naturally associated with dear old ladies like the picture, "Whistler's Mother," also soft, woolly shawls and stoles, exquisite handkerchiefs, bags of lavender, magnifying glasses of purse size, wool slippers, bookmarks, footstools, and lace collars.

MOTHER'S BOOTH—Mother is the easiest one in the family to please; so almost any article can go in her booth, with the exception, perhaps, of a pipe or a pair of roller skates. The collection can be divided into two classes, "Useful Gifts for Mother" and "Elegant Gifts for Mother," with the latter predominating.

FATHER'S BOOTH—A typical and popular father may be persuaded to take the center of the stage in this booth, with the promise that all he will have to do is relax in an easy chair, while his daughters do all the work. In his lounging slippers and smoking jacket, with the evening paper to hide behind, he should make a good drawing card. Here are sold the things that a normal dad really likes, not what his family wants to educate him to like. They include all sorts of gadgets that have to do with radio, smoking, shaving, his car, his hobbies and sports, and so on, not to mention ties, handkerchiefs, scarves, shirts, all chosen by a man shopper. There are also a few books that make light or exciting reading—detective yarns, adventure, humor—and fountain pens and pencils that were obviously fashioned with a man's preference in mind. If picture frames, calendars, and desk furnishings are to be sold, they should have a distinctly masculine cut.

FOR THE HAVES—The young lady in charge of this booth has "that expensive look." This booth should run to the arty gift-shop line of goods—choice novelties from foreign lands, unusual strings of beads, butterfly-wing pictures, imported jewelry, hand-carved treasures, real lace, signed etchings, hand-woven bags, and scarves. Anything, in fact, is sold here that carries with it its own reason for being chosen for the girl who already has everything.

FOR THE HAVE-NOTS—This booth could be presided over by some genial soul who takes a humorous pride in having nothing and boasting of it. This booth could be a sort of glorified white elephant affair, friends being asked to donate some nice new things to which, for some reason, they cannot seem to warm up. These unappreciated treasures should be priced ridiculously low, so that the poor little country cousin can be bought several gifts for the price of one. Luxuries should be especially asked for—handsome dress accessories that don't go with anything the owner wears; strings of good beads that are of awkward length; the purchased-in-Paris bracelet that will neither stay up or down on an active arm; the expensive earrings that seem to make the owner's nose look longer; the too-tight dress ring; the lovely gold shoes that won't stretch—the sort of thing people keep for years because it cost too much to throw away.

LITTLE JANE'S BOOTH—Gifts for the little daughter are sold here—toys and clothes, books and games. Any mother of a little Jane will know exactly what this booth should show. A small girl playing with a doll's house could be the living attraction of this booth.

LITTLE JACK'S BOOTH—Here are sold gifts for the little son, from a tricycle to a dime puzzle. A regular boy, of the lively, freckled, red-haired type, can be stationed in the foreground for as long as he will stay.

FOR CHILDREN OF ALL AGES—An ingenious person will have the time of her life stocking this booth. Here are found riddle books, cross-word puzzles, indoor games of all types, clockwork toys, trick novelties in which somebody gets fooled, the latest amusement fad—anything, in fact, that affords pleasure to that part of every normal person which refuses to grow up.

FOR THE FRIEND WHO ISN'T REDUCING—A nice plump lady may be placed in charge of this booth, which is well stocked with boxes of homemade fudge and holiday candies, preserved fruits, mixed nuts, fruit cakes, plum puddings, jars of home-made dainties and all the hundred and one things a friend who doesn't count her calories can eat.

FOR BOOKLOVERS—The person who loves to read is in the fore-ground of the booth, curled up in a comfortable chair, with a good reading lamp behind her, buried in the latest best-seller. This booth sells not only books for people of varied ages and tastes, but the Christmas issues of magazines. Also gift subscriptions for magazines are taken here. Other gifts that are especially suitable for all who love to read are on display, such as bed lights for those who like to read in bed, bookplates, bookmarkers, bookends, and bookshelves.

FOR MARTHA—In Martha's booth are sold aprons, of course, and all the little kitchen accessories and time-savers that will warm the practical soul of some modern Martha. The booth attendant, in a big apron, sews on a kettle holder in her spare moments. Any article that would be at home in the kitchen is eligible for this booth, from embroidered tea towels to a holly green sponge rubber mat.

FOR THE ELECTRICALLY-MINDED—This booth sells all things electrical, from waffle irons and toasters to the latest appli-ance for rolling away those extra superfluous flesh inele-gantly known as "the middle-age spread." It can easily be the most attractive booth in the bazaar, with all the latest things in illumination, such as novel light fixtures, beautiful floor and reading lamps, and fairy strings of sparkling Christmas tree lights outlining the booth and twinkling all over a big Christmas tree.

FAMILY CONTESTS—No bazaar is complete without its money-making contests. An average family—mother, father, chil-dren—may be placed upon the platform and prizes offered for the closest guesses of their collective weight, then of their collective height, then of their collective ages. Cards for scoring can be sold for a nickel each, with no limit as to number of cards sold to one customer.